18.95 Net

W9-DEH-489

Authority in the Anglican Communion

Authority in the Anglican Communion

Essays Presented to
Bishop John Howe

Edited by
Stephen W. Sykes

Anglican Book Centre
Toronto, Canada

1987
Anglican Book Centre
600 Jarvis Street
Toronto, Ontario
Canada M4Y 2J6

Copyright © 1987 by Anglican Book Centre

All rights reserved. No part of this book may be reproduced, stored in a retrieval system, or transmitted, in any form or by any means, electronic, mechanical photocopying, recording, or otherwise, without the written permission of the Anglican Book Centre.

Typesetting by Jay Tee Graphics Ltd.

Canadian Cataloguing in Publication Data

Main entry under title:

Authority in the Anglican Communion

ISBN 0-919891-61-6

1. Authority (Religion). 2. Anglican Communion
- Doctrines. 3. Howe, John. I. Sykes, S.W.
(Stephen Whitefield). II. Howe, John.

BX5005.A98 1987   262'.8   C87-093014-1

The Rt Revd John William Alexander Howe

Born 1920; educated Saint Chad's College, Durham; ordained 1943 in the Diocese of York; served as curate of All Saints Scarborough 1943–46; chaplain of Adisadel College, Ghana, 1946–50; Vice-Principal Edinburgh Theological College 1950–55; consecrated Bishop of Saint Andrews, Dunkeld and Dunblane 1955; Executive Officer of the Anglican Communion 1969–71; appointed first Secretary General of the Anglican Consultative Council, March 1971; Secretary of the Lambeth Conference 1978. Retired as Secretary General of the Anglican Consultative Council 1982. First ACC Research Fellow 1983-84. Presently Assistant Bishop in the Diocese of Ripon.

Presented to the
Anglican Communion
in recognition of the contribution of
Bishop John Howe
Executive Officer of the Anglican Communion
1969–1971
and
Secretary General, the Anglican Consultative Council
1971–1982
and to
The Lambeth Conference 1978
as an aid to its deliberations on
Authority

ABBREVIATIONS

ACC   Anglican Consultative Council (the meetings of the Council, from 1971 onwards, are indicated thus: ACC-1, etc.).

ARC   Anglican-Roman Catholic Dialogue

ARCIC   Anglican-Roman Catholic International Commission (the first phase of meetings from 1970-1981 is indicated thus: ARCIC I. ARCIC II began in 1983).

BCP   The Book of Common Prayer (1662).

ECUSA   Episcopal Church of the United States of America.

FR   The *Final Report* of ARCIC I.

CONTENTS

FOREWORD

"Anglicans," comments Stephen Sykes in his introduction to these essays "have been seriously exercised about their claim to authority for at least some forty years." An archbishop of Canterbury is better placed than most to appreciate the degree to which this issue is confronting us today. It lies at the heart of so many discussions between churches, as well as of some of the most controversial and sensitive matters which face us all. The nature and exercise of authority will be a vital issue at the 1988 Lambeth Conference.

So I welcome these essays as a timely publication on an important topic. I am especially glad that they bring together contributions from different parts of the Anglican communion with those from an ecumenical perspective. Such breadth of vision is essential if we are to deal adequately with these questions both at the Lambeth Conference and in the daily life of our churches.

That strikes a weighty note, but it is combined with one of gratitude and thanksgiving, since the book reminds us of all that the Anglican communion owes to Bishop John Howe — the first Secretary General to the Anglican Consultative Council. It is impossible to overstate his contribution to the building of coherence and unity within the communion.

I have experienced John's ministry at first hand, and the list of contributors here is eloquent testimony to the respect in which he is held by Christians throughout the world. He is a reminder that there is a profoundly Christian authority in the quiet service of true godliness and faithfulness. In all our debates and discussions that is an authority we must never cease to honour — it is the authority of the Lord we serve.

Foreword by The Most Reverend Robert Runcie,
Archbishop of Canterbury
Essays presented to Bishop John Howe
Edited by Professor Stephen Sykes

Introduction: Why Authority?
S.W. Sykes

This collection of papers focuses specifically on the issue of authority in Anglicanism, and is presented to Bishop John Howe as a token of gratitude and respect on his retirement.

It is significant for our subject that this collection honours a man who served the Anglican communion in a position of great prominence and responsibility but not of much overt power. Of the post of executive officer of the Anglican communion which Bishop Howe held from 1969 to 1971, his predecessor-but-one wrote, in a speech to the 1963 Anglican Congress:

> The Executive Officer is not a master of the Churches, he is their servant. It is the Churches who support him, who direct him in working out their common will. . . . He is not an "assistant to Lambeth Palace" or to the Archbishop of Canterbury. He is an assistant to every archbishop equally, and to every Church. He is obedient to no other person or body than ourselves, collectively, in our separate Churches.[1]

This emphasis on service and corporate obedience carried over in John Howe's person into the new post of secretary-general to the Anglican Consultative Council, which he held from 1971-82. No one who has read his account of those years, and his reflections on general developments in contemporary Anglicanism,[2] will fail to be moved by the note of personal reticence, and, at the same time, by the passion for humility and simplicity which informs the whole book.

A Crisis of Authority?

But *why* the subject of authority? John Howe, who was present at the Washington meeting of primates of the Anglican communion in 1981 and thus participated in the discussion of authority which it initiated, has wise words to say about the fact that authority has again become a matter of concern for Anglicans.

Frequent assertions have been made that Anglicanism lacks authority in adequate measure. This is questionable. An analysis of the position of Christian Churches in general reveals that in most there is more diversity concerning authority than those said to be in authority suppose. Certainly there is not in Anglicanism a universal code or constitution as those terms are normally understood within an organization; nor is there a central jurisdiction. But Anglican appeal to Christ and the gospel, and to faith and order in the apostolic and early Church is well known, although in this, as in any recourse to faith and scripture, the element of human assessment cannot ever be excluded. This is ground that Anglicans and others have gone over many times.[3]

It is correct to say that we have all been here before. To take but one example, in the now well-known 1948 Lambeth Conference document, the question is asked, ''Is Anglicanism based on a sufficiently coherent form of authority to form the nucleus of a world-wide fellowship of Churches, or does its comprehensiveness conceal internal divisions which may cause its disruption?'' (The full text is printed in the Appendix.) As Professor Wright points out in this volume (p.236), the authority of the impressive answer given to this question is not that of the conference as a whole, but of that section of the conference which approved it. The issue is a nice one. It is possible to identify without difficulty resolutions of the whole conference which have fallen dead from the page out of sheer vacuous generality. What is more authoritative can lose authority by disuse. In this case it is evident that what is formally less authoritative has gained authority by use.

Anglicans have, then, been seriously exercised about their claim to authority for at least forty years. Indeed the position given such eloquent expression in 1948 was itself developed over the previous four decades, largely in opposition to the methods employed in the suppression of Catholic Modernism.[4] As Michael Ramsey already correctly pointed out many years ago, it was the work of a generation of men like A.E.J. Rawlinson (who was present at the 1948 Conference), W.L. Knox, T.A. Lacey, J.N. Figgis, and E.G. Selwyn.[5] These were men with very substantial sympathies for what the Catholic Modernists were striving to achieve within the Roman Catholic church by way of freedom of enquiry, if not for each and every theory advanced by the individual Modernists. The sweeping terms of the papal condemnation of Moderism aroused in them both great indignation, and a corresponding confidence that the Anglican communion practised and could articulate an alternative theory. Thus the 1948 Conference document proclaims:

> The positive nature of the authority which binds the Anglican communion together is therefore seen to be moral and spiritual, resting on the truth of the Gospel, and on a charity which is patient and willing to defer to the common mind. (See the Appendix.)

The present volume contains a number of essays which are informed by precisely this conviction, especially those of Professor Skinner, Archbishops Scott and McAdoo and Canon Craston. They are written both from a deep knowledge of and involvement in the practical life of the Anglican communion in the modern world, and also out of immersion in the resources of theological scholarship. Professor Wright, who is properly concerned to prevent an undue smugness from settling upon the references to the 1948 Lambeth document, is at the same time similarly driven to articulate disquiet with recent exercises of the papal power of jurisdiction, which have revived similar apprehensions as those precipitated by the Modernist crisis. It seems that there is still room within world Christianity for the delineation and defense of a now traditional concern of Anglican for ordered freedom.

At the same time we should ask with some persistence, why the subject of authority has returned to the agenda at the present time and with such force? The answer has to do with the fundamental shift in the ecclesiastical ecology, namely the impact of the Second Vatican Council, which has had ramifications in every one of the world communions. If we assume, as we must, that every large organization is in part motivated by concern for its own survival, whatever its overt goals are claimed to be, the survival of non-Roman forms of Christianity has been put in doubt by occupation of what had hitherto been, plausibly, Protestant territory, namely a disposition towards internal reform.

In his recent work on catholicity, the Jesuit theologian Avery Dulles has listed no less than ten ways in which the Council internalized Protestant criticism.[6] The implication is plainly that Protestantism has become redundant; and if Protestantism, then how much more the Anglican communion. Whether or not it is possible to be as sanguine as is Dulles about the character of the internal dialectic now said to be ineradicable within Catholicism, the pressure is plainly upon non-Romans to say why they continue in schism. The act of remaining in schism is evidently an act only justifiable upon the best grounds. Thus the question, But why authority?, presses upon Anglicans with new urgency.

The Grounds of Anglicanism

It is a matter of fact that Anglicans have grown rather unused to self-justification. As an Englishman, one has to say with regret and penitence that this has much to do with an inherited sense of cultural superiority. The monarchy, the cathedrals, the Universities of Oxford and Cambridge, the literary inheritance of the Prayer Book, Authorized Version, and the classic poets seemed like possessions of such transcendent value as to be beyond mere justification. Abroad, the power of the Empire and the reputation of the English gentleman for moderation, courtesy, and fair play undergirded the implicit claim that Anglicanism was an obviously desirable voice in world Christianity — a modest enough claim, it might be thought, but one which regularly infuriated those who perceived in it the cancer of superiority.

But, of course, there were elements of truth in the claim. It would indeed be strange if an ecclesiastical tradition so rooted in reading of the scriptures as Anglicanism had preserved nothing of value. At the same time justification for the continuation of Anglican separation from the papacy had fallen into difficulties, some of Anglicanism's own making, some of a more general character.

Of its own making was the impasse caused by first isolating the theologians of the classic era of Anglican apologetic, Richard Hooker and the Caroline divines, and then ignoring them. Hooker, it was insisted, was a theologian independent of the continental Reformation, and the Caroline divines preserved

Anglicanism from Protestant extremism. But it was, and is, comparatively rare for Anglicans to be learned enough in Reformation studies for this claim to be plausible. And in an era which demanded strenuous new theological work to meet the challenges of Darwin, Marx, and Freud, the *cordon sanitaire* erected around the seventeenth-century fathers seemed increasingly remote, precious, and implausible. Even now, when contemporary Catholic sacramental thought bears so much resemblance to certain strands of seventeenth-century Anglicanism, it is almost impossible to find Anglican scholars with the depth of learning to explore the relationships.

Not of Anglican making, on the other hand, was the general problem about reasoning from scripture. Article VI of the Thirty-nine Articles, together with Articles XX and XXI and the Prayer Book Ordinal, make quite clear that what cannot be proved by scripture cannot be proclaimed as an article of faith necessary to salvation. The appeal to scripture was foundational for the development of Anglicanism, not only since it provided ground for objecting to those additional articles of faith required by the Church of Rome, but also to counter the Presbyterian claim that that church embodied, *iure divino*, the order of ministry found in the New Testament. Specifically against Beza and the practice of the Church in Scotland, the Prayer Book Ordinal insisted in 1662 that it was plain to anyone reading Holy Scripture that there had existed from the apostles' days three orders of ministers in Christ's church, bishops, priests, and deacons. This was, plainly, proving a doctrine by reference to Holy Scripture.

Arguments of that kind, however, have been undermined both by developments in the study of the churches of the New Testament period and by further consideration of the complexity of the relations of scripture and tradition. Although biblical criticism was largely developed in Protestant circles, and was strenuously resisted for more than a hundred years in official Catholicism, the historical concerns of the critics are apparently more damaging to a theological structure supposedly built upon the principle, "by scripture alone." Anglicans have sometimes claimed immunity from this difficulty on the grounds of their deeper respect for the traditions of the primitive church. But candour compels one to add serious qualifications to this claim. The theory propounded by Canon A5 of the Church of England concerning the authority of the fathers for doctrine in that church explicitly restricts its scope to "such teachings of the ancient Fathers as are agreeable to the said Scriptures." And even if one were to discount this Canon as of limited validity in the other provinces of the Anglican communion, the status of the primitive church would remain ambiguous. One must ask not merely how one justifies the apparently arbitrary number of the centuries, or the number of the councils held to embody authoritative voices, but whether there are any considerations which could possibly justify separating the earlier from the later centuries. The reasons which drew John Henry Newman out of the Church of England were not trivial, and call for renewed examination.

That Anglicans have been caught in a difficulty shared by the whole of modern Protestantism is evident when one examines the modifications of the claim, cited above, that the threefold office derives, *expressis verbis*, from the New Testament. The American Book of Common Prayer, for instance, now states in its preface to the ordination rites:

> The Holy Scriptures and ancient Christian writers make it clear that from the apostles' time, there have been *different* ministries within the Church. In particular, *since* the time of the New Testament, three distinct orders of ordained ministers have been characteristic of Christ's holy catholic Church (my emphasis).

A further example of changed expression is found in ARCIC where Anglican members agreed to the following statement:

> The early churches may well have had considerable diversity in the structure of pastoral ministry, though it is clear that some churches were headed by ministers who were called *episkopoi* and *presbyteroi*. While the first missionary churches were not a loose aggregation of autonomous communities, we have no evidence that "bishops" and "presbyters" were appointed everywhere in the primitive period . . . [T]he full emergence of the threefold ministry of bishop, presbyter and deacon required a longer period than the apostolic age. (FR p.32)

Though the conclusions defended are identical, the argument rests now on new grounds. It is not that tradition has been swapped for scripture as the source of authority. That would be altogether a crude misrepresentation of the situation. Rather something which has grounds in "normative principles governing the purpose and function of the ministry" in scriptures has been *effected* by the authoritative decision of the very early church. Exactly the same argument could be deployed to justify the acceptance of the New Testament Canon and the doctrine of the Trinity, both of which are arguably *grounded* in scripture. Scripture is thus not to be isolated as a criterion from the tradition in which it has been read.

The important point for the issue of authority among Anglicans is this: What, if anything, separates us from the kind of reading of the scriptures which has characterized Catholicism from the beginning, namely, the sort of reading which finds grounds in scripture for a universal Petrine ministry and for Mariology. The issues press home not merely in the conservative, but also at the radical end of the spectrum. Given that it could not be held to be sufficient to rule out a certain course of action, for example, ordaining women to the priesthood, simply on the grounds that it was "unknown in the New Testament churches," the controversy which new proposals generate require authoritative judgement. The Anglican communion, or any one province of it, appears to be simply too small a unit and too lacking in the relevant expertise to make a competent decision.

These I take to be among the reasons for a more anxious inquiry into authority at the present time. Whether or not it is adequate to seek to extend the life of a now traditional Anglican theme, that of ordered liberty, in the new context may be variously evaluated. What is certain is the fact that there will be few Anglicans satisfied on reflection with the see-saw view of ecumenism, according to which movement in the direction of Catholic order is thought to threaten Protestant freedom, and vice versa. The dominance of that image is a sure recipe for sociological impasse. If Anglicanism has any business in world Christianity at all, its eyes must be firmly upon the future, and its necessary judgements made without the anxious timidity of an internally unbalanced go-between.

Synodical Government

As I have already suggested, the subject of authority is three-cornered, having to do not merely with theology, but with structures and with practices. A second major theme of this collection of essays relates to the development within Anglicanism of the practice of synodical government, and the locating of the bishop in synodical association with clergy and laity. Bishop Nuttall's fascinating description of the early days of that process in Southern Africa, Canon Chittleborough's research on the concept of bishop-in-synod, and Dr. White's examination of the applicability of the notions of collegiality and conciliarity all focus on what is now a differientiating mark of the Anglican communion.

That things are not well with synodical goverment in the Church of England will be obvious to readers of a recent collection, *The Synod of Westminster, Do we need it?*, in which a variety of contradictory complaints and recommendations come to the surface.[7] What is apparent from this collection, and what Anglicans from other provinces often remark upon, is the English absence of awareness of how synods *outside* England have served the church. The words of John Howe, who has more experience of synods in the Anglican communion than any person alive today, should be noted:

> There is still a long way to go in learning how to use synods, but there should be no limit to thanksgiving that throughout the Anglican communion they exist, and exist because Christian people wanted them.[8]

The historical roots of this practice with Anglicanism are complex, but theologically they are surely connected to the fact, of which the English reformers made so much, that the Bible, the unique criterion of true Christian doctrine, was to be read publicly in the language of the people. At the risk of repeating something I have said elsewhere, it cannot be accidental that the doctrine of the sufficiency of Holy Scripture for salvation found in Articles VI, XX, and XXI, and reinforced in the rituals of the Prayer Book Ordinal, are given explicit support by Cranmer in his explanation of his Prayer Book.[9] In the preface ''Concerning the Service of the Church,'' he commends the patristic practice of reading the whole Bible once every year, not just for the edification of the clergy, but so that ''the people (by daily hearing of holy Scripture read in the Church) might continually profit more and more in the knowledge of God, and be the more informed with the love of his true religion.''[10] The possession by ordinary clergy and by the laity of the gospel in their own tongue, interpreted by, and interpreting the liturgy of the church, is crucial for the Anglican understanding of authority. It means that there actually is a widely distributed source of authority and a means of judging, independently if need be, whether the truth of the gospel is being upheld by those with the most obvious access to the decision-making process.

The same Anglican documents, it should be noted, also affirm quite unequivocally that there is a hierarchy of ministerial order charged with exercising discipline in various matters. The ordained ministry has the authority of Christ (Article XXVI). It is expected that evil ministers will be subject to the discipline of the church (Article XXXIII). Furthermore, bishops are specifically asked whether they will seek a true interpretation of the scriptures when controversy arises, and exercise discipline according to their scripturally bestowed authority.[11]

The combination of a theological empowering of the whole people of God with a hierarchical structure in the church creates in Anglicanism a tension which is now also perceptible in the documents of the Second Vatican Council. Here, especially in the *Constitution on the Sacred Liturgy (II)*, it is made clear that active participation in a vernacular liturgy is seen as a source of enrichment to the laity, who are also encouraged to undertake the study of the scriptures. There are already clear signs that an instructed and active Roman Catholic laity are unlikely to be satisfied with the role of passivity inside the structures of the church assigned them by the unmodified retention of hierarchical government. Here one should draw attention in particular to one response to ARCIC, that of the American Episcopal church, cited by Professor Wright on pp.241-242, which complains of inadequacy in precisely this matter.

Professor Wright points out, with justice, that it was in the United States that the practice of including laity in synods began, and from which it spread to other parts of the Anglican communion. The combination of lay participation with a hierarchy was bound to lead to tension and is not patient of any obvious solution. But Anglicans as a whole have now long experience of what is meant in practice by the phrase, "the bishop in synodical association with the clergy and laity." It was a form of government recommended by William Gladstone to Bishop Selwyn on his creation of a constitution for the "Branch of the United Church of England and Ireland in New Zealand" in 1857, and one which was influential for the constitutions of the Irish church (1870), and the churches of South Africa (1870), the West Indies (1883), Japan (1887), Canada (1889), and China (1921). The inclusion of the laity was, in each case, a matter of principle deriving from the three-fold obligation of the baptismal commission, and not a matter of concession to fashionable theories of representation. A recent writer has held that the origins of synodical government within the Church of England were sociological rather than theological — though the separation of categories is eminently challengeable. The less excusable, therefore, is the Church of England's unwillingness to examine the Anglican communion's experience, and to admit to the comparative immaturity of its own arrangements.[12]

It is, of course, commonly objected that the structure and procedures of synodical government in any given country are frequently modelled on the obtaining political order, especially in England and the United States. The point is an important one, but cannot be regarded as a ground for dismissing synodical government per se. As Bishop Howe has pointed out, the meaning of "synod" is that people set out to find how in Christ's cause they can find a way forward together. The vital factor is that participation relates to the whole people of God; "concern is more with theology than democracy."[13] These words significantly echo the opening paragraph of the report on the position of the laity in the church, produced for the Canterbury Convocation as long ago as 1902, and deserving of careful attention:

The Church of the apostolic age was neither democratic nor despotic. Not democratic: for the pleasure of the multiude was not the ultimate sanction of the office of its leaders. Not despotic: for its officers were not lords over subjects, but divinely commissioned leaders of a divine society of brethren. What it was in general idea may be best expressed by the word ''collective'' or ''corporate''. The life and action of the Church were the life and action of the whole body. The officers acted with, not instead of, the community; and the community acted with, not in mere obedience under, its officers. Still less could it supersede or act apart from them. The priniciple follows directly from the truth that the Holy Spirit was given to the body as a whole. In nothing less than the whole body does the fullness of the Spirit reside — for illumination or for power.[14]

No one denies that such lofty sentiments are far from being achieved. Perhaps the major drawback of synodical government is that, by its very publicity, it affords a splendid theatre for human folly; and there is no practical expression of the exercise of authority immune from folly.

If it should be asked where are the essays relating to the *actual* exercise of authority in Anglicanism, which was the third element of our three-cornered scheme, one is embarassed. Perhaps it should be admitted that no one really knows whether a given church exercises its authority well or not. Part of our difficulty here lies with paradigms of effective leadership. John Howe has shown himself notably reticent about the modern assumption that a bishop should be a leader in the modern executive or commercial sense of that term.[15] Professor Pobee, in this volume, pertinently draws attention to African paradigms of authority (pp. 197-200). Plainly Christians in position of authority are influenced by what their cultures suggest to be the appropriate or desirable ways of exercising that authority. The performance of leaders may be openly evaluated by criteria which have little enough to do with the Christian gospel. But that all those who exercise authority should be open to criticism of it, I take to be a plain implication of the gospel. Modern sociology has developed some acute techniques for unmasking the numerous disguises of power in human structures and relations from which the churches ought to be prepared to learn.

The Future

The intention of these essays is utterly towards the future. Part of that future is the responsible discussion of a series of challenging and original ecumenical documents. Hence as a third section, this book contains essays on ecumenical matters, among which we are delighted to include two from the pens of most distinguished non-Anglicans.

But it is also certain that a future church will need more than sound theology, good structures, and a continuing process of internal reconciliation. It will need also spiritual resources of great depth, if men and women are to be found who will be capable of rising to the religious and ethical challenges of the future of humanity. John Howe has warned us that the last quarter of a century has not been a great spiritual age in the Anglican communion.[16] We should not be tempted, in an understandable concern for structures, hierarchies, and leadership to overlook the fact that tomorrow's occupants of positions of authority are recruited from today's parishes. Patterns of humility, quietness, integrity, and service are learnt early in life. The future exercise of authority is a matter for us all.

Notes

1. Bishop Stephen Bayne, *Report of the Anglican Congress 1963*, 186.
2. John Howe, *Highways and Hedges, Anglicanism and the Universal Church* (London, 1985).
3. Ibid., 97-8.
4. Gabriel Daly O.S.A., in *Transcendence and Immanence, A Study in Catholic Moderism and Integralism* (Oxford, 1980), likens the campaign against the Modernists to that mounted against communists by Senator Joseph McCarthy in the U.S.A., 218.
5. A.M. Ramsey, *From Gore to Temple* (London, 1960), 101-106.
6. A. Dulles, *The Catholicity of the Church* (Oxford, 1985), 150-163.
7. Edited by Peter Moore, London, 1986. The work is notably contradictory on the twin issues of lay involvement in synod, which some do not see as enough of a reality, whilst others think it all too much of one, and of the relationship to the state, which some deplore, and others think has been disgracefully eroded.
8. Howe, 51.
9. *The Integrity of Anglicanism* (London, 1978), ch.7, "Authority in Anglicanism"; "Authority in the Anglican Communion," in *Authority in the Anglican Communion* (London, 1981); "ARCIC and the

Papacy: An Examination of the Documents on Authority," in *Modern Churchman*, xxv (1982), 8-18; "Who has the say in the Church? An Anglican Response," in H. Küng and J. Moltmann eds., *Concilium*, 148 (1982), 32-37; "Authority in Anglicanism, Again," M. Darrol Bryant, *The Future of Anglican Theology* (Toronto Studies in Theology, 17, New York and Toronto, 1983) 167-190.

10. Preface of the 1549 Prayer Book, modelled upon the preface to a breviary commissioned by Pope Paul III, but abandoned for its radicalism. Massey Shepherd points out the remarkable similarities between Cranmer's preface and passages in the Second Vatican Council's Constitution on the Liturgy, esp. 1.21, 1.34-6, 4.91-2; see "The Liturgy" in B.C. Pawley, *The Second Vatican Council, Studies by eight Anglican observers* (London, 1967), 171-2.

11. It is important to emphasize these considerations, whilst recognizing the historical and sociological factors minimizing their force. See K.A. Thompson, *Bureaucracy and Church Reform, The Organizational Response of the Church of England to Social Change 1800-1965* (Oxford, 1970), esp. ch. IV.

12. There is one reference in *The Synod of Westminster, Do we need it?* to the church outside England. This is to New Zealand. Here, it should be noted, the tractarian Bishop Selwyn insisted on lay participation so strongly that he includes it in the church's irrevocable fundamental provisions. See J.H. Evans, *Churchman Militant, George Augustus Selwyn, Bishop of New Zealand and Lichfield* (London, 1964), esp. 138-141, 146-7, and 163-4.

13. Howe, 50f.

14. These words were cited by the evangelical layman whose motion in the Church Assembly in 1953 began the process which led to synodical government in England. See Hugh Craig, "A Question of Confidence," in P. Moore, *The Synod of Westminster, Do we need it?*, 25.

15. Howe, 55.

16. Howe, 215.

Part One
The Theology of Authority

Ideology, Authority, and Faith
John E. Skinner

"If reality is not redemptive, it is not moral." This poignant statement by P.T. Forsyth[1] is one of those remarkable expressions which puts into focus the posture of those who call themselves Jews and Christians. It also may confirm the perspective of many secular humanists who are still living with the inheritance of their Judaeo-Christian past but find it difficult to admit it.

What is implicit in such an assertion? Certain affirmations of faith are involved. The first affirmation is that reality (the created world) has the capacity within it to mediate or convey a salvific or redemptive presence. That which is, also, is ultimately good, has worth and value, and the two, fact and value, cannot be ultimately alienated. The second affirmation is that all derived reality, social constructions of reality, should be media for the creative and redemptive presence implicit in reality itself. When this is not the case, tensions arise between good and evil, fact and value, creation and redemption, which result in various kinds of dualistic explanation.

Such dualisms have been many in the history of thought. One of the most damaging found expression when the source of reality (creator) became alienated from the source of value and worth (redeemer). In this instance the creator was viewed as inferior and evil and needed to be supplanted by a redeemer. A dualism between good and evil, thus, takes on many different forms but is reducible to the ultimate split between creator and redeemer.

Another dualism is the body/soul dichotomy. This can be expressed in a number of ways. For our purposes it may be translated into a dualism between a physical and mental reality. In the modern world this is brought into prominence by the bifurcation associated with Descartes, *res cogitans/res extensa* (thought and extension). Reality becomes identified more and more with mathematical quantification and the subject/object dichotomy develops a novel importance.

From the quantification and reduction of reality to a Newtonian mechanistic universe, the exorcism of any mental reality may be accomplished; as a result, the mental ghost is dissociated eventually from the physical machine. The ghostly mental reality, then, becomes dismissed as emotive and subjective and the dualism is apparently eliminated. Its elimination, however, places all value and worth issues in the subjective sphere and consequently they are alientated from the verifiable, quantifiable reality. A reversal of the early split between creator and redeemer is evident. Now fact is crowned as supreme and value is denigrated. The creator, in this case, the technological reason devoid of any value judgements, supplants the redeemer, affirmations of value and worth implicit in reality and not mere subjective appendages. So in whatever way these dualisms assert themselves, they finally negate the ultimate identification of fact and value which is the essence of Jewish and Christian faith, and is also implied in some expressions of secular humanism.

Ideology

The tilting of emphasis toward the quantitative factual object was bound to have its retractors and resisters. From Pascal's passionate veto of Descartes, from Kant's valiant attempt to rescue value and worth in his concept of the practical reason, from Hegel's imaginative, speculative synthesis of subject and object, to Kierkegaard's violent swing of the pendulum towards subjectivity and its final issue in existentialism, to Marx's subjectification of all reality as an expression of political and economic bias, to the modern sociology of knowledge and its views on the social construction of reality,[2] the redemptive, moral, and value aspects make their mark.

Today a danger exists that all reality will be reduced to ideologies and the complete subjectification of reality will gain supremacy. This can be seen even in the legitimate critique of modern science with its reductionistic tendencies (fact over value),[3] and it is obvious in the passionate expressions involved in social philosophies and theologies of liberation. The obsession with liberation is a reminder of the Gnostics of old who negated the creator in favour of a redemption from the then given reality. This does not mean that no legitimate basis exists for resistance to oppressive regimes and individuals, but the obsession arises when through exaggeration all reality up to the present is perceived as one great conspiracy against the oppressed group.

What began as a legitimate resistance to the reductionism of the technogical reason and the alienation of the moral dimension from factical reality may result in the eventual subjectification of all reality. Facts, then, are wholly subordinate to ideological systems which serve as the only true way to perceive and express what is the case. All history becomes revisionist in the worst sense, because no critical restraint is necessary in reconstructing the past. Through the dictates of an ideological agenda, the butchery of sacred and secular texts, in order to make them less oppressive and to bring them in line with the new redemption which is guaranteed by an ideological conformity, is perceived as legitimate. Thus, all human behaviour is judged in terms of its conformity or lack of it to the reigning ideological system.

Ideology is an attempt to capture the infinite, to enclose transcendence, and to negate all critical thought. Ideology is a value system, alientated from factuality, which then seeks to dominate and to dictate what is the case. Ideology is the subjectification of all reality, the reduction of transcendence to a radical immanence, and the claim to be a total embodiment of all value and redemption. It is the direct opposite of a facticity devoid of value. Concrete evidence for such ideological pretension is abundant. Fundamentalistic religion, secular/political schemes, and tendencies within recent liberationist movements are three examples.

In the Judaeo-Christian tradition, which has had its share of such ideological fixity in its rigid orthodoxies of past and present, the same symptoms can and do appear. A rigid fundamentalism, e.g., the moral majority emphasis in evangelical Protestantism in the United States, is an attempt to capture the infinite, to enclose transcendence, and to negate all critical thought. Rigid fundamentalism is an ideological posture of the worst possible type. It is a subjectification of all reality based on the collective spirit of ecclesiastical groups, and it is an attempt to define all value (redemption) in terms of inclusion or exclusion from its domain.

Hannah Arendt in *The Origins of Totalitarianism* has decribed the way such ideology functions in the secular/political sphere whether its political philosophy is expressive of right-wing fascism or left-wing socialism and communism. The enclosure of all value (redemption) in the political structure is maintained at all costs. The totalitarian system becomes the only source of value and worth. It is the chosen vessel of redemption. Any counter-claims of a chosen people of God are met by extermination of such anomalous vermin. Arendt's evaluation of Stalinism and Hitlerism is a vivid portrayal of a subjectification of reality coupled with the coercive power which accompanies such ideological pretension.

Another example of an ideology of the secular/social type is expressed through the reduction of all value to a production/consumption model. Nothing has worth which does not produce something that can be consumed. All value is reduced in this model in a way similar to the quantification of all factuality in a mechanistic view of reality. Evidence of the influence of this reductionism is now surfacing in our use of language. ''Buy'' or ''own'' are used as synonyms for ''accept'' even in philosophical and theological disputation, and sexual r*eproduction* has put into eclipse sexual pro*creation*. People who do not produce are made to feel guilty about even their own being. Such guilt is felt since there is no value or worth implicit in being itself. Thus each new moment of life must justify itself in terms of what it produces. It produces in order to consume. It consumes in order to produce. As a result, value and worth are restricted to this vicious circle. An example of this is furnished unwittingly by the following statement: ''The women's liberation movement made the non-working woman become professional about shopping in order to justify her existence.''[4] Unless people become a part of this giant production machine, they have no value.

The rise of liberationism is another important development and may serve as an illustration of the alienation of being and worth, fact and value. Liberation philosophies and theologies gain legitimacy from their opposition to dehumanizing structures either in a reduction of reality to a quantified factuality or in the many collective subjectivities which seek to rescue value and worth for some and at the expense of others. The subjectification of reality is at work here in the subtle projections of quasi-objective systems which attempt to enclose all reality and worth and develop gradations of value dependent upon inclusion or exclusion from the power structure. Such inclusions and exclusions are often based on racist, sexist, and elitist criteria. Resistance to this kind of oppression is indeed legitimate and warranted. The foundation for such resistance should be anchored in the fundamental affirmation that fact and value are ultimately one, and that all created reality needs to be included.

Such resistance, however, may develop its own ideologies and may become as oppressive as its enemy. What begins as a legitimate revolution eventuates in oppressive regimes or movements which permit no dissent. How can a person dissent from the total encapsulation of all worth and value in the regime or movement? Such dissent is called counter-revolutionary since the values of revolution and resistance are presumed to be completely conserved in the new redemption, the oppressive regime or movement itself.

Particular expressions of the liberation emphasis can be seen currently in the struggle of blacks and in the women's movement now gaining strength.[5] Racist exclusion is a denial of value and worth to persons simply because of their colour. Resistance here is indeed legitimate. Women have also found themselves subordinated to men in terms of value and worth, and patriarchal distortions are obvious when viewed from a criticial posture and not from the tacit acceptance of the distortions to be a part of reality itself.

Subjectifications of reality which produced such exclusions and distortions are now being resisted by new subjectifications of reality which face the same danger. When confronting racism, the possible creation of an ideology which excludes white people, or which looks upon them as evil, is always a temptation. Tendencies in this direction are usually restrained but break out from time to time with some justification.

Some tendencies in the new redemption being advocated by radical feminists are beginning to surface gradually and may serve as examples of an ideology which assumes that all the past has been dominated by male structures which have denigrated women, and only the future as possibility remains for women since the past is oppressive and demonic. A dualism arises between the female (good) and the male (evil), and all of reality must be recreated in the image of this new good. In theology transcendence is reduced to the masculine imagery of God which is oppressive. Only a radical immanence which negates the past evil tradition and creates in each new moment the value and worth which expresses the good (female value) is possible. The only transcendence is in each future moment which, when it is actualized, perishes into the dead past. Such a radical feminism might eventually become a new religion and attempt to displace what is described as the old, oppressive, patriarchal, male fertility cults of Judaism and Christianity.

It can be concluded from this examination of ideologies of a fundamentalist, secular/political, and liberationist type, that the form or structure tends to be similar in all three; the content of the claims made is different. The ideological system takes the place of transcendence and all possibility is dictated by what is implicit in such enclosures.

When value and worth (redemption) are alienated from fact (creation), the emergence of such conflicting ideologies or collective subjectivities occurs. This is the direct result of the alienation of the individual also. The Cartesian *res cogitans* and the Leibnizian monad are models for an isolated individual subject. When such isolated individual subjects come together in collective subjectivities, ideology arises as a means to gain at least a semblance of value and worth for those contained within the particular collectives. Thus a conflict of gods many, lords many, and ideologies many, is evident.

Is there any solution to this impasse? The only solution arises when an individual subjectivity becomes aware of its finitude, its limits, when confronted by another individual subjectivity. The possibility of breakthrough occurs when an intersubjective dynamic develops which makes possible the discovery of a reality transcending each subject and yet which makes it possible for each subject to relate to the other. Mutual relation is the first step towards a genuine intersubjective dynamic, and a genuine intersubjective dynamic is fundamental in the discovery that transcendent reality discloses itself and can be encountered, but it cannot be ultimately entombed either in a factical reductionism or in an ideological reductionism.

This certainly applies to the conflict between ideological groups who make exclusive claims in regard to redemption, value, and worth. To coin a phrase, they are collective monads, needing to break out of their isolation, to discover their finitude, and to develop a mutual relation with other collective monads. When this happens, they cease to be ideological groups and become genuine human communities open to each other, seeking reconciliation with each other, and also communities which respond to the transcendent reality which discloses itself but can never be captured or entombed.

It must also be said that the reduction of all reality to a quantified factuality devoid of value and worth has become a kind of collective monad itself. The same need to break out of its protective isolation, to discover its finitude, is present. Whenever that happens, the reality, which transcends and is the source of both created fact and value, can disclose itself.

The essence of the Judaeo-Christian tradition that ultimately creation and redemption, fact and value, being and worth, are one, needs to be reaffirmed. P.T. Forsyth is right: if reality is not redemptive, it is not moral. It is also true that redemption must be anchored in reality. If it is not, then, such a quasi-redemption is both illusory and immoral.

Authority

It is axiomatic that when ideology prevails, authority is in eclipse. When social structures, secular or religious, make exclusive claims to be the possessors of value and worth, they become alien to the human moral struggle of those excluded and oppressed by such structures. They become quasi-objective substitutes for reality and they maintain their position through the use of coercive power.

Such power alienates and destroys any possible openness to a transcendence which reveals the finitude both of social structures and of individuals. Ideological systems, therefore, need coercive power in order to enforce their redemption, to protect their value, and to encapsulate their worth. Enforced conformity to the ideological system becomes the equivalent of redemption. Liberation thus is transformed into enslavement.

Legitimate authority is the direct opposite of coercive power. Authority must be anchored in the ultimate identification of fact and value (creator and redeemer). The source of all authority is found in such an ultimate identification.

From the standpoint of the Judaeo-Christian tradition, all authority is derived from God and the revelatory constellation of events which focus ultimacy or transcendence for us. In all revelation both a communal and personal response is a necessary part of a revelatory event. From such a response arise the various symbols and images which mediate the presence of God in the historical situation. Such a communal and personal response is the essence of faith.

For Christians the ultimate source of authority is in the divine revelation of God focused in Jesus Christ. When Christians affirm that disclosure, affirm that the Word which was from the beginning became flesh in a definitive way in Jesus of Nazareth, it is then possible to conclude that the Word of God, the self-disclosure of the Divine Reality, is a creative and redemptive activity which expresses itself both in nature and in history. This creative and redemptive activity, as it is mediated, is a nurturing and liberating presence at work subtly in nature, in history, and in the various cultural and ecclesiastical fabrications of reality achieved through human action and work. Authority, therefore, is anchored ultimately in God, and in its various expressions should reflect the creative and redemptive activity which is its ultimate source.

Roadblocks to such a mediation of authority due to erroneous views of reality, factuality divorced from value and worth, and pretentious claims for the cultural fabric, particular subjectifications of reality claiming to be the exclusive conduits for value and worth, become sinful distortions with a social and personal character. Such distortions result in the disappearance of authority and in the negation of a nurturing and liberating presence. The sheer power of a smothering oppression takes over. Coercion eliminates nurture and liberation.

In an etymological analysis the word, *authority*, has a Latin origin. The Latin verb, *augere*, which means, "to make increase, to cause to grow, to fertilize, to make fertile, to strengthen, to increase, or to enlarge" is the verb root. The noun root is *auctor* which means, "doer, causer, creator of a work of art, the founder of a family, beginner, the leader, maker of a proposal, and author." Both verb and noun roots are reflected in *auctoritas*, authority.

The one word which arises that sums up best both the verb and noun roots is *nurture*.[6] *Augere*, with its emphasis on fertilization, causing to grow, and strengthening; and *auctor*, with its focus on beginning, author, creator, and founder, presuppose nurture as the context within which such activities can happen.

The other Latin word, *imperium*, which is often equated with authority, has a different meaning. It connotes an order, command, power, mastery, government, and also military power. If such power is qualified by *auctoritas*, then, legitimate authority reigns. If such power is alienated from *auctoritas*, then, coercive power ascends the stage and imperial power becomes a synonym for coercion.

Authority must be contrasted to coercive power. Authority as nurture, anchored ultimately in the source of all reality, appears to be the proper meaning of the word. This conclusion occasions the following definition of authority: that kind of structured reality, whether social or personal, which through nurture and cultivation enables individuals to become truly centred selves or persons, and thus, relatively free beings.[7]

This definition needs to be examined carefully in order to determine its accuracy. Structured reality presupposes both a corporate or social dimension to authority, as well as a personal, individual dimension. All reality has structure whether it is found in nature or in the derivative social structures of civilization and culture.

The assumption is that such structures of reality may be legitimate media for the expression of a nurturing and liberating presence derived from the source of all reality, the creator and redeemer. Finite social structures, moreover, have the capacity to mediate the infinite or transcendent (*finitum capax infiniti*). Such an observation is important not only for sacramental theology, but also should include the structures of nature, culture, and church. Furthermore, a structured person is a dynamic human reality which has its life anchored both in transcendence and also has a consistent thread of identity running through the serial moments of its being. It is assumed that such a personal structure also has the capacity to be a medium for a nurturing and liberating presence derived from the creative and redemptive activity of God in nature and in history.

The second part of the definition assumes that this capacity for nurture and cultivation enables human beings, and perhaps other creatures of nature as well in different ways,[8] to become truly centred selves or persons. This means that reality itself is concerned about its emergents and a salvific presence is implicit there for the nurture and cultivation of the emerging new creatures. Structures are not ends in themselves but servants of the nurturing and cultivating process. If particular structures cease to be nurturing and cultivating matrices, alienation results; and they become centres of coercion rather than matrices of nurture.

The result of the nurturing process should be truly centred selves or persons who are relatively free beings. All creatures should have a measure of relative freedom whether they are found in the microcosmic levels of reality or as arising as more complicated structures of the macrocosmic levels. It can be observed that the primary difference between inorganic and organic realities is this degree of relative freedom. Inorganic reality is much more conformal to its reigning structures, while life is a bid for freedom, to use a phrase of A.N. Whitehead. When human life is considered, this affirmation is fundamental. Human beings hover between finitude and infinitude. Finitude represents dependence on nurturing and cultivating structures both for survival and maturation. Infinitude denotes breakthroughs which make it possible for the individual person to be a relatively free being.

It is precisely within such a tensive relationship between dependence and relative freedom that encounters with transcendence are possible. That reality which discloses itself but cannot be entombed serves as the salvific and redemptive anchor both for social structures and persons. The unity between fact and value, creation and redemption, being and worth, is thus both assumed and affirmed.

Such a definition of authority is quite different from popular usage. Authority is erroneously equated with power and usually with various forms of coercion. The person or group with authority is the person or group which wields the biggest stick or has the potential for coercing others into conformity. In contrast, the paradox is that the person or group which possesses genuine authority, which is a nurturing and cultivating matrix, which enables selves or persons to become relatively free beings, needs no coercive power to achieve its ends.

Because of the split between fact and value described in the discussion concerning ideology, is it possible that in our current age there is no such reality as authority? Do only conflicting power structures exist which seek to enclose all of reality within their ken and to alienate whatever does not fit into such enclosures?

Has authority disappeared in the modern world? Are revelatory events, which served both as an historical beginning and also as a definitive focus for transcendence, lost? Is the split between fact and value irreversible? Are we sentenced forever to a warfare between collective subjectivities, in which ideology takes the place of transcendence as conveyed through revelatory events, and the symbols which arise in response to such events? Is authority as nurture and cultivation, as an expression of the creative and redemptive presence of God, forever to be replaced by coercive power in various guises? Are nurture and cultivation to be negated and behavioural conditioning and thought control to prevail? Are collective subjectivities which demand conformity and inclusion wholly within their structures to replace nurturing and cultivating matrices which have as their purpose the emergence of responsible, relatively free, human beings?

These are poignant questions which need to be answered. The answers will determine whether future generations will be slave or free; whether there will be a rediscovery of that authority which is a salvific presence derived from the creative and redemptive activity of God in nature and in history; whether the ultimate unity of fact and value will be affirmed and acknowledged; or whether the warfare of ideologies grasping for quasi-redemptive solutions based on coercive power will continue on its destructive and demonic path.

Faith

Ideology is fundamentally a cloak for unbelief. It hides its failure to acknowledge the ultimate identity of creator and redeemer, fact and value. In a desperate manner, ideology seeks to protect its adherents from the ultimate meaninglessness of a facticity devoid of value through the projection of quasi-objective structures of value and worth offered as opiates for a pervasive despair. Ideology is the expression of human sin. No trust is present which can affirm that the source of all reality is an accepting and redemptive presence. Instead, human fabrications are posited as substitutes for transcendence, and transcendence itself is imaged as enemy, as nothingness, as the ultimate oppressor.

This fundamental lack of belief, lack of trust, lack of acceptance of the implicit redemptive and salvific presence in nature and in history (grace: the ultimate acceptance of all) is covered up by all ideological systems. The "true believers" who are enclosed in such systems are actually the ultimate a-theists, those without genuine faith in the transcendent source both of fact and value, creation and redemption. Ideology thus cloaks a lack of genuine faith with a projected semblance of faith often couched in the language of passionate commitment and firm belief.

Ideology is an idolatrous substitution of what is proximate and finite for what is ultimate and transcendent. Transcendence is viewed as the enemy: the nothingness which swallows all things. Resistance to such an ultimate enemy arises through proximate attempts to protect human beings from transcendent reality itself: the enemy which has no meaning, worth, or value. Such prox- imate structures become enclosures of value and worth for those included within them. An ultimate concern, to use Paul Tillich's phrase, for a proximate collective subjectivity is an idolatrous form of faith which negates genuine faith.

Is there any alternative to such an idolatrous preoccupation with ideological pretensions? The answer of genuine faith expressed both in Judaism and Christianity is an affirmative one. And that faith may also be tacitly present in the perspective of many secular humanists who have become offended by the traditional imagery which mediates that faith, because such imagery has been used as a way of commending particular religious ideologies which are actually a negation of that fundamental faith.

Jews, Christians, and secular humanists need to affirm and reaf- firm the ultimate identification of fact and value, being and worth, and in that affirmation the tacit acknowledgement of a creative and redemptive activity of a benevolent transcendence will be pre- sent. When such affirmations are made, it is then possible to see that such a creative and redemptive presence can be mediated in nature, in history, and in various social, cultural, and eccles- iastical fabrications. Authority as nurture and cultivation resulting in the emergence of relatively free beings can be acknowledged. Furthermore, within the tensive relationship between nurturing and cultivating structures, secular and religious, and relatively free beings who emerge from such matrices, models for a critical faith can be developed.

A critical faith, whether it is expressed as secular or religious, will not attempt to capture the infinite in its work, nor will it con- fuse a legitimate finite or proximate nurturing structure as the complete enclosure of transcendence, nor treat it as a substitute for transcendence. Instead, finite structures will be affirmed as particular media for the creative and redemptive activity of transcendence, and as a result they will be its servants.

The authority of such structures will be found precisely when they serve as conduits for the nurture and cultivation which are explicit actualizations of such creative and redemptive activity. Any attempt to block such a mediation will be seen as a sinful substitution of human action for the grace of God. A critical faith, therefore, entails critical thought which stands in judgement against all ideological sinfulness.

All authority expresses itself as nurture and cultivation, and the matrices of authority are servants of that process. A critical faith insures that such matrices continue to be media of genuine authority rather than outrageous displays of coercive power. The ideal structure of authority, the true servant of creation and redemption, needs no coercive power for its nurturing task. Because of the sinful human condition, a mixture both of nurture and coercion is usually the case. A critical faith has as its principal task the discovery of such pretension in nurturing matrices and the exercise of critical judgement against the presence of coercive elements which inevitably block nurture and cultivation.

A critical faith may find expression in all human civilizing exertions. It should be present in science, art, politics, and in the moral dimension of human action. Ideology, on the other hand, is an erastz faith which expresses itself through a conformity to its own dictates and which assumes that all truth and reality are enclosed in its structures. Science, art, politics, and morality should be servants of transcendence and the nurture and cultivation derived from its creative and redemptive activity, and not instruments of a closed ideological system which uses coercion to insure the necessary conformity. The authority of science, art, politics, and morality is conveyed when such a critical faith is present. It is transformed into coercion when a critical faith is absent and an idolatrous substitute takes its place.

Two examples should suffice. Both science and politics are important nurturing and cultivating matrices in human cultural exertion and may be media for expressing the creative and redemptive possibilities of a benevolent transcendence.

A critical faith anchored in the nurture and cultivation of scientific inquiry should be obvious. Critical thought and scientific thought are often treated as synonyms. The scientific devotion to truth is the ideal for all adherents of this important secular discipline. In fact, scientists may tacitly image transcendence through their devotion to the discovery of dynamic truth. It must be observed, however, that such a critical posture is not always present. Truth can be reduced to what science has discovered or is now discovering. Transcendent possibilities of a dynamic truth may be lost in such a reductionism.

All science works within given paradigms if R.G. Collingwood and Thomas Kuhn are correct in their assessment of the case. A paradigm is a tacit presupposition which sets the limits of inquiry and the direction of all such inquiry. When work is done within the confines of a particular paradigm, nurture and cultivation may occur, and a devotion to truth may be conveyed. But paradigms do shift, are changed, and are replaced by other paradigms: for example, the paradigmatic shift from a Newtonian mechanistic model to the one respresentative of work in physics today. Whether such shifts are major ones or less spectacular, a crisis may arise in scientific inquiry. Resistance may occur to paradigm replacement. Consequently, a reigning paradigm may cease to be a legitimate medium for the discovery of a dynamic truth and instead become the substitute for truth. An idolatrous faith replaces a critical faith and scientific authority is transformed covertly into a subtle coercion. All anomalies are dismissed as irrelevant and conformity is expected of those working in scientific pursuits.

The resistance to paradigm replacement, therefore, becomes an example of the attempt to capture the infinite or enclose transcendence. The desire to rest secure within the limits of the reigning paradigm takes the place of a devotion to truth: the truth which makes a person free; the truth which is an expression of the ultimate identity of fact and value; the affirmation of a benevolent transcendence.

A critical faith articulated in political action is not so obvious as it is in scientific inquiry, but it can be discovered and affirmed. Plato sought a definition of justice in the individual writ large and his speculation about an ideal republic was committed to the discovery of justice both corporately and individually. Justice may be a proper image for the creative and redemptive activity of a benevolent transcendence. The quest for justice entails a critical faith; a faith which remains open to the possibilities of justice, while it attempts to develop finite structures which mediate such justice in particular contexts. Political action needs to be animated by a passion for justice, but should not confuse justice with the passion.

Political structures possess genuine authority when they serve as nurturing and cultivating matrices for the emergence of relatively free beings. A tensive relation between political structure and individual freedom is the *conditio sine qua non* for maintaining a critical faith: a faith in the possibility of justice. Such a tensive relationship also permits genuine authority to express itself in political actions.

The negation of such a tensive relation between politcal structures and freedom results in the transformation of political matrices of nurture into structures of coercion. Structures of coercion dismiss relative freedom and define freedom and justice as conformity to the reigning finite political system. Authority disappears and is replaced by raw power. Transcendent possibilities of justice which would include those outside the political enclosure are blocked. Consequently, a political ideology is blind to possibilities of justice which transcend its collective subjectivity. The raw power of such an ideology cloaks itself in the legitimate images of genuine authority; and authority eventually becomes a synonym for coercive power.

A critical faith derived from the acknowledgement of a benevolent transcendence finds its location and possibility always in the tensive relation between nurturing structures and freedom. The political possibility for the achievement of justice in particular contexts is an emergent from such a critical faith.

It is true, then, to say that a tacit faith is present both in scientific inquiry and in political action when a devotion to truth and justice is present. Truth and justice, as a result, become authentic ways of imaging the ultimate identification of fact and value. It may also be stated that such a faith has had its origins in the traditions of Jews and Christians who have found that the source of all factical reality is also the source of all value and worth: God is One, both creator and redeemer!

The fact that such a faith was discovered and has its origins in Judaism and Christianity makes it imperative that Jews and Christians exemplify both in teaching and in practice what that faith entails. Faith is the communal and personal response to revelatory events which focus definitively the creative and redemptive activity of God in nature and in history. That creative and redemptive activity should be mediated as nurture and cultivation in the religious institutions which have arisen as a result of that response to such revelatory events.

The authority of such institutions is precisely identified with possibilities for nurture and cultivation resulting in relatively free human beings who then may encounter a benevolent transcendence through the images and symbols which make up the nurturing matrix. The tensive relation between nurturing structures and freedom is thus the location for a vibrant, living, and critical faith.

Both Judaism and Christianity have served as media for the creative and redemptive activity of God. Their authority as servants of God rests on whether or not they continue to be a transparent medium for such creativity and redemption. The history of Judaism and Christianity confirms that such a genuine response of a critical faith has taken place from generation to generation. Such history also reveals that those servants of God have fallen short, have missed the mark, and have identified the medium for God's gracious activity with that activity itself. The temptation to capture the infinite, to enclose transcendence, is always with us, and particularly, does it hover in the background for all the institutions of religion.

Revelation is a universal possibility because of the creative and redemptive activity of God in nature and in history. The communal and personal response to such revelation occurs in particular, concrete, historical situations and events which bear the marks of the cultural situation within which they take place. The treasure, therefore, is conveyed through earthen vessels.

A critical faith must be able to discern the difference between the treasure and the earthen vessel which mediates that treasure to human beings. The development of any living, dynamic tradition is due to the tensive relation between these two factors. Since such a tensive relation is fundamental for a critical faith which can encounter transcendence without capturing it, all authority must reflect this kind of tensive relationship: an authority which is servant rather than master.

The authority of Judaism and Christianity rests upon the ability to mediate the creative and redemptive activity (grace) of God through the particular matrices of nurture and cultivation which result in relatively free human beings. The relationship between Judaism and Christianity should also reflect such a posture.

When Judaism is the transparent medium for the grace of God expressed through nurturing and cultivating matrices, it is indeed what Christians call the "new" Israel. The dynamic authority of a prophetic, critical faith is present and the grace of God is not blocked but served. When Christianity is the transparent medium for the grace of God expressed through nurturing and cultivating matrices, it is also the "new" Israel. When Judaism or Christianity are not such transparent media, they are indeed the "old" Israel. The difference is determined by the presence or absence of a dynamic prophetic and critical faith living within the aforementioned tensive relationship. The absence of such a prophetic and critical faith results in the emergence of a religious ideology.

It is imperative that both Judaism and Christianity resist disintegrating into ideologies in conflict with one another. The conservation of each particular tradition and the way it has developed in history is of the utmost importance. Jews are Jews and their identity as Jews should be conserved and respected. Christians are Christians and their identity as Christians should also be conserved and respected. Both traditions, however, are servants of God, not substitutes for God. Jews and Christians should love one another as servants of God. In so doing the ultimate identification of fact and value, creation and redemption, is upheld. Jews and Christians, as servants of God and of one another, will avoid the temptation of becoming religious ideologies who have deified their own corporate spirit and who have turned their back on God. They thus will be redeemed from worshipping their respective golden calves: idols of their own making!

For Christians Jesus is the definitive revelation of a benevolent transcendence. In Jesus it is possible to affirm the ultimate identity of creation and redemption. In Jesus, whom Christians call Lord, may be found the decisive qualification of all power. Jesus is the king who is the servant; Jesus is the prophet who faces the world's judgement; Jesus is the priest who is also sacrificial victim. The servanthood of Jesus ultimately qualifies power and the unique concept of authority as nurture and cultivation may be derived from the gospel of Jesus Christ. This pattern of servanthood, this paradigm of authority for all Christians, should prevail in our relationships with one another.

The development of corporate structure in the church has been necessary in order to conserve the identity of the Christian person and in order to determine what is distinctive about Christian existence. Corporate structure which is often called "catholic order" has a long history. It has contributed to the nurture and cultivation of individuals in many different centuries and it has been the transparent medium for the grace of God mediated through Jesus as Lord.

This mediation of the grace of God, when it is present, authenticates the authority of ecclesiastical order. But a paradox arises. No order in itself is fully catholic or universal. To mistake a finite structure for a universal possibility is to flirt with the temptation of reducing the transcendent God to the finitude of the structure which is supposed to serve God. Catholic order should mean a particular, dynamic structure which nurtures and cultivates relatively free human beings, which affirms the tensive relation between nurturing structures and freedom, and within that tensive relation remains open to and affirms the catholic or universal possibility of God's creative and redemptive activity in nature and in history. Catholicity thus is an image representing universal possibility rather than a static enclosure of all that is transcendent within itself.

Catholic order needs to affirm within itself a principle which criticizes its own tendencies towards the enclosure of transcendence. Catholic order, which is the servant of God, and not a substitute for God, needs to be animated by a critical and prophetic faith. Such a critical faith will avoid the transformation of a corporate structure which serves God into a religious ideology which serves only itself. These observations are valid when considering any principle of ecclesiastical order which has emerged during the history of the Christian response to the grace of God focused definitively in Jesus of Nazareth.

The Second Vatican Council served as a vibrant affirmation of a critical faith and it corrected the tendencies of the post-Tridentine Roman Catholic church which confused a finite ecclesiastical structure with the universal or catholic possibilities of the grace of God. Because of the impact of that Council, the relationship between various churches has taken a new direction. This direction may result in the development of genuine tensive relationships between various Christian churches.

In the specific discussions between Anglicans and Roman Catholics, new horizons have arisen which offer important possibilities for the future. A few suggestions need to be made based on some of the conclusions reached in this essay.

In the first place, Christian unity should be affirmed in terms of our faith in Jesus Christ and the possibilities for the future that such faith involves. This possibility for unity is anchored in the image of a servant church whose authority is derived from its capacity to nurture and cultivate relatively free human beings: such nurture and cultivation itself being an expression of the gracious activity of God.

In the second place, no church should claim catholicity exclusively for itself. Catholicity should be a symbol for the universal possibility of revelation, the creative and redemptive activity of God in nature and in history, and the particular, finite, ecclesiastical structures should be understood as potential media for the grace derived from God. Catholicity thus becomes an image for transcendence in the same way that Truth and Justice are such images. If catholicity is understood in any other way, religious ideology is the harmful result.

In the third place, intercommunion is an important step for the churches to take. Christian churches should not be collective monads, alienated from one another. Instead, they should be genuine communities of faith engaging in an intersubjective dynamic which opens up the dimension of transcendence. This means the conservation of the dynamic particular traditions which have developed in history, and at the same time it involves the recognition in a pluralistic manner of the catholic possibility implicit in such communion and intercommunion. Such intercommunion would be the opposite of isolation and alienation.

In the fourth place, no need is demonstrable for a giant, super church which absorbs all of the smaller bodies into itself, and which then might presume that catholic possibility has been fully actualized in such a mammoth ecclesiastical establishment. Universality can never be fully actualized in finite structures. The danger is in the sinful human desire to capture the infinite and enclose transcendence. Ideology is a lurking temptation for all human beings and Christians are no exception. Totalitarian pretension is not negated even when it is cloaked with the imagery of the One who is servant of all.

Genuine authority rests in the tensive relation between nurturing structures and relative freedom. Such authority is the actualization of the universal possibilities of creation and redemption in nature and in history. When this authority prevails, whether it is expressed in scientific and political exertions of a secular culture, or whether it is discovered in the communities of Judaism and Christianity, or whether it is found in other religions outside the Judaeo-Christian tradition, all nurturing structures become servants of transcendence and not substitutes for it; and the ultimate identification of fact and value, being and worth, is acknowledged and celebrated.

Notes

1. P.T. Forsyth, *The Principle of Authority* (London, 1952), 129.
2. See Peter L. Berger and Thomas Luckman, *The Social Construction of Reality* (Garden City, New York, 1966).
3. See Thomas S. Kuhn, *The Structure of Scientific Revolutions* (Chicago, 1970). And also Michael Polanyi, *Personal Knowledge* (New York, 1964).
4. Pamela Reynolds, "Going to Market," *The Boston Globe*, August 11, 1984, 8.
5. My sympathies here are a matter of public record. See my book *The Christian Disciple* (Lanham, Maryland, 1984).
6. The Latin root word for nurture is most likely *nutrire*. It means literally, "to nourish, suckle, or feed." It may also have a broader meaning in terms of, to foster, bring up, rear, support, or cherish. In its usage by Horace, *mens rite nutrita*, "the mind properly nourished," it comes close to what is involved in education. It should be obvious that nourish does relate closely to the meanings of *augere*, and helps to distinguish *auctoritas* from *imperium*.
7. See my book *The Meaning of Authority* (Lanham, Maryland, 1983), 6.
8. See my essay "An Incarnational Spirituality," *Anglican Spirituality*, edited by W.J. Wolf (Wilton, Connecticut, 1982), 135-161.

The Grace of a Holy God: P.T. Forsyth and the Contemporary Church

R.C. Craston

Has a Congregationalist theologian dead some sixty years anything relevant and illuminating to contribute to Anglican thinking on the problem of authority today? The thesis of this chapter is that he has. P.T. Forsyth has been described by such theologians as Emil Brunner and J.K. Mozley as the greatest dogmatic theologian Great Britain has given to the church in modern times; by A.M. Hunter as a great man born before his time; by several as "a Barthian before Barth" but "greater because of his belief in reason, whereby he maintained the essential liberal theological principle."[1]

Appreciation of Forsyth's contribution to the church has grown since his death. Indeed during his lifetime he won few followers. For, although R.W. Dale of Birmingham could ask, while Forsyth was still in his forties, "Who is this P.T. Forsyth? He has recovered for us a word we had all but lost — the word Grace,"[2] the mood of his time was against him. Liberalism was on the crest of the wave. It was not, however, the whole of the liberal approach to Christianity that Forsyth reacted against. As A.M. Hunter maintains, the mature Forsyth remained a liberal

in his demand for intellectual liberty, in his insistence on the right and value of biblical criticism, in his refusal to rest content in the ancient creeds with their obsolete categories, in his concept of theology as Christian faith giving a reasoned account of revelation. The liberalism which he early espoused, and on which he later came down like a hammer, was that version of Christianity which so sought to accommodate it to the modern mind as to make shipwreck of the historic faith: which stressed evolution rather than revelation, viewed the kingdom of God as a human creation rather than a divine invasion, minimised human sin and guilt, scaled down the New Testament Christ and his cross to all-too-human dimensions, and regarded Paul as the perverter of an originally simple gospel about God's fatherhood and man's brotherhood.[3]

Forsyth believed himself to be contending for the truth of the gospel against the greatest threat to the church since the Gnosticism of the early centuries. And he saw the heart of that struggle as concerned with the principle of authority. "The principle of authority is ultimately the whole religious question."[4] For him Christianity was a religion of authority or it was nothing. Its objective was the establishment of the ultimate authority for mankind for belief and life. The reference to life needs emphasizing. Not merely personal behaviour, but life in the family, in the church, and in society depended on recognition and acceptance of that authority.

> An authority of any practical kind draws its meaning and its right only from the soul's relation to its God. That is so not only for religion strictly so called, nor for a Church, but for public life, social life, and the whole history and career of humanity. [5]

Forsyth maintained that submission to the ultimate authority, of which the gospel was the medium, was the way of true freedom. If man is made for God, he can only find his own freedom when freed to live for God.

The Anglican Debate

Several factors combine to put authority at or near the top of the Anglican agenda in the 1980s. The ARCIC discussions, with the need for a formal response of the whole communion at Lambeth 1988, focus largely on the matter, not just because the *Final Report* of ARCIC I has sections on authority in the church, but also because differences on the other subjects, found within and in reaction to the report, inevitably raise the question, "By what authority?"

Then, a unique contribution the Anglican communion has to make to the world family of churches relates to the exercise of authority. Being an episcopal and a synodical church, allowing for and expecting bishops in the historic succession to give leadership yet at the same time providing for criticism as well as co-operation from clergy and laity (a provision that may be traced back to the Reformation Settlement), the Anglican church has experience to show how in the exercise of authority that tension can be creative — and more, how the tension can be worked out in different cultures across the world. That is not to claim outstanding or uniform success. Travel within the communion soon convinces one of much progress still needing to be made; but yet, of Anglicanism being on the right road.

Furthermore, current debate and developments within the sources of authority in the Anglican communion — the establishment of the Anglican Consultative Council and its evaluation process from ACC-5 onwards, the reconstitution of the Primates' Meeting from 1979, the continuation of the Lambeth Conference and the developing role of the archbishop of Canterbury — have revived interest in the concept of "dispersed authority" highlighted at Lambeth 1948 (see the Appendix).

It is when one attempts to unpack the meaning of "dispersed authority," however, that awareness of different interlocking strands of meaning arises. Authority can relate to centres of power at local, diocesan, provincial, or international level, the places and the process of decision making. It is evident that authority in that sense is dispersed in Anglicanism. As the *Report* to the 1948 Lambeth Conference affirms, such dispersal can be accepted as a divine provision "against the temptations to tyranny and the dangers of unchecked power." But when the authors of the report spoke of "dispersed authority" they were not just thinking of decision-making bodies. They had in mind the elements that shape belief and practice for Anglicans, and listed scripture, tradition, creeds, the ministry of word and sacraments, the witness of saints, and the *consensus fidelium*. Here we move into another, but related, realm of authority. Here the question is, What is God's word for the faith and order of the church? and, be it noted, his word today? At the different levels of decision making in varying degrees that question has to be faced.

When, however, these different strands of meaning of authority have been explored there remains a further strand, a primary concern, which has not been faced. And it is here that Forsyth has a crucial, an essential contribution to make, in the judgement of this writer. It may be introduced thus: "Why should I believe?" "What in the final analysis makes me believe as a Christian?" and more, "What ultimately motivates me to want and strive for a change of life, style, and purpose, that as well as joy occasions pain and sacrifice?" These questions are about *The Principle of Authority*, the title of Forsyth's longest book.

The Principle of Authority

What is the ultimate authority for belief and life? The question is about conviction of the intellect, the conscience, and the will. Forsyth was dissatisfied with the various answers around in the church.

Could ultimate authority be found in an infallible book? Forsyth had a high doctrine of scripture, but biblical criticism had made it impossible to read the scriptures as in former centuries. "To the Bible as the Reformers read it we can never, indeed, return."[6] Forsyth also had a high doctrine of the church. Indeed, in an age when in his own Protestant tradition the doctrine of the church was in eclipse, he was writing of the unity, mission, and essence of the church in terms that sound very relevant today. He could not, however, locate ultimate authority in an infallible church.

If Forsyth could not locate ultimate authority in the external infallibilities of Bible and church still less could it be in the religious experience, whether moral sense or rational intuition, of the liberalism of his day. That way ended in an anthropocentric religion.

> But the God of the Church's revelation is not an anthropocentric God. Heaven is not humanity glorified, even by a God. The public is not the tribunal of the Church. The revelation in Christ entrusted to the Church reveals God for whom man exists, rather than man for whom God exists.[7]

Here may be detected a hint of the reason why Forsyth perceived the prevailing theology of his day as the greatest threat since Gnosticism.

Bible, church, reason, religious experience, and the other elements listed in the *Report* to the 1948 Lambeth Conference, tradition, creeds, the ministry of word and sacraments, the witness of saints, and the *consensus fidelium*, all have their place, a derived or secondary place, in the principle of authority, as Forsyth frequently affirms in around twenty major works. But the ultimate authority must be something beyond, behind, underlying these media. Confronted with any or all of them the question still has to be faced, Why do I believe what I find in the Bible, or what the church teaches, or what the creeds say, or what the preacher declares? The question retains its validity even for such as cling to the concept of infallibility in Bible or church.

The Nature of Authority

Forsyth emphasizes that authority cannot simply be external to man — whether a book or a church or a creed — nor can it be simply internal, subjective.

> Of course, empirically, educationally, we do depend on external authority in the first part of our discipline. . . . It is a necessary stage of our growth. . . . We depend on statements about religion made by other people who are in some historic position of religious authority over us — parents, teachers, churches, or Apostles. That is to say, our most direct contact at that stage is not with the object of religion but with the people produced by that object.[8]

As he puts it, "the order of time is not the order of reality."

It may be observed in passing that churches, particularly where long established, may have many members stuck in that preliminary stage of spiritual development Forsyth describes. They either lack or appear very uncertain about "direct contact with the object of religion."

According to Forsyth, final authority must be recognized as external, objective to the soul, and yet known directly within it.

> The seat of authority . . . is one thing, the source and sanction of it is another. The seat of it, of course, is subjective to us. Real authority is a thing that must be experienced, but it is not the experience, which is but a mode of ourselves.[9] A real authority . . . is indeed *within* experience, but it is not the

authority of experience, it is an authority *for* experience, it is an authority experienced. All certainty is necessarily subjective so far as concerns the area where it emerges and the terms in which it comes home. The court is subjective, but the bench is not. Reality must, of course, be real for me. It must speak the language of my consciousness. But it makes much difference whether it have its *source* in my consciousness as well as its *sphere*. . . .[10]

The Holy God

We have already noted Forsyth's emphasis on ultimate authority as being for life as well as thought. In the words of one of his commentators,

> . . . the ideals and purposes by which we live can never be the product of the impartial intellect alone. They stand for judgements of value which involve the will as well as the reason; they are therefore *moral* judgements and not simply intellectual. Thus the nature of reality, in so far as it is a matter of human experience at all, is a matter of moral experience, and man's interest in reality is a moral interest.[11]

It is impossible to exaggerate the significance of the moral dimension in Forsyth's theology. For him, the final authority for man, and indeed his whole destiny, was in his relationship with God as holy. Another commentator, assessing Forsyth's stance within the thought of his own time, maintains, "There is no one point at which Forsyth stood so alone as in his conscious, explicit relating of all doctrine to a fundamental understanding of God as holy."[12] As he consistently maintains, it is only as the biblical testimony to God as Holy Father, the Holy One, "our Other" is fully accepted that God as Love can be rightly appreciated. Unless we take seriously the holiness which is absolute moral perfection and goodness, our understanding of God's love will degenerate into a sentimentality indifferent to the moral gulf between man and God. Forsyth speaks of God—

> as self-complete and absolute moral personality, the universal and eternal holy God whose sufficiency is of Himself, the self-contained, and self-determined moral reality of the

universe, for which all things work together in a supreme *concursus,* which must endure if all else fail, and must be secured at any cost beside.[13]

A further quotation shows how Forsyth sees holiness working itself out in love.

> For the creature to be holy is *to be for God*; for God himself to be holy is *to be God*. His holiness is the complete accord of his will and his nature. It is not an attribute of God; it is his name, and being, and infinite value. But if the holiness do not go out to cover, imbue, conquer, and sanctify all things, if it do not give itself in love, it is the less holy. It is but partial and not absolute. As holy he must subdue all and bless all. God's holiness is the fundamental principle not of our worship only, but of his whole saving revelation and economy of love. It is the moral principle of both love and grace. It is love's content, it is what love brings or grace gives. . . . For only the holy can love for ever and for ever subdue the loveless; only the holy can thoroughly forgive so as to make his holiness dear.[14]

The holiness of God makes a total claim upon man, a claim he may recognize but completely fail to meet. And so the effective establishing of God's authority in man must solve that dilemma. "The truth of Christianity," Forsyth says, "must rest on a view of life which starts with the primacy and finality of the moral, recognises the wreck of the moral, and presents the grand problem as the restitution of the moral."[15] The restitution of the moral starts, as he sees it, with the vindication of God's holiness. We do well at this point to note that holiness in God is no abstract morality. Because it ever expresses itself in holy love it is ever within interpersonal relationship. Holy love is principally the Holy One in communion with himself in the life of the Trinity. And when the Holy One moves out to his fallen creature, man, it is to restore relationship and to establish in man that holiness on which communion with a holy God must be based. "You shall be holy, for I am holy." So Forsyth declares,

> Authority is a personal relation and a moral, the relation of two wills and consciences. It is the authority of an absolute, holy person . . . the holy is the absolute conscience. So this

divine authority is exerted upon a conscience. But on a conscience which, as soon as it realises the holy, realises itself in
the same act as sinful and lost. . . . It is therefore the authority of a Saviour who effects a new creature, with the absolute
right over it that creation always must give. It is the new-
creative action of the perfectly holy conscience of God on the
helplessly guilty conscience of man.[16]

Forsyth adds a footnote to indicate that by helplessly guilty he
does not mean totally corrupt.

Revelation as Redemption

If the situation between creature and Creator is to be described
in terms of gulf and guilt — and by the latter Forsyth is not so
much concerned with a *sense* of guilt as the *state* of guilt in being
in rebellion against a holy Father — then man is in need not
merely of illumination but of redemption. The significance of this
for apologetics, mission, and evangelism will be noted in due
course. For the present we may sum up Forsyth's emphasis in
the words of G.O. Griffith: ''The gulf that is fixed is that which
stretches between sinfulness and Holiness. It is not man's
dullness or backwardness that marks the separation, but his self-
will, his rebellion.''[17] Truths about God, even a faithful presentation of God as holiness and as love, can never be adequate to
the reality of the situation, nor constitute an effective final authority in and for man.

> God in Christ is the maker of his own revelation. It was God
> himself that came to us in Christ; it was nothing about God,
> even about his eternal essence or his excellent glory. It is God
> that is our salvation, and not the truth about God. And what
> Christ came to do was not to convince us even that God is love,
> but to be with us and in us as the loving God for ever and
> ever. He came not to preach the living God but to be God in
> our life; yes, not to preach even the loving God but to be the
> love that God for ever is.[18]

In this typically uncompromising way Forsyth directs attention to the very heart of God's solution, the Cross, where Incarnation culminates in Atonement. John H. Rodgers sums up Forsyth's understanding of the Cross thus:

> Atonement is that act of God in Christ whereby he judges sin unto destruction and satisfies his own holy nature in the sacrifice of the Son, doing this in such a way that man is placed again in communion with himself as a penitent recipient of grace.[19]

The Word of the Cross

The Cross is from first to last an act of God. Its sacrifice is rendered within humanity but by no third party; it is by himself in his Son. It vindicates and satisfies his own holiness. As A.M. Hunter puts it, ''The real objective element is that God made the atonement and gave it finished to man.''[20] Forsyth will have no understanding of the atonement that undermines the unity of the Godhead or suggests the placation of the Father by incarnate Son.

For Forsyth the Cross — he often seems to use the word as theological shorthand for Jesus Christ, incarnate Son of God, crucified and risen — is the gospel. The title of one of his books, *The Cruciality of the Cross*, suggests that. Criticism has been levelled against his neglect of other great biblical themes, creation, convenant, the teaching of Christ, and so on. Recognizing his avowed intention within the controversies of his day, however, the supreme emphasis on the Cross may be well understood. But, in any case, a church that puts the eucharist at the heart of its worship and fellowship must go along with Forsyth in testifying to Christ crucified and risen as God's Word, final and complete, to man.

God's Word to man! But how can the Cross be a Word, a revealing Word, if, as Forsyth would have us believe, the atonement is essentially within the Godhead? The bloody crucifixion on Calvary was seen by some, but its meaning hidden. If no Word is heard at or through the Cross, how can it constitute a final authority for man? Forsyth's answer is to stress the essential place of the *kerygma*. It would not have been sufficent for God merely to have acted in the Cross.

> The mere crucifixion of Jesus was no revelation. Many people saw it to whom it meant nothing more than an execution. It does not reach us as a religious thing, as revelation, till it receives a certain interpretation. . . . Therefore besides God's act we must have God's version of his act. God must be his own interpreter.[21]

It is to the apostolic witness we must look for God's interpretation of the Cross, Forsyth maintains. He places the greatest weight on the promises of Jesus before his crucifixion that the Holy Spirit would guide his disciples into all truth. Referring to their presentation of the good news, the *kerygma*, he writes:

> This is not an article of theology, nor a tentative interpretation by apostles of a vast, vague, spiritual impression that they felt, without positive features of its own; but is their inspired statement of the Gospel of God's act and gift, the marrow of Christian religion, the object and content of faith. To leave that living tradition and experience of the Spirit is to adopt another faith.[22]

In summing up Forsyth's position, John H. Rodgers speaks of the act of the Cross and the *kerygma* of the Cross forming the fact of the Cross, which called into being the New Testament, through which the fact is handed on.

A further quotation from Forsyth will be helpful, both for the way it emphasizes the relation between revelation and redemption and leads into the key issue, namely, how God's authority is effectively established in man.

> Revelation then may be defined as the free, final and effective act of God's self-communication in Jesus Christ for man's redemption. It is not simply an act of manifestation, or even of impressive representation, but it is a historic and eternal act of deliverance, prolonged in an infinite number of acts *euisdem generis* in the experience by Christian people of their redemp-

tion in Christ. It is a free act as being wholly marvellous and unbought. It is a final act because it embodies in an aforesaid sense, the whole purpose of God with man. And it is effective because it is only completed by its return on itself in man's experience and response. A sound returns void, but not a word, not a revelation. . . . It is impossible to separate revelation from redemption. Revelation has no real and final meaning except as the act of redemption to the experience of being redeemed. . . .[23]

The act of deliverance in the Cross is prolonged in an infinite number of acts of the same kind in the experience of people. That, according to Forsyth, is how God establishes his authority in man, that is the principle of authority. He calls it "the evangelical experience."

The Evangelical Experience

Nothing can create faith but God's actual coming in Son or Spirit, His actual contact and action in a soul. Nothing else can be a final authority for faith.[24]

It is the experience of the *evangel*, in which the Christ of the Cross, the Christ of history, is the centre and controlling factor, thus establishing him as king, which constitutes primary authority. Understood in a narrow, party sense the phrase, "the evangelical experience," could suggest such categories as decision, commitment, repentance, faith, conversion. Without denying their validity, Forsyth would not place the major emphasis on human response but rather on the action of God in the soul. Final authority is the holy God coming to man in Christ, redeeming and renewing him through the Cross, coming to the soul, breaking it down in grace and restoring it in grace, thus subduing and liberating in the same act. That experience is an experience *sui generis*, we must affirm.

The last authority of the soul for ever is the grace of a holy God, the holiness of His gracious love in Jesus Christ. And this is the last reality of things, the last rest of all hearts, and the last royalty of all wills.[25]

Forsyth can speak of Christ coming to the soul or the Holy Spirit coming. He uses the expression, "the Holy Spirit of the Cross," because the Spirit takes of Christ and brings him to men. He is the presence of the living Christ.

> The ministry of the Spirit was not to supersede the historic salvation, and yet it was to do more than merely transmit it. It was to be at once its continuity, its amplification, and its individualization — all three. . . . The Holy Spirit is thus inseparable from this work of Christ and from the word of it in the apostolic preaching which is crystallized in the Bible.[26]

Certain questions about Forsyth's identification of man's ultimate authority in the "evangelical experience" are worth asking, but one thing may be said now. He is testifying to an authority that is effective. An authority is not just that which *ought* to rule a man, but actually *does* rule him. A World Council of Churches report[27] has stressed that authority is nowadays accepted only where it proves itself. Of the secondary or derived authorities, Bible, church, creeds, etc., all of which have their essential part, as Forsyth is most concerned to demonstrate, the "ought" may well be claimed. But it is not to them we look when answering the question, What in the final analysis does rule a Christian believer? It is the actual operation of the redeeming and renewing God in the soul, described in one word, *grace* — the word R.W. Dale said Forsyth had recovered for the church in the late nineteenth century.

Questions

Is Forsyth too individualistic in his approach to the principle of authority when locating it in the "evangelical experience"? Undoubtedly he believed that "individual men have to enter upon that reconciled position, that new covenant, that new relation, which already, in virtue of Christ's Cross, belonged to the race as a whole."[28] But an individualistic approach to Christianity was abhorrent to him. The Christ experienced was the Saviour and Lord known in the church from the beginning. Individual experience of him is transcended in the common experience of the church. And to know, or rather be known by, Christ is to be in the church, which Forsyth saw as the earnest of a saved humanity, a new humanity in the making. For, ''. . . it was a race that Christ redeemed, and not a mere bouquet of believers. It was a Church he saved, and not a certain pale of souls. Each soul is saved in a universal and corporate salvation.''[29]

Did Forsyth understand the ''evangelical experience'' as a unique, ''Damascus road'' type of experience? There is no evidence to think he did. Indeed his own history and spiritual development suggest a gradual work of God in him. And even where the ''Holy Spirit of the Cross'' appears suddenly to open up the life to an awareness of God in Christ, the understanding of the meaning of it is a life-long process, never complete.

If the Word of the Cross, that is, of Christ incarnate, crucified, risen, coming to the soul in subduing and renewing grace, is the final authority in the believer, how are secondary authorities to be seen? Space forbids anything like adequate treatment but one or two quotations may indicate the line of Forsyth's thought.

> The Gospel, thus experienced, has the secret of salvation of the future only because it has the authority before whom we are not our own at all, to whom we owe our delivery from perdition and impotence and not from mere backwardness or waywardness, and to whom our absolute obedience is our only freedom. . . . Everything else, Church or Bible, is authoritative for us in the proportion in which it is sacramental of the final and absolute authority of the Creator as Redeemer, the authority not merely of God but of a God of grace. Authority reflects a dying King.[30]

> If the Gospel of Christ's grace is the one authority set up among men, the seat of that authority is the Bible, and the witness is the faithful Church.[31]

A Word for Today?

The opening sentence of this study posed the possibility of Forsyth's understanding of authority having relevance to Anglican thought today. This writer would offer the following observations in support of that thesis.

First, and obviously, if in inter-church discussions, and particularly with Rome where authority is a key issue, we do not begin from a sound base clearly understood, confusion must arise. The various strands of meaning of authority must be unravelled. If Forsyth were alive and permitted to advise, he would undoubtedly ask both the Anglican and Roman communions in the context of the ARCIC discussions, "How do you define man's ultimate authority in faith? What in the final analysis creates faith?"

Then, attention to Forsyth's works could clarify our understanding of grace. Maybe it is not a word in need of recovery, as suggested in his day, but is it a clear and dominant theme in teaching and preaching? John H. Rodgers speaks of a tendency to distort the concept of grace in two ways, "as an impersonal power or virtue and as sentimental love."[32] Anglicans, at any rate in England, when discussing moral issues — a recent debate on the marriage in church of divorcees is an example — can be strong in law, but less clear on grace, in the view of this writer. The answer to God's law broken is not just compassion, nor even forgiveness, but the primacy of grace. Grace triumphs, or all are lost, and grace is only possible because God assumes in himself at infinite cost the consequence of broken law, vindicating his holiness and redeeming the transgressor.

A further line of enquiry touches the realm of apologetics and evangelism. How do we commend the faith to modern man? How may the church witness so that God's authority is established in human lives influenced by scientific thought and secularism? The problems for belief in a loving Creator have doubtless intensified since Forsyth's day, not least through the researches of astronomy and physics and the threat of global destruction — though his *Justification of God*, written in the midst of the Great War, still has relevance in a world where violence abounds. So the church must look to its theologians to interpret the faith in the thought-forms of the age. Forsyth insisted on the necessity of this — creeds and doctrine were tentative, never possessing finality. But the theology of Forsyth presses two major, and in my view indispensible, considerations on the apologist and the evangelist.

First, creation of faith is not simply a matter of intellectual conviction. God's action in the soul concerns "the wreck of the moral" and "the restitution of the moral." He is not only mystery, but holiness. And man needs to be convicted and converted as well as intellectually convinced. Indeed, unless the primacy of

the moral is recognized, the apologetic process may so accommodate the faith to man's questions as to evacuate it of saving
value. Forsyth quotes "that searching Christian genius
Kierkegaard, the great and melancholy Dane," thus:

> For long the tactics have been: use every means to move as
> many as you can — to move everybody if possible — to enter
> Christianity. Do not be too curious whether what they enter
> *is* Christianity. My tactics have been, with God's help, to use
> every means to make it clear what the demand of Christianity
> really is — if not one entered it.[33]

Forsyth recognizes the statement as extreme, but pointing the way
to salvation. When all possible efforts have been made to interpret belief in God to modern man, the scandal of the Cross
remains, if it is the Christian gospel we proclaim.

The second consideration is closely related. The experience of
the Holy Spirit's working in the life alone can establish the validity
of the Christian claim. "We may take it that the authority of a
holy Gospel cannot be proved to the natural man. The offence
of the Cross has not ceased. It must first capture him and make
him a supernatural man."[34]

A.M. Hunter summing up a magisterial treatment by Forsyth
of "the autonomy of the Christian claim," writes:

> The man who has never experienced this divine act (God's cen-
> tral act in Christ) in his own life has no rights to judge it by
> methods which, however valid in other fields, do not apply
> to the experienced fact of grace. In short, the Christian gospel
> cannot have anything else for its criterion. It is spiritually
> autonomous.[35]

This emphasis accords with a clear strand of New Testament
teaching. "Father, I thank you because you have shown to the
unlearned what you have hidden from the wise and learned . . .
this is how you wanted it to happen."[36]

St. Paul in 1 Corinthians 1:18 - 2:16, building on Old Testament insights, expands on the theme that experience of the Spirit
is the prerequisite of spiritual understanding. If it be argued by
an unbeliever that on this thesis he stands no chance unless God

unbidden come to him, one could imagine Forsyth responding thus: "Put yourself with humble and open mind where the Word of the Cross can be heard, that is, in the fellowship of faith created by that Word."

A Word of Testimony

It is fitting, in conclusion, to allow Forsyth's own explanation of his theology.

> Might I venture here to speak of myself, and of more than thirty years given to progressive thought in connection for the most part with a pulpit and care of souls? . . . There was a time when I was interested in the first degree with purely scientific criticism. Bred among academic scholarship of the Classics and Philosophy, I carried these habits to the Bible, and found in the subject a new fascination, in proportion as the stakes were much higher. But, fortunately for me, I was not condemned to the mere scholar's cloistered life. I could not treat the matter as an academic quest. I was kept close to practical conditions. I was in a relation of life, duty and responsibilty for others. I could not contemplate conclusions without asking how they would affect these people, and my word to them in doubt, death, grief or repentance. I could not call on them to accept my verdict on points that came so near their souls. . . . It also pleased God by the revelation of his holiness and grace, which the great theologians taught me to find in the Bible, to bring home to me my sin in a way that submerged all the school questions in weight, urgency, and poignancy. I was turned from a Christian to a believer, from a lover of love to an object of grace. And so, whereas I first thought that what the Churches needed was enlightened instruction and liberal theology, I came to be sure that what they needed was evangelization, in something more than the conventional sense of that word.[37]

In humbler circumstances, more than thirty years of parish ministry have convinced this writer of the validity of Forsyth's discovery and created an abiding gratitude for an introduction to his writings while in training for ordination.

Notes

1. Quotation from a letter in A.M. Hunter, *P.T. Forsyth — Per Crucem and Lucem* (London, 1974), 13.
2. From a Memoir by Forsyth's daughter in P.T. Forsyth, *The Work of Christ* (London, 1948), xv.
3. Hunter, *P.T. Forsyth*, 15.
4. P.T. Forsyth, *The Principle of Authority* (London, 1952), 2.
5. Ibid., 2, 3.
6. P.T. Forsyth, *Faith, Freedom and the Future* (London, 1955), 132.
7. Ibid., 286.
8. Forsyth, *The Principle of Authority*, 19.
9. Ibid., 49.
10. Ibid., 75.
11. Gwilym O. Griffith, *The Theology of P.T. Forsyth* (London, 1948), 31.
12. John H. Rodgers, *The Theology of P.T. Forsyth* (London, 1965), 30.
13. P.T. Forsyth, *Positive Preaching and the Modern Mind* (London, 1949), 241.
14. P.T. Forsyth, *This Life and the Next* (London, 1953), 28.
15. P.T. Forsyth, ed. M. Anderson, *The Gospel and Authority* (London, 1971), 107.
16. Forsyth, *The Principle of Authority*, 58.
17. Griffith, *The Theology of P.T. Forsyth*, 34.
18. P.T. Forsyth, *The Person and Place of Jesus Christ* (London, 1948), 354.
19. Rodgers, *The Theology of P.T. Forsyth*, 54.
20. Hunter, *P.T. Forsyth*, 62.
21. P.T. Forsyth, "Revelation and Bible," *Hibbert Journal* (1911-12), X, 242-3.
22. Forsyth, *The Principle of Authority*, 259.
23. P.T. Forsyth, "Revelation and the Person of Christ," in *Faith and Criticism, Essays by Congregationalists* (London, 1893), 116-17.
24. P.T. Forsyth, *Theology in Church and State* (London, 1915), 13-14.
25. Forsyth, *The Principle of Authority*, 419.
26. Forsyth, *Faith, Freedom and the Future*, 11-13.
27. *Ecumenical Review* 21, 150-66.
28. Forsyth, *The Work of Christ*, 86.
29. P.T. Forsyth, *The Church and the Sacraments* (London, 1955), 43.
30. Forsyth, *The Principle of Authority*, 299.
31. P.T. Forsyth, "The Evangelical Churches and the Higher Criticism," *Contemporary Review* 88, 591.

32. Rodgers, *The Theology of P.T. Forsyth*, 258.
33. Forsyth, *The Work of Christ*, xxxii.
34. Forsyth, *Positive Preaching and the Modern Mind*, 34.
35. Hunter, *P.T. Forsyth*, 54.
36. Matthew 11: 25-27: cf. Luke 10: 21-23.
37. Forsyth, *Positive Preaching and the Modern Mind*, 192-3.

The Authority of Love
Edward W. Scott

In recent years there has been much discussion and concern about "authority" in the church. It is right that this should be an area of concern because Christians are called to live under authority — the authority of God. My concern, however, is that it is all too easy to relate the authority of God to the authority of the church, and then it becomes too easy to substitute the exercise of authority for the responsibility to live under authority. I believe it is extremely important to examine the nature of the authority of the Christian community and the way in which that authority is exercised as revealed in the biblical record; and then to reflect upon the way in which the church tends to exercise authority today. This is of particular importance for Anglicans who maintain that while the Bible is the book of the church but that the church always stands under the judgement of scripture.

In the New Testament there are a variety of words used to designate power and authority. But there is a distinction to be drawn between those usages which refer to the source of all power in God and the divine life, and those which refer primarily to the world of order, of structure, of lines of responsibility in structure, and to responsibilities of persons who hold office.

As I reflect upon discussions about authority in the church today, most of them seem to relate to authority in the realm of organization and structure, and to lines of responsibility and accountability. When issues about the "integrity" of organizations are raised, they seem to relate primarily to this area of concern.

Both as a human being and as one who holds office in the Anglican communion — who is a member and representative of an "order" in the church — I respond to many of the issues being raised. I like to have things orderly and tidy. I feel much more secure when orderliness exists and I feel much more "in control" in a structure where I can keep things in order. Even as I recognize these realities, I am aware that the line between keeping "order" and exercising "control" is a fine line but that there is a fundamental difference between maintaining order and controlling. I am driven, therefore, to ask questions about the nature and purpose of authority as revealed in scripture, particularly as it is revealed in Jesus Christ, the Word made flesh. Is authority used to control, or to liberate?

Even as this discussion takes place, I am very aware of a parallel concern which goes deeper than the issue of organization. More and more people are asking, implicitly and explicitly, "Does the church as a community still possess power to renew? Is it still a living channel of the creative energy of God?" If renewal of the church is to take place, I am convinced that it will come from an exploration of this question, an exploration of the nature of divine power rather than from an exploration of structures of authority.

Here I believe it is useful to examine the way in which Jesus exercised authority. This is particularly important when we recall that on two occasions in John's gospel he said that even as the Father had sent him, so he was sending his followers into the world. If we take this seriously, surely we should seek to exercise authority as he exercised it.

In his first recorded address at the synagogue in Nazareth after his baptism, Jesus indicates his understanding of his mission, by applying to himself the reading from Isaiah:

> The spirit of the Lord is upon me because he has anointed me;
> he has sent me to announce good news to the poor,
>   to proclaim release for prisoners and recovery of sight for the blind;
>   to let the broken victims go free,
>   to proclaim the year of the Lord's favour. (Luke 4:18-19)

In the course of his ministry on several occasions, after he had taken action, Jesus was asked by what authority he did things. This was a question he never answered verbally; he answered it by the way he lived. Martin Bell in *The Way of the Wolf* (p.107) writes:

> There he is in the temple again, causing trouble. The broken one who cuts through our most stubborn defences and demands that we place our lives on the line. The fugitive who

confronts us with *direct authority*. Make no mistake about it. This is a dangerous man.

What is the nature of this "direct authority" which Jesus exercised and which the common people recognized? Is it not the authority of God? The authority of love incarnate? This is not an orderly, tidy, controllable thing. (Words used with reference to the Holy Spirit such as wind and fire are not particularly tidy words!)

This tough, hard, accepting, challenging love, expressed by Jesus Christ, is not a tidy thing. It leads to change, to transformation, to renewal. It is, surely, the energy of the loving God expressed in action.

If we reflect further we find support for this linking of divine power with God who is love. The great commandments focus attention upon love for God and love for neighbour in response to love from God. Jesus calls us to love enemy as well as neighbour. Why? "That we may be the children of God" who loves all. He also gives a new commandment "That we should love one another as He has loved us." The life and teaching of Jesus illustrate the authority of love, the power of love.

Jesus made no claim to set forth an intellectual statement of what was "truth." He set up no organizational structure as a means of exercising authority. He did say, "I am the Way, the Truth and the Life," and in so doing makes truth more than intellectual statements. Truth and love are inextricably linked and cannot for Christians be separated. The direct authority which Jesus exercised held truth and love intertwined; nothing is really true unless love is involved in it.

Paul in his reflections on "the more excellent way" (in 1 Corinthians 12 and 13) affirms that three things abide, "faith, hope and love, and that the greatest of these is love."

It seems clear, then, from reflection on these scriptural references, that for followers of Jesus Christ the supreme authority should be that of love as this was the supreme authority for Jesus.

This is easy to say but what does it mean in action and emphasis? It seems to follow that the church will only be able to act with authority as it becomes an accepting, loving, supportive, challenging community, a community held together by "bonds of affection." Such a community requires some structure, order, and form, which are not ends in themselves, but the means that enable the church to be and to do what it is called to be and do.

If, therefore, we are to examine the issue of authority in the church creatively, I believe we must start not by examining structures but by reflecting and seeking to clarify our understanding about how the church can become more of a loving, serving, transforming community; how it can come to be a channel for the loving energy of God to flow into the life of the world. Only after we get greater clarity about this will we be in a position to know what forms and structures and relationships will be most appropriate.

In the meantime, the present realities of structures, forms, and relationships continue to exist. My belief is that we must seek to use them "to loose" rather than "to bind," and so to provide a more open, reflective community where there is greater freedom to explore and to initiate, where the wind and fire of the Spirit can more easily be at work, so that new divine power can bring new life.

Authority in the Church: Spiritual Freedom and the Corporate Nature of Faith

H.R. McAdoo

A survey made in 1981 claimed that 57.9 per cent of Anglican clergy and laity in the dioceses of the United States of America are so by decision and adoption.[1] What has drawn them from other churches, or from none, and what does Anglicanism give us all? What are the gifts which, in company with our fellow gift-bearers, we hope to bring in humility to what Theodore Wedel called "the coming Great Church"?

Various answers will be made depending on the personal experience and the ecclesial background of those who become Anglicans. I suspect that for many it may be the attraction, either clearly grasped or dimly perceived, of a spiritual freedom within the parameters of "the faith once for all delivered" (Jude, v.3). People sense a desired or experienced reality for their lives somewhere deep down within that creative tension between the truth which makes one free, between the glorious liberty of the sons of God, and that *hapax*, that once-for-allness of the Father's revelation in the Son made effective in the present for the Family through the Spirit. At its best, Anglicanism has striven to express this both in its concept of authority and in the instruments and instrumentalities of that authority within the life of the *koinonia*. The point is taken up in an interesting comment from a current journal:

> The Anglican way, the Via Media, holds together the claims of the individual to freedom, a freedom which can annihilate all real unity, and of the church to authority, an authority which can annihilate the free development of the individual. When this balance passes into the intellectual sphere, it is seen as limiting the extent of the conflict between authority and private judgement. Charles Gore, the great exponent of a positive and dynamic understanding of the Via Media, wrote that:

> The extremes are represented by a dogmatism which crushes instead of quickening the reason of the individual, making it purely passive and acquiescent, and on the other hand by a unrestrained development of the individual judgement which becomes eccentric and lawless just because it is unrestrained. (*Roman Catholic Claims*, 1889, 6)
>
> Stephen Neill has stressed that the Anglican way is demanding; it leaves a man with full moral and intellectual freedom, but it rests on a confidence that has been rarely found in Roman Catholicism, a confidence in the ability of the truth to make itself known. With such confidence, a universal primate, preserved from error by divine grace, may seem to be superfluous luxury. We should not be too quick to write off the idea of Via Media as negative, irrelevant or useless in the contemporary dialogue.[2]

This is how it struck Emmanuel Amand de Mendieta as he reflected on his later experience as an Anglican from within the Church of England. He saw this spirit as a quality differentiating the Anglican from the Roman and Orthodox communions with which it nevertheless shares so much in common: ''This emphasis on spiritual freedom has coloured the whole ethos and expression of Anglicanism. There is no other Church in the Catholic tradition . . . which so passionately believes in spiritual freedom, and which so positively demands it from clergy and laity alike.''[3]

Like William Temple, he recognized the inherent dangers but felt them to be outweighed by the gain which Temple saw as coming from this freedom in terms of ''a fullness of individual apprehension and appropriation''[4] — in a word, *maturity, the goal of responsible and responsive membership.*

Clearly, it is precisely this attraction which led Bishop Michael Marshall to become an Anglican and to see world Anglicanism as ''a provisional prototype of the reunited *Ecumene*'' (to quote the Roman Catholic Van de Pol). This comes across in Marshall's book *The Anglican Church Today and Tomorrow* and he has some very pertinent things to say in this connection about authority, to which we may return.[5]

Centuries ago, and in a different setting, Archbishop Laud was conscious of the need to reconcile the *hapax* and spiritual freedom when, in the preface to his *Conference*, he wrote that catholicity was not to be confined within "a narrow conclave" and so he desired "to lay open those wider gates of the Catholic church, confined to no age, time or place; not knowing any bounds but that faith which was once (and but once for all) delivered to the saints."

This same freedom/authority tension remains embedded in the very concept of membership in the church and is at the centre of the ecumenical dialogue. To speak of spiritual freedom when the freedom you are talking about is Christian freedom, created by the Truth, is inevitably to find oneself ultimately talking also about Christian authority and about the *hapax*. The paradox is inescapably at the heart of Christian believing and Christian behaving so that St. James can even write about "the perfect *law* of *freedom*" (James 1:25). And anyway, can Christians talk about freedom and authority without talking about the Spirit's abiding in the church? All the time, the institutional church which is "a witness and a keeper of Holy Writ" (Article XX: *Of the Authority of the Church*) has to present the content of the *hapax* in such a way that each generation can understand in its own idiom and appropriate to itself the message of salvation in terms real for its own day: "*Interpréter un dogme, c'est lancer un pont entre deux mondes, celui dans lequel il a été formulé et celui dans lequel nous vivons.*"[6] It is here at this point of perception that the member of the church becomes aware of the limitation of this Christian freedom and of the nature of this Christian authority.

Successive Lambeth Conferences

Lambeth 1978

The 1978 Lambeth Conference requested the primates to institute a study of authority, its nature and exercise, within the Anglican household of faith. Resolution 11 reads:

> The Conference advises member Churches not to take action *regarding issues which are of concern to the whole Anglican Communion* without consultation with a Lambeth Conference or with the episcopate through the Primates' Committee, and requests the Primates to initiate a study of the nature of authority within the Anglican Communion.

While no doubt it was the disciplinary aspect of the ordination of women by some Anglican provinces which was the catalyst here, the final clause indicated a desire for some solid thinking on the meaning, purpose, and implementation of authority within our world-wide church. The 1978 *Report* underlines the need at two points. The first is the comment on episcopal authority and synodical government which begins by declaring that "all authority comes from God and that which is given to the Church involves all the people of God *in responsibility and obedience.*"[7] Neither bishop (nor synod) receives authority "by any succession independent of the Church." Incidentally Laud said the same thing about councils which have no power or assistance "but what is in and to the Church." That assistance is given "when they suffer themselves to be led by the Blessed Spirit, by the Word of God."[8] The 1978 *Report* likewise refers to "awaiting the continuing judgement of the Holy Spirit expressed by the *sensus fidelium*" and to "the authority of a) Holy Scripture and b) tradition." It adds: "The guardianship of the faith is a collegial responsibility of the episcopate. Synodical government should make provision for this responsibility to be fulfilled." This, in fact, has been incorporated in the constitution of the Church of Ireland where the House of Bishops is provided with a power of veto in the proceedings of the General Synod (*Constitution*, Ch. I, 19-21).

Here, in a brief aside, the Lambeth *Report* plunges us into the heart of the problem — the purpose of authority in the church, the instruments and instrumentalities of authority, its relation to the corporate body of believers and to the individual believer, and above all the relation of the objective of authority, the maintenance of the church in the truth of the gospel, to the work of the Holy Spirit abiding in the church.

I venture to offer here a summary I wrote elsewhere which may help to concentrate ideas at this juncture.

In summary, therefore, Anglicanism has a concept of authority which relates directly to authority's primary function of maintaining the Church in the truth. It has an instrument or instrumentality which can apply the theological criterion (i.e., the appeal to Scripture, to tradition comfortable to Scripture, and to reason) authoritatively, and which has also administrative and legislative functions in respect of the life, worship and mission of the Church. This instrumentality is the episcopate and the bishops in synodical association with the clergy and laity. It is a concept of the nature and exercise of authority which, while fully capable of acting on behalf of the whole Church in matters of doctrine, sacraments and discipline, nevertheless leans to an emphasis on process rather than on the juridical. One suspects that what undergirds this is a deeply-rooted Anglican conviction that the Spirit's guidance is not irresistible and that the Church in history has not necessarily at all times been perfectly responsive to its infallible Guide (cf. Article XIX). As E.J. Bicknell pointed out long ago, what was promised to the Church was not infallibility but an infallible Guide, the Holy Spirit.[9] This raises the important aspect of how this authority ensures the Church's permanence in truth — is the Chruch as such infallible or indefectible? Is it an uninterrupted or an ultimate reliability which is at issue?[10]

In this way the Anglican model works out in the local church and provincial church setting *but what of authority in a world-wide communion?* This is the source of the anxiety and unease which prompted Resolution 11 and it was to this that the then archbishop of Canterbury turned in a speech to the 1978 Conference.[11] This constituted the *Report's* second underlining of the urgency of this problem for Anglicans. Strictly speaking the archbishop's intervention has to do not with authority in itself but with the instrumentality of authority in the Anglican communion, a search, as he put it, "to find out where the centre of authority is." The problem as he saw it is how to construct an instrumentality of authority for a world-wide communion of twenty-five churches which would enable the achieving of a "common mind on main issues . . . at the same time maintaining the independence of the member Churches themselves." The problem is a typically Anglican one and by no means separable from that deeper strain of spiritual freedom in the Anglican ethos. It makes real difficulties, however, in the quest for what Randall Davidson, in the run up to the Lambeth Conference of 1897, termed a "central tribunal of reference, for disputes on doctrinal or even disciplinary questions." So he had written to the American Bishop Doane, going on to dismiss as unacceptable to the Conference "anything in the nature of a Canterbury *Patriarchate*."

In his observations to the Conference of 1978, Archbishop Donald Coggan took the same line that this suggestion did not accord with "the genius of Anglicanism." He similarly rejected a legislative Lambeth Conference, or an Anglican Consultative Council transformed into a central authority. Positively, he held that we are now trying to learn how to maintain the healthy and health-giving episcopacy/synodical government tension (some Anglicans have been engaged on this exercise for more than a century!). So "*where*," in the archbishop's view, "*is authority to be found?*" He thinks that such a centre of authority may be created through regular meetings of the primates of the world-wide communion. The primates "as they meet, should be in the very closest and most intimate contact with the Anglican Consultative Council." The archbishop concluded that

> on lines something like these — without a rigidity which would be foreign to our tradition — we should move towards a maturity in the exercise of authority which would be to the good of our Communion as a whole and might well be the means through us of our making a contribution to the whole Catholic Church of God.

That is well said. It chimes with the "It seems good to the Holy Spirit and to us" of the first Christian Council of apostles, presbyters, and the whole church (Acts 15). It meshes with the Anglican authority-process of the continuous appeal to scripture, tradition, and reason. Such meetings, the archbishop thought, "should be held perhaps as frequently as once in two years." Anglicans will hope and ask that this model, the only one so far proposed, will be used in the most effective and structured way possible. If systematically and regularly used, and if the member churches are made aware of its function and encouraged to call on its services, this could be extremely valuable. Since the Lambeth Conference, the primates have met three times, once in conjunction with the ACC Standing Committee and this is proposed again for 1986. The Anglican churches, through their respective primates, should make a habit of bringing major matters before such a body, thus making it a normal and accepted process and channel of consultation. We ought to be aware, however, that the objective can be achieved only through the exercise of forebearance, charity, and fraternal consultation on the part of each and every Anglican province. "Going it alone" is, of course, the legislative prerogative of each General Synod (within the accepted parameters of faith and order as set out, for example, in the Lambeth Quadrilateral). It can even at times be prophetic action but such must surely go hand in hand with "love of the brethren" lest its effects be simply divisive rather than challenging to the communion as a whole.

Lambeth 1968

If Lambeth 1978 was chiefly concerned with a possible structure for the exercise of authority, the preceding Conference had something to say concerning the nature of authority in the church. Again, the matter arose in connection with something else, the role of the Thirty-nine Articles in the Anglican communion as a whole.

The Addendum (*Report*, pp. 82-3) is concerned with relating authority in the church to the corporate nature of faith. In fact, it identifies authority with the inheritance of faith and comments on how this ethos is creative of an "ordered liberty" — a further resonance of the relation of spiritual freedom to the corporate faith of the Spirit-led community:

> The inheritance of faith which characterizes the Anglican Communion is an authority of a multiple kind and . . . to the different elements which occur in the different strands of this inheritance, different Anglicans attribute different levels of authority. From this foundation arises Anglican tolerance, comprehensiveness, *and ordered liberty*. . . .

The Addendum then describes the inheritance of faith along the familiar Anglican lines of scripture, tradition, and reason.[12] The first strand is the Holy Scriptures also "proclaimed in the Catholic Creeds set in their context of baptismal profession, patristic reasoning, and conciliar decision." The second strand consists of the Church of England's "witness of its own to Christian truth, particularly in its historic formularies." The third strand is the continuing "responsible witness to Christian truth" through Anglican preaching, worship, and

> the writings of its scholars and teachers, the lives of its saints and confessors, and the utterances of its councils. In this third strand, as in the Preface to the Prayer Book of 1549, can be discerned the authority given within the Anglican tradition to reason, not least as exercised in historical and philosophical enquiry, as well as an acknowledgement of the claims of pastoral care.

This is an underlining of the classical Anglican position and how it relates to the spiritual freedom of the individual must be endemic in any concept of mature or responsible membership. This is brought out further by the Addendum's description of authority:

> To such a threefold inheritance of faith belongs a concept of authority *which refuses to insulate itself against the testing of history and the free action of reason.* It seeks to be a credible authority and therefore is concerned to secure satisfactory historical support and to have its credentials in a shape which corresponds to the requirements of reason.

Interestingly, echoes of this relation between spiritual freedom and the corporate nature of faith may be heard in the preamble to the same Conference's section on renewal in faith.[13] It is alive to the mutual interaction of freedom and the *hapax* where it speaks of the need for "a deeper awareness of the deposit of the faith once delivered to the saints" and "for an attitude and an approach that combine Christian assurance with a bold exploration of theology and society." It is also aware "that recent theological discussion, while it has been liberating to some, has been thought by others to be destructive of faith." So far, this is simply a setting out afresh of the *status quaestionis*, occasioned in this instance by the then current "debate about God" and this is further elaborated on in the course of the section report.[14] The group responsible for the theme "renewal in faith" was clearly alive to the problems of communicating the faith in a time of change and of free questioning in Western society. It was conscious of an apparent clash between "new exploration (which) can in the end be fortifying and enriching" and "the impression . . . sometimes given that the whole basis of Christianity is undermined." It called for more understanding between those engaged in academic and those engaged in pastoral ministries. *Plus ça change* — the very same situation has arisen this year in connection with statements attributed to the bishop of Durham. If the *Report* was somewhat euphoric in connection with the "beneficial reformulations of the Christian faith (which) have often arisen out of conflicts" there is something further of value in the phrase, "We also remember that the Church and Christian tradition cannot truly be themselves if they are *static.*"[15]

The last word is significant, for it is in this area of movement and insight, of interpretation and translation of the given faith which the church guards and proclaims, that the relation between corporate faith and freedom is seen to have its inevitable interactions. This is reflected also in the section on "Renewal in Ministry" where the bishop is called on to exercise an authority which is rooted in the authority of the risen Christ, Servant and Lord. The bishop's service "is developed in his work of teaching and *safeguarding the faith.* . . . As a teacher he must try to evoke the creative thinking of his people."[16]

In other words, the gospel is dynamic, not static. Its proclamation demands communication in a way appropriate to a generation or a culture while at the same time its content must be "safeguarded," neither diminished nor explained away.

Something of all this has been particularly well expressed in the ARCIC statement, *Authority in the Church,* 1, 15:

> The Church's life and work are shaped by its historical origins, by its subsequent experience, and by its endeavour to make the relevance of the Gospel plain to every generation. Through reflection upon the word, through the proclamation of the Gospel, through baptism, through worship, especially the eucharist, the people of God are moved to the living remembrance of Jesus Christ and of the experience and witness of the apostolic community. This remembrance supports and guides them in their search for language which will effectively communicate the meaning of the Gospel.

All generations and cultures must be helped to understand that the good news of salvation is also for them. It is not enough for the Church simply to repeat the original apostolic words. It has also prophetically to translate them in order that the hearers in their situation may understand and respond to them. All such restatement must be consonant with the apostolic witness recorded in the Scriptures; for in this witness the preaching and teaching of ministers, and statements of local and universal councils, have to find their ground and consistency. Although these clarifications are conditioned by the circumstances which prompted them, some of their perceptions may be of lasting value. In this process the Church itself may come to see more clearly the implications of the Gospel. This is why the Church has endorsed certain formulas as authentic expressions of its witness, whose significance transcends the setting in which they were first formulated. This is not to claim that these formulas are the only possible, or even the most exact, way of expressing the faith, or that they can never be improved. Even when a doctrinal definition is regarded by the Christian community as part of its permanent teaching, this does not exclude subsequent restatement. Although the categories of thought and the mode of expression may be superseded, restatement always builds upon, and does not contradict, the truth intended by the original definition.

ARCIC is saying that in its mission of proclaiming God's saving work in Christ, the church, as it strives to build up the new community of Christian life, has found "creeds, conciliar definitions and other statements of belief indispensable. But these are always instrumental to the truth which they are intended to convey."[17]

Returning to the 1968 Lambeth *Report* in its section on renewal in faith, we encounter this same concern for building up a community committed in faith and obedience to the active expression of God's love in Christ the Servant. Right at the beginning of the section we meet the affirmation:

This faith, which is set forth uniquely in the Scriptures and is summed up in the Catholic Creeds, develops and grows under the guidance of the Holy Spirit within the life of the Church, the Body of Christ. The mission of the Church is to bear witness to Jesus Christ as Lord and Saviour of the world, who offers all men the true fulfilment of their longings and their hopes.[18]

Here is an assertion of the dynamism of faith under the tutelage of the Spirit abiding in the church, a concept constantly referred to also in the Agreed Statement, *Authority in the Church,* 1. This is a vital element in the assessment of Christian authority bearing as it does on the church's indefectibility and on the Spirit's guidance to the Christian community which is thus "enabled by the Holy Spirit to live out the Gospel and so to be led into all truth."[19] In addition to the affirmation already quoted one may note the preamble to the same section of the Lambeth 1968 *Report,* (p. 63):

To say that the Church needs renewal is to say that it must show itself to be a *fellowship of the Holy Spirit, the giver of all newness of life and truth.* The Church always needs a renewed awareness of the Gospel, the good news of God's love and grace in Jesus Christ; *a deeper awareness of the deposit of the faith once delivered to the saints;* a fresh awareness of the things that cannot be shaken. Without renewal, Christian theology and Christian institutions become as dry bones; with the renewal of the Spirit they become the lively expression of a transforming vision. We recognize, however, that recent theological discussion, while it has been liberating to some, has been thought by others to be destructive of faith.

No assessment of authority in the church is possible without giving full value to the role and function of the Spirit and the scriptures. By stressing this, Lambeth 1968 contributes to our attempt to carry out Resolution 11 of Lambeth 1978 "to initiate a study of the nature of authority within the Anglican Communion." As William Laud put it three and a half centuries ago, the councils of the church must "suffer themselves to be led by the Blessed Spirit, by the Word of God." His *Conference* with Fisher represents a typical Anglican statement on the relative authority of scripture and of tradition in the life of the church. So is his relating

of the authority of conciliar judgements to the guidance of the
Spirit and to the scriptural criterion in the context of the church's
indefectibility.

Here is where twentieth-century Anglicans must put to
themselves certain questions concerning the corporate nature of
faith if we wish to do some honest self-examination on how we
understand authority in the church, its nature and functioning.
Where is doctrine to be found? What constitutes the essential faith
of the church? What are the fundamentals and what guarantees
a doctrine as authentic Christian teaching? What are the legitimate
limits of diversity and what legitimizes them?[20] To this we shall
return but first can we see a lead-in contained in the phrasing
of the affirmation already cited from the section report of Lambeth
1968?

To my mind, the passage contains a hidden agenda when it
describes the faith "uniquely set forth in the Scriptures" as a faith
which "*develops and grows* under the guidance of the Holy Spirit
within the life of the Church." What does this mean? If the faith
is *hapax paradotheise,* once for all delivered, then in what sense
can it be said to "develop and grow" — even under the guidance
of the Spirit abiding in the church? *Development* — shades of J.H.
Newman and J.K. Mozley! At once one senses the stirrings of
a long-dormant Podsnappery: "I knew it from the first. Development. No. Never with my consent. Not Anglican." (With
apologies to Charles Dickens and *Our Mutual Friend.*)

For, in fact, the hidden agenda in the passage quoted *is* development, and the question is, What does it mean for Anglicans, for
all Christians, in relation to revealed truth? Is not "revelation"
closed and does not "development" represent a method of
adding to revelation — under the counter, so to speak? Here we
need to attempt a clarification by asking ourselves what is meant
to be conveyed by both concepts, revelation and development,
and how they bear on the criteria by means of which the church
can answer the question, What is your authority for asserting that
this or that is part of authentic Christianity?

In the first place, tedious argument and misunderstanding can
be avoided if we distance ourselves from any propositional concept of revelation. God did not unveil a series of propositions but

revealed himself in Christ and continues to do so through the Spirit abiding in the church. Certainly, revelation is "closed" since "in this final age he has spoken to us in the Son" (Hebrews 1:2), but because he continues to communicate with us in Jesus, the living Lord, through the Spirit, then revelation has a dynamism of life and carries with it the unceasing requirement of constant re-presentation of the nature and being of God, of the truths of the Incarnation and of the Paschal Mystery, if the revelation is to be proclaimed and appropriated through all the changes of history and in a variety of human cultures.

This process of apprehension and reflection involves an element of development. One may instance the fourth-century development of the Catholic doctrine of the Trinity or the medieval, Reformation, and later theories of the Atonement. In either case it can be shown that the later church, accepting revelation as did the early church, accepted it differently and with a wider and deeper understanding of certain concepts, such as the concept of sacrifice. This can fairly be described as development. But one thing also stands out: it is development *from* the facts, the content, of revelation, not development away from them or independent of them. Thus the reality of the Father, Son, and Holy Spirit, experienced in the life of the new community of faith, asserts itself throughout the New Testament, though nowhere does the word *Trinity* occur, to say nothing of the word *homoousios*. The same is true in the case of the Atonement but could not similarly be claimed for the dogma of the Assumption. So what we are saying is that there is continuity of doctrine and there is historicity so that development must have criteria. These are contained primarily in scripture, but also in the living tradition conformable to scripture and in the life and worship of the church. Without these historical checks, development can become what R.P.C. Hanson describes as "A virtually uncontrolled doctrinal space flight."[21] The result can then be a dogmatic super-structure with little foundation or a reduced Christianity bearing little resemblance to the faith of the ages. Are we then to be forced back to a new fundamentalism in our investigation of the nature and the working of authority? Not so, writes Hanson in his admirable *The Continuity of Christian Doctrine,* while claiming that "it is highly unsatifactory to

emancipate the development of doctrine from all historical checks
. . . and when we speak about historical checks we realize at once
that there can be only one primary check, Holy Scripture."[22]

Interestingly, it is this concept of "checks" and "mutual checking" which underlies the 1948 Lambeth Conference's explication
of authority in the Anglican communion. Hanson maintains that
scripture must be used as a norm, but with flexibility, and tradition must remain as a criterion, but open to reassessment. In his
view development does not take place in a straight line by "ever-
increasing growth and articulation of a vast unending system of
doctrinal elaboration and speculation. It should have and will
have its periods of reduction, retrenchment, reformation, and
reconsideration as the anchor-line of Scripture pulls back the
adventurous ship of development."[23] Elsewhere in his Tuohy
Lectures, Bishop Hanson likens development to a boat moored
to a fixed buoy; "There is a point at which the cable attached to
the buoy always checks its course, not always pulling it back to
the same point, but always preventing it moving any further on
its existing course."[24]

Lambeth 1948

Hanson's evaluation of the place and function of the criteria sends
us back with revived interest to the 1948 Lambeth Conference's
committee report on the Anglican communion and in particular
to the section on "The Meaning and the Unity of the Anglican
Communion," wording significant in itself for our subject. A good
case could be made for maintaining that no Lambeth Conference
has so far produced anything better on the nature and instruments of authority as understood by Anglicans. It should be
recommended reading for all students of Anglican theology.[25]
The reader is referred to the text of the statement quoted in full
in the Appendix.

The answer which this report gives to the question whether
Anglicanism is based on a sufficiently coherent form of authority is to a remarkable degree echoed in the Agreed Statement,
Authority in the Church of ARCIC I, 26. Authority is from Christ,
and scripture is normative for corporate faith. There is mention
of continuity of doctrine, conciliar authority and reception, the
church's task of representing and re-interpreting, the authority

of the Christ-like life, and the role of the ministry — all are present in both documents. Had Charles Gore lived another sixteen years to 1948, his approval of these Lambeth sentiments would have sounded out loud and clear. Here then is one example of how Anglican theology, seeking to understand authority in the church, faced the inbuilt tension between spiritual freedom and corporate faith, endeavouring to avoid the dilemma of extremes to which Gore referred in the extract quoted at the beginning of this chapter.

Lambeth 1888

A quick glance at the Lambeth Conference *Report* of 1888 will conclude this section. It was the year of the Lambeth Quadrilateral — not, of course, that the Lambeth fathers had produced it there and then out of a hat.[26] It was in reality a distillation of all that *Ecclesia Anglicana* had learnt over the centuries of worship, work, and witness and in the writings of unnumbered theologians. Yet the importance then and since of the Quadrilateral has dimmed the memory that the Conference also discussed and reported on authoritative standards of doctrine and worship.[27] Consideration of the subject was evoked by growing ecumenical contacts and by Anglican expansion throughout the world. It was a world of Empire and of an ebbing tide of liberalism in continental Europe. It was an ecclesiastical world in which what Garrett Sweeney has called Italianism contributed generously to the 1870 decree of Vatican I, *Pastor Aeternus*.

> Salvation, both in Church and State, lay in strong centralized governments, dominating unified and obedient populations. It was no mere coincidence that the definition of the Primacy came within the same twelve months which saw the proclamation of the German Empire and the unification of Italy; came shortly after the United States had asserted its unity in the Civil War; and was to be followed in a few brief years by Victoria's crown of Empire, and liberal England's brief excursion into Imperialism.[28]

In such a climate, a conference of a world communion might fairly be expected to reflect in its deliberations a desire to express itself on such a vital subject as authority. But it is altogether to the credit of Lambeth 1888 that its motivation was quite different and its expression of the principle never lost sight of the fundamental Anglican concept which governs all the communion's thinking on this matter.

> We declare that we are united under one divine Head in the fellowship of the one Catholic and Apostolic Church, holding the one faith revealed in Holy Writ, defined in the Creeds, maintained by the Primitive Church and reaffirmed by the undisputed Ecumenical Councils.

Its motivation in declaring Anglican adherence to the faith once for all delivered is to make clear the basis of corporate faith for the benefit of younger Anglican churches and as a starting point for conversations with Old Catholics and Orthodox, as well as for what the Conference called "Home Re-union." This is apparent from the succession of resolutions following Resolution 11 (which sets out the terms of the Lambeth Quadrilateral — scripture, creeds, the sacraments of baptism and eucharist, and the historic episcopate).

But tucked away in the paragraph on authoritative standards in the encyclical letter is a phrase which makes clear that the fathers, even then at that time in history, were determined not to lose sight of that spiritual freedom which is part of this Anglican inheritance.

> It is of the utmost importance that our faith and practice should be represented, both to the ancient Churches and to the native and growing Churches in the mission-field, in a manner which shall neither give cause for offence nor *restrict due liberty,* nor present any stumbling-blocks in the way of complete communion.[29]

In a move which, for a century ago, was decidedly liberal and promotive of "due liberty," the Conference followed this up by declaring that newly constituted churches abroad "should not necessarily be bound to accept in their entirety the Thirty-nine Articles of Religion," provided they receive "from us Episcopal Succession, (and) that we should first receive from them satifactory evidence that they hold substantially the same doctrine as our own."[30] In this connection and in view of recent developments in respect of the "desire of both the Lusitanian and Spanish Reformed Churches to become fully integrated members of the Anglican Communion" (Resolution 14 of Lambeth 1978), Resolution 15D of Lambeth 1888 is of interest ". . . we trust that they [reformers in these countries] may be enabled to adopt such sound forms of doctrine and discipline, and to secure such Catholic organisation as will permit us to give them a further recognition."[31] The Church of Ireland's role in supporting these churches from the time of Lord Plunkett, archbishop of Dublin (1885-1897), onwards can now be seen as prophetic and courageous.

Finally, the Conference of 1888, while favouring the suggestion of a manual of church doctrine, declined to treat any such "as an authoritative standard of the Church" and firmly rejected the idea "that any new declaration of doctrine should, at the present time, be put forth by authority."[32]

As one passes in review the recorded deliberations of a century of Lambeth Conferences as these bear on the subject of authority in the Anglican communion, there can be clearly discerned a marked consistency in setting out the framework, the bones, so to speak, of a position. The position was constantly maintained but successive Lambeth Conferences did not permit the bones to fossilize. They have not been insensitive to the transition through which men's minds have been passing, in times of war, in social revolution, and in theological upheaval. In changing conditions, they have tried, if with varying success, to be aware both of the needs of the faithful and of the queries of the seekers, and to "ensure that tradition is not fossilized in historic formularies, but available in a living and continuous stream."

The Perfect Law of Freedom

So then, authority's judicial function in the church is to be declarative of the truth. The church is "God's household, that is, the Church of the living God, the pillar and bulwark of the truth" (1 Timothy 3:15). The church, says Article XX, is *testis et conservatrix* and the primacy of the scriptural criterion of saving faith is merged in the Article's description of the authority of the church. The deposit is to be guarded (1 Timothy 6:20) but "with the help of the Holy Spirit dwelling with us" (2 Timothy 1:14),

implying not a continuous revelation but a continuous interpretation through the Spirit abiding in the church of what has been
"once for all delivered" (Jude 3). The authority-process works
in a range of ways, varying from general councils, synods,
episcopates, to the consent of the universal church and to the
multiple authority of the inheritance of faith, and all the time certain norms are operative to ensure that the fundamental objective content and quality, "the truth of the Gospel" (Galatians 2:5),
may be maintained in its purity and power. So far, one can say
that institutionally and in its formularies and official statements,
Anglicanism has never lost sight of all this, but what happens
to that spiritual freedom of which Amand de Mendieta was so
proud, and *what kind of freedom is it?*

The question, for some members of the church, will often be
about how one's own spiritual freedom relates to the commitment which all the baptized and confirmed make to the corporate
faith of the church. Some find no difficulty in a total acceptance,
while for others there will be areas opposite which they see
question-marks. It is not a new phenomenon — how could it be
since the reflective capacity is part of being human? Archbishop
Laud, as we saw, was strong on the corporate faith of the people
of God, but he also contended that "grace is never placed but
in a reasonable creature." Just as clearly as any modern he
recognized the need and the impulsion in the human spirit: "man
. . . is still apt to search and seek for a reason why he will
believe." Nothing, in Laud's view, could or should prevent him
from weighing all "at the balance of reason" even "the tradition
of the Church, the inward motives in Scripture itself."[33] For him,
this freedom is part of being human and, equally, acceptance of
the parameters of the *hapax* is part of being an Anglican. Three
or four years later the publication of *Religio Medici* showed how
a cultivated layman handled this dynamic interaction between
spiritual freedom and corporate faith which has always been
recognized by Anglicans as a fact of life and membership. Sir
Thomas Browne was a totally committed Anglican with a
generous attitude to other Christians which was well ahead of
the times. He writes of:

> The Church of England to whose faith I am a sworne subject,
> and therefore in a double obligation subscribe unto her articles,
> and endeavour to observe her Constitutions: whatsoever is

beyond, as points indifferent, I observe according to the rules of my private reason, or the humour and fashion of my devotion. . . . In brief, where the Scripture is silent, the Church is my Text; where that speakes, 'tis but my Comment, where there is a joynt silence of both, I borrow not the rules of my Religion from Rome or Geneva, but the dictates of my own reason.[34]

The plain fact is that men like Laud and Browne accepted "the revelation" and accepted that in consequence there was a sense in which, for the Christian, corporate faith limits individual spiritual freedom; that if you wished to call yourself an Anglican you could not exempt yourself from the requirements of the corporate faith of the church and continue to claim membership.

What then of today? As it seems to me, the heart of the matter from a practical point of view lies in the area of comprehensiveness, as was indeed pointed out by Lambeth 1948. Stephen Sykes has some very pressing questions here and some telling criticisms.[35] While, for reasons adduced elsewhere[36] I would not go along with all his conclusions, I think that he has put his finger on the nub of the problem, for the problem is that, if authority's function is to maintain the church in the truth, then authority is called on from time to time to assert the limits of comprehensiveness. Part of the thrust of this chapter has been the attempt to show that these limits have been set out in our formularies and endorsed by successive Lambeth Conferences, never losing sight of the continued Anglican stress on reason and free enquiry, a tradition stretching from Richard Hooker, John Hales, the Tew circle, and the Cambridge Platonists to the present day.

Here one comes to realize something of the complexity of the human and theological situation in which comprehensiveness, diversity, freedom, historicity, and criteria are all seen to be valid elements. As far as comprehensiveness is concerned, Lambeth 1968 took note of the interplay of these elements when it made three statements: "Comprehensiveness demands agreement on fundamentals . . . comprehensiveness is not compromise. It is not a sophisticated word for syncretism . . . comprehensiveness implies a willingness to allow liberty of interpretation."[37]

Behind this lies the continuing Anglican insistence from Jewel onwards on the *hapax*, "the faith once for all delivered," something inseparable from belief in which historical checks, particularly that of Holy Scripture, operate. In other words, as we have maintained in the first part of this chapter, there are parameters. The present archbishop of Canterbury wrote that "it is quite alien to original Anglican thought that there could be logically opposite expressions of faith in fundamentals. To be an Anglican is not to be content with self-contradiction." He went on to relate this to a description of comprehensiveness as "the achievement of unity in diversity through the distinction of the essential from the non-essential by means of the Holy Scriptures interpreted by Tradition, in the light of Reason, all expressed in and through the corporate worship of the Church."[38] It was T.S. Eliot, himself a convert to Anglicanism, who wrote, "A Catholicism *without* the element of humanism and criticism would be a Catholicism of despair."[39] A.M. Allchin comments that Eliot found in the classical Anglican theology

> a willingness to question, to recognise the uncertainties which surround even our deepest certainties . . . not that the willingness to leave many questions open and unsettled implies any denial of the reality of man's knowledge to God. The apparent openness of seventeenth century Anglicanism does not proceed from a lack of commitment in the fundamental areas of Christian faith. To recognise our own uncertainties can be a mark of realism and humility, and can make us in the end more willing to acknowledge the great but mysterious certainties of God.[40]

What we are seeing here is the perennial quality of the traditional Anglican theological method, the appeal to scripture, tradition, and reason — perennial because it belongs to the spirit of Anglicanism in every generation. Twenty-five years ago Archbishop Michael Ramsey adjudged that "the times call urgently for the Anglican witness to Scripture, tradition and reason," a theme which he developed in his Hale lectures.[41] Last year, the same theme was convincingly developed for our own times by Bishop Michael Marshall in his candid and appreciative analysis of the Anglican ethos in *The Anglican Church Today and Tomorrow*.[42] Comprehensiveness springs, says Peter Baelz, "from a proper recognition of the *complementarities* of the Christian response to the gospel, not from an easy-going accommodation and compromise.''[43] The Anglican church is both catholic and reformed and has absorbed the insights of the Renaissance. Anglicanism is saying that evangelical and catholic views are not alternatives but that in scriptural faith both are one. Anglicanism is saying that ''here is the one Gospel of God; inevitably it includes the Scriptures and the salvation of the individual; and inevitably the order and sacramental life of the Body of Christ, and the freedom of thought wherewith Christ has made man free.''[44]

As far as this freedom through which Christ makes men free is concerned, what emerges in the spirit of Anglicanism is neither permission to treat the household of faith as no more than a theological debating society nor a demand to toe a literalist line. Rather, is it the case that we are being led to understand in matters of faith, corporate and personal, that *freedom* has a perfect *law*?

If we accept Marshall's assertion that ''at its best, Anglicanism has been a strong ally of the human quest,''[45] must we not also agree that the living context of this Christian freedom is membership through baptism in the eucharistic fellowship of apostolic faith: ''they that gladly received his word were baptised . . . and they continued steadfastly in the apostles' doctrine and fellowship, and in breaking of bread, and in prayers'' (Acts 2:41-2). In other words, Christian freedom cannot be divorced from the implications of membership in the household of faith or considered apart from that given faith which consititutes the church as an identifiable society. This is seen as central to the problem by Anthony Harvey in his essay in the Doctrine Commission's Report:

> As an individual I am of course free to believe what I like. . . . But in so far as I am a member of the Church, I associate myself with a ''corporate believing'' which consists in a recognition of, and a constantly changing response to, ''the authority of Scripture.'' There may be no point at which this ever-moving response to the historic given-ness of Christianity can be caught, immobilized and presented as a still shot, a systematic statement of belief (though an important part of the response itself will consist of personal attempts by the theologians to do precisely this). But this does not prevent any individual who

consciously associates himself with the Church from recognizing that, by so doing, he is making his own personal understanding of the faith to a certain extent subservient to the collective activity of attention to, and interpretation of, Scripture which is an essential part of corporate believing.[46]

Are we being led to discover a fresh content and context for that favourite term of our forbears — "obediential faith"?

A valuable aspect of the Report of the Doctrine Commission is the way in which many of the essays face up to what Basil Mitchell calls, "the problem of how to reconcile individual thought with corporate commitment."[47] Space forbids anything more than a selective condensation of some of the points raised, a précis which must surely send us back to study the Report, one of the more honest, perceptive, and often profound of such documents in recent times. Into the discussion come such matters as living with declared doctrine; the limits of development; the difference between doctrine and theology and the relation of both to corporate believing; the exercise of the freedom through which Christ makes men free and the duty of the theologian both to the tradition and to the community; the distinction between forebearance and compromise; the current exaggeration of individualism which ignores the role of corporate believing in the formation of the individual's view, even by reaction; the importance of a recognizable adherence to declared doctrine which is "part of the Church's struggle to *be* the Church";[48] the right of church members to expect not only honesty but loyalty from their teachers. One could continue but it would be fair to say that throughout the Report's handling of its theme, the corporate nature of faith and how this bears on individual freedom in the ethos of Anglicanism, there runs "the conviction that there is an underlying unity of belief, and that this underlying unity is best safeguarded by a strong tradition whose stability nourishes the faith of individuals, while their freedom to question prevents it ossifying."[49]

In other words, what is surfacing in the Report and throughout this investigation is a growing realization that Lambeth 1968's comprehensiveness and ordered liberty is no chimera. Rather it is a reality factually experienced in truth by Anglicans as a total attitude authentically arising from the three-fold appeal to scripture, tradition, and reason. One grows weary of the rather smug throw-away remark fashionable in some Anglican circles, "Of course, it's not tidy." That's as may be, but what one wants to say is that it is an experienced reality which holds and draws many people to the Anglican ideal. Nor is it any more adequate to talk in terms of pragmatism, "In fact, it works." Again, that's as may be, but the truth is that comprehensiveness and ordered liberty don't just happen fortuitously. They are the outcome of that organic process of growth and interplay, of mutual checking, as men's reason reaches out to the mystery of faith, questing and yet knowing that "the voice of the city, the Church and household of Christ" has resonances for them even in their very questioning.

But the conclusion of the whole matter is not the cosiness of claiming Abraham as our father. Anglicans must not be found lighting candles to Pangloss as our patron saint and muttering the *mantra*, "All is for the best in the best of all possible churches." Yet neither should we be apologetic for this ordered freedom and its anomalies or for being seen to wrestle at times with the clarifying and deepening of the relationship between reason and the declared doctrine which ensures our corporate identity within the living stream of the faith uniquely set forth in scripture, defined in the creeds, and in continuous theological study, mediated in the ministry of the word and sacraments, and verified in the witness of saints and in the *consensus fidelium*.

There is more to the traditionary process than the institutionalization of the past experience of the living church in believing and behaving. Tradition has a forward momentum also, as the living church, guarding the apostolic testimony, deepens and widens its awareness in the present of the implications, the application, and the exposition of the apostolic faith. The traditionary process involves a dynamism of belief which is channelled and directed, as Archbishop Laud put it long ago, by the Holy Spirit and the Word of God. Neither the role of reason in matters of believing nor the working of the tradition can be considered or understood apart from the work of the Spirit who guides the church into all the truth. Perhaps in our own day we are being led to rediscover the implications for authority and freedom of the Spirit's abiding in the church. Perhaps we are in today's context being led to ask ourselves what the Cambridge Platonists really thought was implied for theology when they kept reminding their own generation that the Spirit in man is the candle of the Lord.

Notes

1. Information supplied by the Management Information Systems of the Executive Council of the Episcopal Church notes: "As far as the laity are concerned, in a typical year (1983) we acquired 7,000 members by reception from the Roman Catholic Church and Orthodoxy. We acquired 21,500 from Protestant and undesignated groups."
2. Martin Dudley in *Insight*, I, No. III (March 1983) 27.
3. Emmanuel Amand de Mendieta, *Anglican Vision* (London, 1971), 63.
4. W. Temple, *Essays in Christian Politics* (1927), 201-2.
5. (London, 1984.) The former bishop of Woolwich is now director of the Anglican Institute, St. Louis, U.S.A.
6. *La Revue Novelle*, Tome XLIX, Numéro 5-6, (1969), 487.
7. In the section "The People of God and Ministry," *Report*, 76-77.
8. See *A Relation of the Conference* (1639), Sect. XXXIII.
9. *A Theological Introduction to the Thirty-Nine Articles*, 242-3.
10. H.R. McAdoo, "Anglicanism and the Nature and Exercise of Authority in the Church," in *New Divinity* VII, No.2 (1976), 87-88.
11. See *Report*, 122-4, Appendix 3.
12. For an examination of this "theological method" of interpreting and proclaiming "the faith of the ages," see H.R. McAdoo, *The Spirit of Anglicanism* (London, 1965).
13. *The Lambeth Conference Report 1968*, 63-4.
14. Ibid., 69-70.
15. Ibid., 69.
16. *Report of the Lambeth Conference 1968*, p.108.
17. Ibid., 14.
18. *The Lambeth Conference Report 1968*, 64.
19. *Authority in the Church I*, 2.
20. On this aspect of the question cf. Stephen Sykes, *The Integrity of Anglicanism* (1978) and H.R. McAdoo, *The Unity of Anglicanism: Catholic and Reformed* (1983).

21. R.P.C. Hanson, *Continuity of Christian Doctrine* (New York, 1981). The Walter and Mary Tuohy Lectures at John Carroll University, 77.
22. Ibid., 77.
23. Ibid., 83.
24. Ibid., 29.
25. *The Lambeth Conference Report* 1948, 84-86.
26. Resolution 11 of the Conference.
27. Randall T. Davidson, *The Lambeth Conferences of 1867, 1878 and 1888* (1896). On the Conference of 1888 and the report of the Committee on Authoritative Standards, see 352-358.
28. Garrett Sweeney, "The Primacy: The Small Print of Vatican I," in *The Clergy Review*, LIX, No. 2. (1974) 106.
29. Davidson, 274.
30. Ibid., 284 (Resolution 19).
31. Ibid., 282.
32. Ibid., 358.
33. *A Relation of the Conference* (1639), L.A.C.T. ed., 48-9.
34. *Religio Medici* (1642/1643), i.5.
35. See his *The Integrity of Anglicanism* (London, 1978).
36. See my *The Unity of Anglicanism: Catholic and Reformed* (1983).
37. *The Lambeth Conference Report, 1968* 140-1.
38. *Rome and Canterbury — Unity, Diversity & Comprehensiveness* (1981).
39. *For Lancelot Andrewes* (London, 1928), 140.
40. *The Dynamic of Tradition* (London, 1981), 58.
41. Arthur Michael Ramsey, *From Gore to Temple* (London, 1960), ix.
42. Michael Marshall, *The Anglican Church Today and Tomorrow* (London, 1984).
43. Quoted in Marshall, ibid, 131.
44. A.M. Ramsey, *The Gospel and the Catholic Church* (London, 1936), 208, 209.
45. Ibid., 80.
46. *Believing in the Church; The Corporate Nature of Faith* (London, 1981), 44.
47. Ibid., 9.
48. Ibid., 138.
49. Ibid., 6.

The Judicious Mr. Hooker and Authority in the Elizabethan Church

J.E. Booty

It is commonly understood that whereas sixteenth-century Puritans, such as Thomas Cartwright, claimed that there was but one authority by which humans were to be guided in this life, and that was scripture, Richard Hooker (1554-1600), the judicious theologian of the Elizabethan establishment posited three: scripture, tradition, and reason. Richard Church, the nineteenth-century Tractarian and dean of St. Paul's Cathedral, London, was more accurate when he wrote:

> To what he considered the fundamental mistake of the Puritans, an exaggerated and false theory of the purpose and function of Scripture as the exclusive guide of human conduct, he [Hooker] opposed his own more comprehensive theory of a rule derived not from one alone, but from all the sources of light and truth with which man finds himself encompassed.[1]

The picture that Hooker presents, as in his description of the universe of laws, is that of God from whom come all of the diverse guides to human conduct, working through the created order (the moral law of reason), through such law as is necessary to govern human societies (positive human law, international law), and through that special revelation provided to correct the imperfections of other laws (the revelation of God in Christ as transmitted in and through scripture and tradition).[2]

Hooker would not, in my opinion, in spite of his pre-modern understanding of scripture, disagree with Stephen Sykes's assertion: "There is only one source of authority which is the freedom and love of the Triune God." I am less sure of his agreement with Sykes's further statement: "In human life, in scripture, in the creeds, in the decisions of councils, in the liturgical order and canon law, in church leadership, there is only the discovery of authority, not its embodiment."[3] But Hooker does at times come close to such an understanding, as will be apparent further on in this essay.

Indeed, Hooker, at the outset of the *Lawes*, focuses attention on God when refuting the suggestion that God wills to do this or that for no reason. The God he acknowledges is the ultimate source of all that is and what God does is not done arbitrarily, but always for some reason, although the reason may not be apparent to us. This provoked in Hooker a sense of awe and an attitude of worship as he wrote, beginning with Paul in Romans 11:33:

> *O the depth of the riches both of the wisdome and knowledge of God, How unsearchable are his judgements, etc.* That law eternal which God himselfe hath made to himselfe, and thereby worketh all things whereof he is the cause and author, that law in the admirable frame whereof shineth with most perfect bewtie the countenance of that wisedome which hath testified concerning her self, *The lord possessed me in the beginning of his way, even before his works of old, I was set up, etc.* That law which hath bene the patterne to make, and is the card to guide the world by: that law which hath bene of God, and with God everlastingly: that law the author and observer whereof is only one God to be blessed for ever, how should either men or Angels be able perfectly to behold? The booke of this law we are neither able nor worthie to open and looke into. That little thereof which we darkly apprehend, we admire, the rest with religious ignorance we humbly and meekly adore. (I.2.5)[4]

It is important to note here Hooker's concentration on God, the Triune God, and the fact that, not unlike the Cappadocian fathers, and Euagrius their friend, he assumes and emphasizes what was for him the basic meaning of theology. For him *theologia* was both the study of God and the contemplation of God, study which issues in worship and worship which contributes toward study. In Hooker's theology thought and feeling are not strangers to one another.[5] We should also note the suggestion that there is in God one source for a diversity of authorities. This God, whose ways so often exceed our understanding, does all according to reason, to some ultimately rational end or purpose. And what God does is done through many means, not just one.

In the second book of the *Lawes*, Hooker considered the Puritan claim, *"That Scripture is the onely rule of all things which in this life may be done by men,"* and in particular, the first proof, taken from Proverbs 2:9. The biblical citation was understood by Thomas Cartwright to mean "that the word of God containeth whatsoever things can fall into any part of man's life," inferring that nothing can be done in this life without scriptural warrant. Lacking such warrant human actions are sinful. Hooker reacted against the narrowness of this point of view and concluded:

> Whatsoever either men on earth, or the Angels of heaven do know, it is as a drop of that unemptiable fountaine of wisdom, which wisdom hath diversely imparted her treasures into the world. As her waies are of sundry kinds, so her maner of teaching is not meerely one and the same. Some things she openeth by the sacred bookes of Scripture; some things by the glorious workes of nature: with some things she inspireth them from above by sprituall influence, in some thinges she leadeth and trayneth them onely by worldly experience and practise. We may not so in any one speciall kind admire her that we disgrace her in any other, but let all her wayes be according unto their place and degree adored. (II.1.4)

God's wisdom is imparted in various ways, in and through works of nature, through scripture, the activity of the Holy Spirit ("spiritual influence"), and through tradition and custom. Thomas Cartwright's statement could be interpreted to apply to all things that humans do, sacred or secular, although the things chiefly contested were the ecclesiastical laws governing the church's policy and its authorized forms of worship. Hooker was more careful. Focusing attention on God and the diverse laws proceeding from the first law eternal, Hooker viewed each of the ways by which God's wisdom was imparted in relation to the end or purpose for which it was given.

According to this account scripture is but one of the means by which we are guided in our lives, but Hooker had the highest regard for the canonical books of the Old and New Testaments. He wrote that "the ende of the worde of God is *to save*, and therefore we terme it the word of life" (V.21.3). Furthermore, "we are to knowe that the word of God is his heavenlie truth touchinge matters of eternal life revealed unto men; unto prophetes and apostles by immediate divine inspiration, from them to us by theire bookes and writinges" (V.21.2). This did not mean that what scripture says is always clear, always reasonable. Hooker acknowledged that there are things "obscure and darke" in scripture requiring time and effort to be understood. And he believed that if we lay up in our memories hard places "for a tyme, judgement afterwardes explaneth them. Scripture therefore is not *so harde* but that the *onlie readinge* thereof may give life unto willinge hearers" (V.22.14). Nevertheless it was evident to Hooker, regarding scripture and its authority from the point of view of the person receiving guidance, that scripture "presupposes" the ability to think and thus the operation of the law of reason, scripture presupposes the operation of positive human law, the law of societies possessing legislative power, scripture presupposes the operation of human authority and reason for the confirmation of scripture and for its interpretation.[6] Indeed, Hooker argued that where the polity of the church is concerned laws are made in accordance with what humans working together discern as God's will expressed in natural law as well as scripture. The complexity of the matter was expressed by Hooker when he wrote:

Scripture comprehending examples and lawes, lawes some natural and some positive: examples there neither are for al cases which require lawes to be made, and when there are, they can but direct us as precedents onely. Naturall laws direct in such sorte that in all thinges we must for ever doe according unto them; positive so, that against them in no case we may doe any thing, as long as the will of God is that they shoulde remaine in force. Howbeit when scripture doth yeelde us precedents, how far forth they are to bee followed; when it giveth naturall lawes, what particular order is thereunto most agreeable; when positive, which waye to make lawes unrepugnant unto them, yea though all these shoulde want, yet what kind of ordinances would be moste for that good of the Church which is aimed at, al this must be by reason founde out. (III.9.1)

When we consider authority from the perspective of mankind, the importance of reason for Hooker is inescapable. Indeed, W.D.J. Cargill Thompson has argued that, in spite of the evidence concerning the Calvinist Puritan Thomas Cartwright in the *Lawes*, Hooker understood natural law, and reason, substantially as did all of the leading Reformers of the sixteenth century. He was not teaching a peculiar doctrine. "Where Hooker differs most significantly from the orthodox Reformers," wrote Cargill Thompson, "is in the much greater degree of respect he shows for the power of human reason."[7] Scripture presupposes the operation of reason and was given to make up the defects of reason, not to replace or destroy it. Reason and revelation work together and where reason is as it should be there can be no conflict between the two.

What is this reason? "Goodnesse is seen with the eye of understanding. And the light of that eye is reason" (I.7.2). Reason comes from beyond the individual. It is God's reason: "the lawes of well doing are the dictates of right reason" (I.7.4). But in so far as reason indwells us, illuminating the understanding, it is the human ability to discern the good. "There is not that good which concerneth us, but it hath evidence enough for it selfe, if reason were diligent to search it out" (I.7.7). And yet, in his *Answer* to Travers, Hooker avers that the reason to which he appeals is not "mine own reason":

> but true, sound divine reason, reason whereby those conclusions might be out of St. Paul demonstrated, and not probably discoursed of only; reason proper to that science whereby the things of God are known; theological reason, which out of principles of Scripture that are plain, soundly deduceth more doubtful inferences, in such sort that being heard they neither can be denied, nor anything repugnant unto them received, but whatsoever was before otherwise by miscollecting gathered out of darker places, is thereby forced to yield itself, and the true consonant meaning of sentences not understood is brought to life. This is the reason which I intended.[8]

The reason to which he refers is not, then, his own reason. It is not, because it is that in him that partakes of divine reason, the "light of that eye" that perceives goodness, that eye that is human understanding. There is a sense in which I feel drawn to Jeremy Taylor's definition at this point: "by 'reason' I do not mean a distinct topic, but a transcendent that runs through all topics."[9] Or one might say that reason is that gift of God to human nature that directs human understanding (my own reason) so that it is capable of knowing the things of God, principally that which is good, enabling us to will and thus to choose the good, although the willing is another thing.[10]

In the *Lawes*, however, Hooker seems to make no distinction between understanding and reason as he proceeds with his argument. He speaks, as in Book III, of the Holy Spirit working secretly within us, leading "us into all truth and directing us in all goodnes," whose working we may "gather by reason from the qualitie of things beleeved or done" (III.8.15). Further on in the same chapter Hooker wrote:

> we have endevoured to make it appeare, how in the nature of reason it selfe there is no impediment, but that the selfe same spirit, which revealeth the things that god hath set down in his law, may also be thought to aid and direct men in finding out by the light of reason what lawes are expedient to be made for the guiding of his Church, over and besides them that are in scripture. (III.8.18)

It is possible that Hooker understood the activity of the Holy Spirit to be that which, through word and sacrament, repaired reason in the individual so that reason could then perceive the things of God, including the activity of the Holy Spirit. In any case, Hooker believed that there was that in redeemed humanity that scripture presupposed and that dare not be ignored when considering authority. We are justified in speaking of reason as that something in man that scripture presupposes, reason working as empowered by God through the activity of the Holy Spirit. There it is not "mine own reason."

Hooker provides some further explanation when in his Preface to the *Lawes* he speaks of the Puritan claim to being led to the Genevan polity as *the* scriptural polity by the Holy Spirit. He first insists that the spirits be tested, referring to 1 John 4:1, and then explains that there are two ways that the Holy Spirit leads us to all truth. The one is extraordinary, belonging to but a few people whom we may rightly regard as prophets. This way is that of revelation. The other way is common, applying to all the people of God. This way is that of reason. If the Puritans have been led by the Holy Spirit through revelation to discover the Genevan polity in scripture, they must all be prophets — which is absurd.

> *Or if reason be the hand which the Spirite hath led them by, for as much as perswasions grounded upon reason are either weaker or stronger according to the force of those reasons whereupon the same are grounded, they must every of them from the greatest to the least be able for every severall article to showe some special reason as strong as their perswasion therein is earnest.* (Pref. 3.10)

There must, therefore, be consultation, discussion, reasoning together in the community of the faithful. Furthermore, history must not be forgotten or rejected. Attention must be paid to tradition and custom, the wisdom of especially gifted men conferring together in the past and arriving at solid conclusions. Hooker warns against ignorning the principal pillars of the church (II.7.4), encourages consultation which takes into consideration past wisdom and shares with others of the English reformers a high respect for the ancient church.

Hooker is cautious when dealing with the authority of councils. If it is possible to locate "one demonstrative reason" or "one manifest testimony cited from the mouth of God himself" contrary to what councils have decreed, then the conciliar decrees are not to be treated as authoritative. But then he goes on to say:

> Howbeit in defect of proofe infallible, because the mind doth rather follow probable perswasions, then approve the thinges that have in them no likelihood of truth at all; surely if a question concerning matter of doctrine were proposed, and on the one side no kinde of proofe appearing, there should on the other be alleaged and shewed that so a number of the learnedest divines in the world have ever thought; although it did not appear what reason or what scripture led them to be of that judgement, yet to their very bare judgement somewhat a reasonable man would attribute, notwithstanding the common imbecilities which are incident into our nature. (II.7.5)

Hooker insists that the quest to understand whither God is leading us takes place not alone or primarily in the isolated individual, but in relationship to others in the community of the faithful. In his "Sermon on Pride" Hooker established a fundamental principle concerning human nature and all of the created order, writing, "God hath created nothing simply for itself: but each thing in all things, and of every thing each part in other have such interest, that in the whole world nothing is found whereunto any thing created can say, 'I need thee not.'"[11] In Book V he states that none can be in God without being in the church (V.56.7). Furthermore, those that are in "the mysticall bodie of our Saviour Christ" — including all in the fellowship of saints, divided into many generations — "are . . . coupled everie one to Christ theire head and all unto everie particular person amongst them selves, in as much as the same Spirit . . . doth so formalize unite and actuate his whole race" (V.56.11).

It is in this context of the individual participating in the community of the faithful that scripture and tradition are commonly communicated to Christians and their authority realized. It is in this same context that reason is renewed and empowered by the Spirit to discover that which is authoritative, in communion with others. Liturgy looms large in Hooker's understanding, for it is in worship that the community finds its true identity and its necessary focus. It is through baptism that the Christian is incorporated into Christ, his merits being imputed to us for our justification and the Holy Spirit being infused in us.[12] It is through the Holy Communion that we are empowered along life's way toward sanctification.[13] It is in the context of such public worship that the word is read and preached. Furthermore, the liturgy is not something devised for the moment. As Cranmer pointed out, the Prayer Book is scriptural through and through. It has a history and is the bearer of that tradition (encompassing scripture) that is in itself authoritative.

Hooker viewed worship as personal and dialogical. In one place he wrote of angels descending with doctrine (scripture and tradition) and ascending with prayer. Thinking of corporate worship, he asked: "For what is thassemblinge of the Church to learne, but the receivinge of Angels descended from above? What to pray, but the sendinge of Angels upward? His heavenlie inspirations and our holie desires are as so many Angels of entercorse and commerce betwene God and us" (V.23.1). Hooker wrote of the superiority of corporate worship to private devotions, speaking of the "vertue, force, and efficacie" of the public liturgy, "to help that imbecillitie and weakenes in us" (V.25.1). That help is there in part because, unlike Puritan forms of worship, the reading of scripture is "a parte of our litourgie, a special portion of the service which we doe to God" (V.19.5).[14] Indeed, perhaps thinking of angels descending with doctrine and angels ascending with prayer, Hooker sees great value in the mingling of scripture lessons with prayers in the liturgy of The Book of Common Prayer. Thus he wrote:

> for as much as effectuall prayer is joygned with a vehement intention of the inferior powers of the soule, which cannot therein longe continewe without paine, it hath bene therefore thought good so by turnes to interpose still somewhat for the higher parte of the minde the understandinge to worke upon, that both beinge kept in continewall exercise with varietie, neither might feele any great wearinese, and yeat each be a spurre to other. For prayer kindleth our desire to behold God by speculation; and the minde delighted with that contemplative sight of God taketh everie where newe inflammations to pray, the riches of the mysteries of heavenlie wisdome continuallie stirring up in us correspondent desires towardes him. (V.34.1)

Thus was Hooker sensitive to the interaction of intellect and feeling, doctrine and prayer in liturgy. His intention was to describe how effective the authorized liturgy was in forming and reforming Christians.

In another passage, defending the responsive reading in the morning office and the litany in particular, Hooker pointed to the ways in which the interchanges increase the bonds between pastor and people and amongst the people in relation to one another. He had in mind the vocal participation of people in corporate worship, in their saying "Amen," in the exchange of versicles, in *kyrie* responses to the Ten Commandments, and the like, including the *Sursum corda* of the Holy Communion, the priest saying "Lift up your hearts," the people responding, "We lift them up unto the Lord," the priest saying, "Let us give thanks unto our Lord God," the people responding, "It is meet and right so to do." Hooker asked: "these interlocutorie formes of speech what are they els but most effectuall partlie testifications and partlie inflammations of all pietie?" (V.39.1). Elizabethans may not have understood the sacraments as drama in exactly the way the early Eastern fathers did; time past and time present may not have merged exactly in the way they did in the worship of the early church,[15] but Hooker for one did seem to believe that in their participation in the liturgy people were involved in the sacred drama, the remembrance of things long past being present realities to them. John Barton and John Halliburton cite the passage from Hooker above and conclude:

Of course it was never in doubt for Hooker that the Bible is addressed from God to man; but he was open to the possibility that, in its liturgical function, it can become a word spoken by man in the presence of God: a word by which the worshipping community sustains and transmits its faith as it confesses its identity with the people of God in Scripture.[16]

The explanation for this may rest, at least in part, in the meditative style prevailing in Hooker's day and most evident in the sermons of Jewel, Andrewes, and Hooker.[17] The intent, as in rhetoric, was to reach through the intellect to move the affections of the faithful. The emphasis tended to fall on moving the affections, bringing about a state of contrition, leading to repentence and amendment of life. Hooker praised sermons "as keyes to the kingdom of heaven, as winges to the soule, as spurres to the good affections of man, unto the sound and healthie as foode, as phisicke unto diseased mindes" (V.22.1). Preaching in sixteenth-century England was biblical, opening with a text and prayer, then proceeding to explication and exposition of the text, with proofs, and culminating with the application of text and exposition to the lives of those listening, to the end that their affections might be aroused to good purpose. Hooker's sermon on Jude, 17-21, provides an example. Having laid a preliminary foundation, Hooker asked, "Which of you will gladly remain or abide in a mishapen, a ruinous, or a broken house? And shall we suffer sin and vanity to drop in at our eyes, and at our ears, at every corner of our bodies, and of our soules, knowing that we are temples of the Holy Ghost?'' After developing this thought for some time, Hooker concluded:

> Blessed and praised for ever be his name, who perceiving of how senseless and heavy metal we are made, hath instituted in his Church a spiritual supper, and an holy communion to be celebrated often, that we might thereby be occasioned often to examine these buildings of ours, in what case they stand. For sith God doth not dwell in temples which are unclean, sith a shrine cannot be a sanctuary unto him; and this supper is received as a seal unto us, that we are his house and his sanctuary; that his Christ is as truly united to me, and I to him, as my arm is united and knit unto my shoulder . . . therefore ere we put forth our hands to take his blessed sacrament, we are charged to examine and to try our hearts whether God be in us or no. . . .[18]

This sermon was preached in the context of public worship, perhaps in the course of the Holy Communion, where the intent was to involve the people, inviting them, as the scripture was read and exposited, to use their reasons, and moving their affections toward amendment of life. Some might think that this was a subtle way of conditioning people to think and to do as officialdom directed, perhaps making them docile in the presence of arbitrary power exercised by the crown, but Archbishop McAdoo has presented another point of view.[19] He suggests that in the "reformed" church the pulpit took the place of the confessional, the sermons of the Caroline divines setting forth and interpreting the scripture to the gathered people, the people exercising their reasons, imbibing the Word in the words and making judgements concerning specific behaviour, not in isolation but in relation to others and as guided by the totality of instruction received. In addition to the scripture there was the regular catechizing of the congregation and there was exercise of discipline in accordance with canon law, the activities of ecclesiastical courts, and the rubrics of the Book of Common Prayer. In so far as moral theology was concerned the aim was to avoid legalism and to regard law in relation to spiritual development. At its best Caroline moral theology held in tension "lawful authority" and "just liberty"[20] and regarded scripture, tradition, and reason as presupposing one another, although "Holy Scripture is the one charter of conscience."[21]

George Herbert expressed his understanding of scripture in his poem "In S. Scripturas," a Latin poem in his *Sacred Grove*. He viewed the Bible not so much as a book of laws, but rather as God's Word, an enlivening spirit penetrating him, traveling through

All the dark nooks and hidden pleats
Of the heart, the alleys and the curves
Of flying passion. Ah, how wise and skilled you are
To slip through these paths, windings, knots.[22]

Scripture thus understood is not to be viewed as a legal text which gives or withholds warrant for doing or not doing anything and everything in this life. Scripture is a divine gift for the formation and the reformation of people. One way of putting it is to say that living in relation to the scripture the faithful are open to the working of the Holy Spirit and are enabled to make decisions affecting their lives, decisions that are not without ambiguities, but decisions which are nevertheless responsible and responsive to God's will as revealed in and through that living Word, Jesus Christ, to whom the scripture bears witness. This is to live a life imbued with contrition, repentence, and newness of life.

The Holy Communion itself, which provides the context for the reading and the preaching of God's word, itself directed attention to that which is for the Christian central to the understanding of God in the New Testament. As it was known in the sixteenth and seventeenth centuries this sacrament preserved something of medieval piety, picturing Christ crucified, the now victorious Son of man and Son of God then dying on the cross that those who repent might have new life, everlasting life.

If at the time of Hooker there was any particular focus of scripture and its authority as represented in the New Testament it was to be found in the passion of Christ as that was presented in the Holy Communion. Hooker, in his central chapter on the Holy

Communion,[23] pointed to Christ on the cross. Believing that he was citing Cyprian of Carthage, but actually echoing the twelfth-century abbot Arnold of Bonneval, Hooker said:

> the verie letter of the worde of Christ giveth plaine security that these mysteries doe as nailes fasten us to his verie crosse, that by them we may draw out, as touchinge efficacie force and vertue, even the blood of his goared side, in the woundes of our redemer wee there dip our tongues, wee are died redd both within and without, our hunger is satisfied and our thirst for ever quenched. . . . (V.67.12)

Looking at sermons, poems, and devotional writings of the sixteenth and early seventeenth centuries, it may be suggested that although E.C. Ratcliff was right in distinguishing the ways in which ancient Christians viewed the sacraments as sacred drama in contrast to the ways in which the English Reformers understood the sacraments, yet they shared something of vital importance. Hooker viewed the sacraments in relation to the Western tradition of meditation as modified by the *devotio moderna*. In this tradition there was a strong emphasis on the passion and death of Jesus Christ, the events being carefully depicted in and through the Holy Communion, especially in the canon or communion prayer. This can be viewed as drama, the sacraments being such that they made present again *(repraesentaverunt)* to the devout worshipper, "with all their saving potency, the divine acts from which those sacramental rites took their origins and efficacy."[24] The passion of Christ was brought to mind in baptism, along with Christ's own baptism, when it was recalled that "for the forgiveness of our sins," Christ "did shed out of his most precious side both water and blood," the water of baptism and the blood of the sacrament of Christ's body and blood, when the child was signed with the sign of the cross and when, the child having been dipped in the water *(baptismos*, deluged, drowned), the prayer is made that the child "being dead unto sin, and living unto righteousness, and being buried with Christ in his death, may crucify the old man . . . that as he is made partaker of the death of thy Son, so he may be partaker of his resurrection."[25] The "dipping" of the child in the water and the raising of the child up out of the water, to sign him with the sign of the cross, was done with the death and resurrection of Christ in mind. It was all drama. And, the remembrance of Christ's passion was central in the 1559 Prayer Book Holy Communion, the great prayer of thanksgiving beginning:

> Almighty God our heavenly Father, which of thy tender mercy didst give thine only Son Jesus Christ, to suffer death upon the cross for our redemption; who made there (by his one oblation of himself once offered) a full, perfect, and sufficient sacrifice, oblation, and satisfaction for the sins of the whole world; and did institute, and in his holy gospel command us to continue, a perpetual memory of that his precious death, until his coming again.

The *anamnesis* occurred in order that by his oblation the faithful might be empowered to offer themselves, their souls and bodies as ''a reasonable, holy, and lively sacrifice'' and spend their lives in sacrificial service to their fellow men and women.[26] And this too was drama, the spectators being effected in such ways that they become participants in the focal dramatic action.

Scripture was read in accordance with the lectionary of the Elizabethan Prayer Book and in the context of the church year which was structured in terms of Christ's life and death. All scripture was read with the reiterated emphasis on Christ's passion, death, and resurrection, at the heart of the public worship of the church. Thus did Christians at the time of Richard Hooker come into vital relationship with scripture, and thus did they experience the authority of scripture. And it was here, in the context of public worship, that the faithful were expected to use their God-given powers of understanding and make judgements through the use of right reason. Tradition too was involved; the liturgy itself was a primary bearer of tradition and custom. The liturgy was, as Cranmer claimed, thoroughly biblical, but it was also influenced by the wisdom of the ages as liturgies evolved and were reformed. Liturgy was also a primary vehicle for the transmission (*paradosis*) of scripture and its authority. Indeed, liturgy itself came to constitute an authoritative influence, scripture, tradition and reason operating as a seamless whole in and through the Book of Common Prayer.[27]

These considerations lead us back to where we began. Hooker and others of his era, were not so much interested in distinguishing the various sources of authority (scripture, tradition, reason) as in focusing attention on the encounter between God and man. Since to be in God was to be in the church and since being in the church involved, for Hooker, daily participation in public worship, liturgy itself was the chief enabler of that ongoing, dynamic relationship of God and man that was necessary for salvation, and for life itself. It is not too much to say that the Book of Common Prayer for Hooker was an unified entity, a whole, in which scripture, tradition, and reason worked in various and ever-varying ways. Through the liturgy there were provided doctrine and prayer in relation to which the faithful discovered that which was authoritative guiding them, not in narrow, arbitrary ways, but in nurturing, sympathetic ways to do and to be that which they were created to be — humanity made in the image of God.

Taking into consideration all that we have reviewed concerning Hooker's understanding of authority, four further comments seem to be in order.

1   Hooker viewed the state as authoritative in relation to God's universe of laws, and specifically in relation to positive human law, such law as encompasses not only the state but also ecclesiastical government, including the authority of bishops. As Hooker understood it, government was provided for the protection of humans against the wicked and malicious as well as for the promotion of general happiness (I.10.2-3). That was Aristotle's understanding, as embraced by Hooker. Government was also provided on account of the Fall and because people have need of the supernatural law that teaches not only supernatural duties but also "such natural duties as could not by the light of Nature easily have been known" (I.12.3). Government exists to promote true religion to such ends. This does not mean that Hooker believed in or taught the seventeenth-century doctrine of *divine right*. In fact, he subordinated the English crown to law. When Book VIII is read in relation to the newly discovered notes that Hooker made in preparation for that book, Hooker is seen to separate the spiritual from lay jurisdiction and to conclude that "*Kings* have dominion in *Ecclesiasticall* causes but according to the lawes of the *Church*."[28] That separation of spiritual and lay jurisdiction assumed by law is vitally important to preserve

the necessary tension between "lawful authority" and "just liberty" and to allow for the appropriate operation of the scripture/ tradition/ reason complex in critical areas of doctrine and conduct without inappropriate interference from the state.

2   Hooker's understanding of authority reflects something of the times in which he lived and worked, and yet there is also a central and more permanent thread running through all of his discussions. Differentiating between the God of arbitrary will and the God who presupposes the operation of a universe of laws, each linked to the operations of the others, Hooker takes a position akin to a view held by some twentieth-century theologians. John Skinner, for instance, distinguishes between coercive power and authority as the gospel in the New Testament presents it. He writes:

> Authority is derived from God, derived from his nurturing and liberating presence in nature and in history. Consequently, all authority should express itself as both a nurturing and liberating presence reflecting its ultimate source in the creative and redemptive activity of God. The Gospel of Christ, as a result, becomes the criterion for the Christian in order to determine whether authority is present, or only organized power parading as authority.[29]

In the light of this, Skinner arrives at a definition, admittedly not in Hooker's terminology but nevertheless Hookerian, as I see it. Authority is:

> *That kind of structured reality, whether societal or personal, which through nature and cultivation enables individuals to become truly centered selves or persons, and thus, relatively free human beings.*[30]

This is Hookerian in the sense that the focus is not on abstractions but on persons and on the dynamic relationships that function to nourish individuals and enhance their fundamental humanity. For Hooker that relationship between human beings in community which he identifies in terms of participation in God (or in Christ) involves growth or cultivation in the process of sanctification. Authority in this context is not coercive but nurturing and liberating for the end or purpose of authority is the end or purpose that God has for all his creatures and that, in Hooker's terms, is their participation in Christ from whence comes "a true actuall influence of grace whereby the life which wee live accordinge to godlines is his, and from him wee receave those perfections wherein our eternall happiness consisteth" (V.56.10).[31]

3   This view of authority depends upon our ability to see things whole. Hooker began his *Lawes* with an affirmation of the wholeness of creation. As Richard Church has said, for Hooker,

> Law is that which binds the whole creation, in all its ranks and subordinations, to the perfect goodness and reason of God. Every law of God is a law of reason, and every law of reason is a law of God. Laws, which are of God, cover the whole field of nature, moral as well as physical, and that by which they are ascertained, and their authority is recognised, is reason. All this is antecedent to Scripture. . . .[32]

And lest one conclude that authority viewed as divine law, expressed in various laws, is coercive and arbitrary, Church, summarizing Hooker's teaching, says: "there is no authority without reason, no just authority which cannot give its reason: no authority which is not at last based on reason which can be tested and verified. The will of God is the supreme authority, but (Hooker) utterly rejects the notion of arbitrary will. . . ."[33] Laws are not to be viewed in and of themselves alone, but as emanating from God whose character is revealed in and through Jesus and those acts of God in which Jesus was the chief actor. It is of vital importance, therefore, that laws be viewed in relation to one another and all as emanating from the one source whose will is not arbitrary. Furthermore, the laws are understood not only in terms of their source, but also in terms of their ends or purposes. Mutable laws which do not serve the ends for which they were given are to be ignored or reformed, the action being taken by lawful authority, responsible persons using their reasons in concord, taking into account other laws both immutable and mutable. This way of thinking is definitely holistic.

The holism of Hooker's thought is contrary to much modern understanding. Post-industrial Westerners tend to view reality as fragmented. As Richard Wollheim puts it: "We think on the assumption that the world is like a vast jig-saw puzzle which can be taken to bits and studied fragmentarily. . . ."[34] We should, perhaps, go even further and state that to the modern mind reality *is* fragmented, was never whole, and will never be whole. Only those deprived of the superior knowledge of the scientific world-view would think otherwise. But then there is the theoretical physicist, David Bohm, who views fragmentation as a kind of modern sickness and lays the blame on our assumption that our perceptions of reality are accurate. To the contrary, Bohm asserts, "what should be said is that wholeness is what is real, and that fragmentation is the response of this whole to man's action, guided by illusory perception, which is shaped by fragmentary thought."[35] Bohm does not then begin quoting Hooker, nor does he espouse a Christian understanding of reality based on doctrines such as those of creation, providence, and last things. But Christians should be prompted by Bohm and others to take Hooker seriously, without, however, adopting his fundamentally medieval world-view.

Where authority is concerned, the danger in fragmentary thought consists in the possibility of our viewing things (scripture, tradition, and reason) and persons (ecclesiastical officers, civil officials) in isolation from one another. The challenge Hooker puts to us is to view particulars in relation to one another, in relation to the whole, and with the recognition that "There is only one source of authority which is the freedom and love of the Triune God."[36] This one source finds expression in and through a number of instruments (scripture, tradition, reason, bishops, civil authorities, assemblies, parliaments, canon law, liturgy, etc.). It is incumbent upon the discoverer of authority in any and all of these instruments to take a receptive yet critical stance toward them,

testing the spirits, testing the particular expression of authority in relation to the one source of all authority as we understand it, conferring with others, conferring with the past and
concerned for the purpose or end for which any authority
is given. Indeed, in the spirit of Hooker we need to be
prepared for the reformation of the instruments of authority, or the re-interpretation of received traditions of authority
for doctrine and for life. This, too, is of vital importance.

4   Finally, having stressed the importance of liturgy as an instrument of authority and thus, in a sense, an authority itself,
we must agree that the reform or revision of liturgy is not
simply a matter of aesthetics, nor is liturgy to be revised simply in order to revive third-century norms for twentieth-
century practice.[37] Liturgical revision should be the concern
of all people and certainly of theologians anxious to work on
and work out the problems concerning authority in our time,
the application of doctrine to life and work. The fact that
liturgical change seems destined to be a centre of controversy points to the importance it has for the Christian *ecclesia.*
Such controversy is not to be avoided for the sake of peace,
but is to be entered into with the expectation that the Holy
Spirit is in the midst of the furor effecting encounters that
are productive for the life of the church.[38] We engage in the
difficult processes of liturgical change with the assurance that
none of the instruments of authority is perfect and that all
reflect in various ways, various complementary ways, the one
source of all authority, our steadfast God.

Notes

1. Richard Hooker, *Of the Laws of Ecclesiastical Polity*, Book I, ed. R.W.
    Church (Oxford, 1882), xvi.
2. See, ibid., xviii, xix, and Gerald R. Cragg, *Freedom and Authority,
    A Study of English Thought in the Early Seventeenth Century*
    (Philadelphia, 1975), 98-99.
3. Stephen W. Sykes, *The Integrity of Anglicanism* (New York, 1978), 98.

4. Quotations from Hooker's *Lawes* are from *The Folger Library Edition of the Works of Richard Hooker*, ed. W. Speed Hill. Four volumes of six have been published. Vol. 1: *Of the Laws of Ecclesiastical Polity, Preface, Books I to IV*, ed. Georges Edelen. Vol. 2: *Of the Laws of Ecclesiastical Polity, Book V*, ed. W. Speed Hill. Vol. 3: *Of the Laws of Ecclesiastical Polity, Books VI, VII, VIII*, ed. Paul Stanwood. Vol. 4: *Of the Laws of Ecclesiastical Polity, Attack and Response*, ed. John E. Booty (Cambridge, Massachusetts, 1977). References in parentheses are to book, chapter, and section in this edition.

5. See Andrew Louth, *Discerning the Mystery: An Essay in the Nature of Theology* (Oxford, 1983), 3-4, for a discussion of the separation of thought and feeling, theology and spirituality, in the twentieth century.

6. See III.8.13, and John E. Booty, "Hooker and Anglicanism," *Studies in Richard Hooker, Essays Preliminary to an edition of his Works*, ed. W. Speed Hill (Cleveland and London, 1972), 217.

7. W.D.J. Cargill Thompson, "The Philosopher of the 'Politic Society', Richard Hooker as a Political Thinker," *Studies*, ed. Hill, 31.

8. *The Works of Mr. Richard Hooker*, ed. John Keble, 7th ed. rev. by Church and Paget (Oxford, 1888), 3:594-595.

9. Jeremy Taylor, *The Whole Works*, eds. R. Heber and C.P. Eden (1850), 7:372.

10. See John E. Booty, "The English Reformation: A Lively Faith and Sacramental Confession," *The Anglican Moral Choice*, ed. Paul Elmen (Wilton, Connecticut, 1983), 28-31, for a discussion of "Hooker and Moral Choice."

11. Hooker, *Works*, (1888), 3:617, and see, John E. Booty, "Richard Hooker," in *The Spirit of Anglicanism*, ed. W.J. Wolf (Wilton, Connecticut, 1979), 35.

12. It is important to note here Hooker's understanding of salvation as set forth in his *Learned Discourse of Justification*, sec. 21 (*Works*, 1888, 3:507-508) and related to the sacraments in *Lawes*, V.56.11, and specifically to baptism in V.60.2. See Booty, "The English Reformation," in *The Anglican Moral Choice*, ed. Elmen, 24-28.

13. See V. 67.1, and John E. Booty, "Hooker's Understanding of the Presence of Christ in the Eucharist," in *The Divine Drama of History and Liturgy*, ed. Booty (Allison Park, Pennsylvania, 1984), 131-148.

14. See John Barton and John Halliburton, "Story and Liturgy," in *Believing in the Church: The Corporate Nature of Faith*, A Report by

the Doctrine Commission of the Church of England, (Wilton, Connecticut, Toronto, Canada, 1981), 98, for a discussion of Hooker and scripture read before service by Puritans and during service by those loyal to the Book of Common Prayer.

15. E.C. Ratcliff, *Liturgical Studies*, eds. A.H. Couretin and D.H. Tripp, (London, 1976), 131.
16. Barton and Haliburton, "Story and Liturgy," in *Believing*, 99.
17. See John Booty, "Joseph Hall, *The Arte of Divine Meditation*, and Anglican Spirituality," in *The Roots of Modern Tradition, The Spirituality of Western Civilization*, Jean Leclerq, intro., ed. E.R. Elder, (Kalamazoo, Michigan, 1984), II, 215-228, "Meditation and Anglican Spirituality."
18. Hooker, *Works* (1888), 3:686-687.
19. H.R. McAdoo, *The Structure of Caroline Moral Theology* (London, 1949), 16.
20. Ibid., 4.
21. Ibid., 42.
22. George Herbert, *The Latin Poetry of George Herbert: A Bilingual Edition*, trans. Mark McCloskey and Paul R. Murphy (Athens, Ohio, 1965), 84.
23. In my reconstruction of the original Book V of the *Lawes*, in an introduction to be published in Vol. 6 of *The Folger Library Edition of the Works of Richard Hooker*, chapter 67 is regarded as a part of the original Book V. Chapter 68 appears to have been added later by Hooker.
24. Ratcliff, *Liturgical Studies*, p. 131.
25. *The Book of Common Prayer 1559: The Elizabethan Prayer Book*, ed. John E. Booty (Charlottesville, 1976), 274-275.
26. Ibid., 263-264.
27. See the Preface to the *Book of Common Prayer*, ibid., 14.
28. VIII.3.3. See A.S. McGrade, "Richard Hooker and the Medieval Resistance to Modern Politics," an unpublished paper exploring the relationship between Book VIII and the Dublin Notes for Book VIII, 11, where he cites the quotation and adds, Hooker "concludes strongly, in terms which would have gained unmistakable content if his reader had been able to refer them to a treatment of spiritual jurisdiction based on the Dublin notes: 'Whither it be therefore the nature of *Courts* or the forme of pleas, or the kinde of governours or the order of proceedinges in whatsoever spirituall businesses for the received lawes and liberties of the *Church*, the *King* hath supreme authoritie and power against them none' (*Laws* VIII.2.17. . .)."

29. John E. Skinner, *The Meaning of Authority* (Washington, D.C., 1983), 4.
30. Ibid., 6.
31. Hooker here cites Rom. 8:9 and Gal. 4:6.
32. Hooker, *Book I*, ed. Church, xviii.
33. Ibid., xviii-xix.
34. Richard Wollheim, "F.H. Bradley," 47, cited in Peter G. Ellis, "T.S. Eliot, F.H. Bradley, and Four Quartets," *Research Studies* 37:2, 94.
35. David Bohm, *Wholeness and the Implicate Order* (London, Boston, and Henley), 7.
36. Sykes, *Integrity*, 98.
37. See, ibid., 99: "decisions made about worship are crucial to the integrity of faith. And decisions are unavoidable because liturgical arrangements must change. Because decisions involved in change rest upon judgements, which are necessarily controversial, it is essential to the health of the church that it learn how to conduct controversy constructively and openly.'
38. See John V. Taylor, *The Go-Between God: The Holy Spirit and the Christian Mission* (Philadelphia, 1973), 17-18.

Part Two
Anglican Structures and Usage

A Family Affair: The Pattern of Constitutional Authority in the Anglican Communion

Philip H.E. Thomas

"The Anglican family holds together — and let no one underestimate the reality of cohesion — through the faith that is shared, through much history in common, and — again let no one underestimate the reality of the cohesion — through sheer affection or love." That was the way Bishop John Howe introduced a discussion of inter-Anglican relationships to the Anglican Consultative Council's meeting in 1979, and for him it was the image of family life that most readily described the nature of the Anglican communion.[1] His evaluation of each meeting of the Council was measured as an expression of family feeling; the work of the Council as a whole was seen as promoting understanding and articulating the concerns of a very diverse family of churches; and he could look back on his ministry as a time during which Anglicanism had come into a new understanding of itself, as a "world-wide family of equals."[2]

The metaphor of the family can sometimes intrude too quickly into a discussion of ecclesiology. It lacks conceptual clarity and at the same time possesses an emotive force which encourages a sense of communal well-being by distracting attention from issues under dispute. It can be used to cover up sincerely held differences within the church rather than encouraging an honest resolution of them. The church of God is certainly more than a debating society, but a premature closing of ranks, the determination to keep things within the family, is not really an expression of faith, hope, or love. It certainly does not help it in the pursuit of truth or an understanding of its mission.

John Howe's experience of the Anglican family was never sentimental, however. For him the "cohesion" discovered by the Anglican Consultative Council was found amidst a renewed awareness of the diversity of nationalities, races, and cultures of churches which make up the Anglican communion. It was tested by a willingness to face the implications of that diversity as they affected questions as varied as the proper Christian response to institutionalized racism, to the internal questions posed by the decision of some Anglican provinces to ordain women priests. Under Howe's leadership, the ACC found its function — and the Anglican communion its universality — by learning "to listen to its member churches . . . and to describe consensus as it forms."[3]

It was precisely because Anglicanism has faced so many changes and challenges to this quest for a consensus that a closer examination of the ties that bind the Anglican churches into a communion has proved necessary. When the 1978 Lambeth Conference located the question of authority as underlying a number of the other problems that troubled it, it ultimately fell to Bishop Howe to organize a response. [4] As part of the study which he initiated and to which this volume contributes, the bishop encouraged the present writer to open some of the "black boxes" in the ACC archives in order to trace from their constitutional history the flight plans of various Anglican provinces towards their theological self-identity.[5] This essay returns to the substance of that research.

A collection of constitutions and canons, statutes and regulations, may seem to be an unlikely source of evidence about the faith of a church, and it is true that on the surface such documents do not make inspiring reading. However, one of the principal difficulties of Anglican studies is precisely the problem of locating agreed statements of church belief and practice, and the constitutional material from each of the autonomous Anglican provinces does at least provide a record of the way in which each church has sought to define the underlying features of its faith and order. A comparison of these provisions can give insight into the character of the Anglican communion. In particular it enables an understanding of the similarities and differences that exist between one province and another. It provides an indication of the way authority functions within and between the different provinces. It demonstrates the kind and extent of communion that Anglicanism possesses. In short, it gives substance to the claim that faith, history, and a sense of mutual affection provide real "cohension" for the Anglican family.

Constitutional Material in the Anglican Communion

To readers whose experience of Anglicanism is limited to that of the Church of England, attention to an easily identified collection of constitutional papers may seem surprising. As an established church, the constitution of *ecclesia Anglicana* is found in the whole range of history, precedent, legislation, and literature which makes up the constitutional story of the English nation. The church, it is properly assumed, is part of the state and at one with its governmental processes. This assumption is not shared by the rest of the Anglican communion. Whenever Anglicans, for one reason or another, have found themselves to be beyond the protective embrace of the English establishment, they have been forced to define the beliefs and character of their Christian experience and to make provision for the future well-being and organization of their church. The members of the Anglican communion may have drawn inspiration and guidance from the Church of England, but they have not inherited automatically its laws or doctrine or patterns of liturgy.[6] To organize their corporate life beyond the shores of England, Anglicans have had to start from first principles and lay down what it is that holds them together and gives substance to their hopes and ideals. This they have accomplished by means of voluntary association in synods and through a system of self-government under constitutional formularies. To this extent at least, the provincial constitutions of the Anglican communion give testimony to the way Anglican churches have struggled to establish and maintain the integrity of their faith.

This being so, it is surprising that Anglicans have given so little attention to the contents of the constitutional materials within the communion. A definitive study was carried out by a former archbishop of Melbourne, Henry Lowther Clarke, in 1924, but at that time there were only nine provinces outside the British Isles, and most of them had quite different geographical boundaries from their present-day descendants. In 1948, G.W.O. Addleshaw, then a canon of York, reviewed the situation while a retired American lawyer, Spencer Ervin, began a comprehensive survey of the polity of individual provinces in 1964.[7] Of course the last thirty years have seen a spectacular proliferation of self-governing Anglican provinces and Ervin's death meant that his project was cut short with only five studies complete. Since then no systematic attention has been given to the subject. When the 1978 Lambeth Conference asserted that an examination of the constitutional documents "reveals a marked resemblance between member Churches of the Anglican Communion" there was in fact no supporting examination which could sustain the claim.[8]

The sort of comparison which could test the bishops' confidence and at the same time advance the argument of this paper will inevitably be selective. It will not be possible to revise Lowther Clarke's province-by-province survey but a briefer composite analysis can still draw out the fundamentals of the material under review without totally ignoring the differences within it.

Provincial constitutions vary in their format. For that matter, there is no such thing as a typical province. There are various ways by which dioceses are associated. Some provinces — for instance England, Ireland, the United States, Canada, and Australia — utilize a sub-structure of "regional provinces." In other areas, a number of dioceses combine as councils even though they are located in quite independent nations. Examples are found in East Asia, Latin America, and the South Pacific. To confuse the terminology still further, a number of national churches in South America combine to form a province which calls itself a council. In general, however, a province is never less than national in extent, and its validity is not measured by physical size or numerical extent but by the way it seeks to find an adequate basis for self-sustaining Christian organization and mission. This fact further enhances the importance of provincial constitutions for an understanding of modern Anglicanism and its claims.

The composition of individual constitutions reflects the diversity of geographical setting and historical context in which each of the provinces has begun its corporate life. This varied background can provide the basis for a preliminary classification of the constitutional materials into three groupings.

Most obviously, the colonial churches of the nineteenth century can be associated together. It was their realization that they were legally isolated from the Church of England that provoked the newly independent bodies to make provision in constitutional form for the proper management of their affairs. This they did in the sonorous tones of Victorian jurisprudence. The South African constitution typically relates:

> Whereas it is expedient that the members of a Church, not by
> law established, should, for the purpose of its due government,
> as well as the management of its property and the ordering
> of its affairs, formally set forth the terms of the compact under
> which it is associated . . . .

and proceeds to offer a statement on the faith and doctrine of
the church, provisions for its due interpretation, and an outline
of the structure and functions of synodical organization. Although
aware that they were breaking new ground as far as the Church
of England was concerned, the colonial churchmen were not
acting without precedent. The association of the Scottish
Episcopalians under canons after the year 1727 provided the first
example of constitutional and synodical Anglicanism, and the
North Americans used this example to develop their own ecclesiastical ideals in the atmosphere of freshly won independence
after 1789. Victorian bishops of the overseas churches were well
aware of these events and Bishop Selwyn of New Zealand, the
leading spokesman for the colonial churches in the mid-
nineteenth century, was in regular contact with leaders of the
American church at critical points of his career.[9] The colonial
churches followed suit.

A second category of constitutional material is that belonging
to provinces formed during the last twenty-five years, not because
independence was thrust upon them but because it became
necessary for particular churches to assume responsibility for their
own life within their own regional setting. Here the newer African
provinces are typical. The way in which national churches have
been formed out of the old Province of East Africa during the
1970s, or the composite Province of West Africa, itself formed in
1970, sub-divided to create a separate Province of Nigeria in 1979,
might be seen simply as a reflection of nationalistic rivalries. At
best though, it also expresses a sense of self-awareness and self-
reliance. The formation of the francophone Province of Burundi,
Rwanda, and Zaire in 1979 demonstrates the way in which a
church responded not just to the political problems of administration in the former Province of Uganda, but also to the realization
that a different cultural setting called for a distinct organizational
basis for the church in its mission. A proper sense of independence can also be seen in the way the Sudan assumed its
own metropolitical rights which had previously been exercised

by the See of Canterbury (1976), or when Melanesia established its own identity after a century of dependence on the Church of the Province of New Zealand. Understandably, such close connections of time and place lead to similarities between the constitutional forms adopted during this period. Certainly John Howe in his role of consultant and advisor to the churches encouraged them to follow a recognizable pattern in their legal formularies.[10]

The third category of provincial constitutions exemplifies the way in which independence can be woven together with the interdependence of a universal faith. For most of the world, Christianity in general and Anglicanism in particular is a minority faith. While national identity is an important factor it is not the fundamental unit of Anglican ecclesiology. When considerations of distance or numerical size appear overwhelming it is important for self-governing churches to be aware that they are not alone. The Province of the Indian Ocean provides an example of how various dioceses met the first problem — that of distance; Jerusalem and the Middle East associates churches which are very aware of their minority status; the regional councils of South America, East Asia, and the South Pacific present attempts to meet both problems at the same time. And when a province or council is made up of dioceses from more than one nation (as in Central Africa, West Africa, South America, East Asia, the Indian Ocean, Jerusalem and the Middle East, and South Pacific, the West Indies, and Burundi, Rwanda and Zaire) it is a hopeful reminder of the way in which Christian community transcends national boundaries. The Australian constitution which was only instituted in 1955 is another example of the way regional churches have to find the most appropriate basis for partnership. So too is the existence of extra-provincial dioceses within the Anglican communion and the way in which Anglican fellowship has been extended by agreements of intercommunion with the Old Catholics (1932), the Philippine Independent Church (1961), the Iberian Churches (1963), and the Mar Thoma Syrian Church (1974).

From these diverse backgrounds come constitutions of various forms, but certain elements can be taken as characteristic of them all. In most cases, a preamble identifies or names the church concerned and often details the circumstances of its founding or the situation which has given rise to the present constitutional formulation. This introduction then gives way to a prominent statement outlining the sources of faith and order which the church will observe. Typical details from these statements are the subject of the next section of this essay, but the fact of their existence and the manner in which the declarations are made is of interest in itself. Anglican theology is perhaps notorious for its apparent flexibility, but the churches of the communion all seek to provide permanent way-markers for the course of their doctrinal development. These are often given in the form of fundamental clauses which are taken to be virtually unalterable (e.g., Australia, Central Africa, Melanesia, New Zealand, Nigeria, Scotland, South Africa, and West Africa). Others profess a Solemn Declaration (Canada) or offer a Statement of General Principles (Japan). Virtually all the other provinces give a distinct paragraph which states their beliefs concerning doctrine and worship. Some churches (e.g., Sudan, Central Africa, Indian Ocean, Kenya, Melanesia, South Africa, and Uganda) specifically disclaim the right to modify their fundamental standards, while others emphasize that alterations to statements on doctrine or worship can only be carried out under the most stringent conditions. These provisions are qualified by some exceptions which would allow, at least in matters of worship, such changes as: may from time to time be made by the Church of England (Central Africa, Indian Ocean, Kenya, New Zealand, Nigeria, South Africa — where any alteration to the creeds is explicitly rejected, Sudan, Tanzania, Uganda, and West Africa); may be required to meet the requirements of local conditions (Australia, Canada, Central Africa, Indian Ocean, Jerusalem, Kenya, Melanesia, and New Zealand — the latter two distinguish between what they see as an unchanging faith and the possibility of varying forms of worship or discipline, Nigeria, South Africa, Sudan, Tanzania, Uganda, and West Africa); or, may result from the authority of some higher synod (South Africa). Some churches also include a statement to the effect that while they are bound by universal standards of doctrine, they are bound to no interpretation of those standards other than those of their own tribunals, (Indian Ocean, Kenya, and Nigeria).

The only exceptions to this pattern of doctrinal definition are in the regional councils which, initially at least, define their faith as that of their member churches; the church in Wales which adopts the standards of the Church of England as foundational;

and the Episcopal Church of the United States of America, (ECUSA), which simple refers to its formularies as expressing the one, holy, catholic faith, and being agreeable to the Word of God.

Following the articles on faith and order the principles of worship and procedures for church government generally follow. The exercise of ecclesiastical discipline is dealt with — sometimes at considerable length — by a system of judgement and appeal provided, although quite often this is covered by canons or regulations independent of the constitution proper. The question of metropolitical authority is alluded to in the same way.

It is because the different constitutions set out to resolve the same sort of ecclesiological questions rather than any suggestion that they share similarities of form or language, that they can be subject to comparison and contrast between one or another. As such a procedure is appropriate it is possible to examine the constitutions in order to observe the degree of family likeness in faith and history that exists between members of the Anglican communion.

The Shared Faith of the Anglican Communion

Anglican faith and order is defined by reference to two standards in the provincial constitutions. First, there is an insistence that Anglicanism reflects the universal faith of the church, and secondly, it acknowledges that this faith is expressed within a particular historical tradition. The universal referrent gains attention first.

The dogmatic sections of Anglican constitutions focus upon the claim that the church concerned is part of the one, holy, catholic and apostolic church (Australia, Canada, Scotland, Melanesia, China, and Japan — although the last two omit the specific reference to unity); that it is a "fellowship within" that church (United States of America); or is a current embodiment of "the Ancient Catholic and Apostolic Church" (Ireland). Alternatively, churches profess "the Christian faith" (Australia, and South America); "the Faith of Christ" (Central Africa, Indian Ocean, Sudan, and Tanzania); "the Faith of our Lord Jesus Christ" (South Africa, and West Indies); or some variant of the formula "the faith, doctrine, sacraments and discipline of the Lord" or "the Church of Christ" (New Zealand, Nigeria, and West Africa).

Some (e.g., Australia and Melanesia) utilize a combination of credal and christological forms.

More particularly the universal faith is apprehended within an Anglican framework. Some provinces see this as an inevitable result of their historical or missionary origins (China, Japan, Ireland, and New Zealand). Other provinces because they hold, receive, or retain communion with the See of Canterbury and the Anglican communion (Canada, Central Africa, Indian Ocean, Ireland, Jersusalem, Kenya, Nigeria, South America, Sudan, Tanzania, United States of America, and West Africa). Scotland simply lists the churches with which it holds full communion. The Anglican perspective is also described as a consequence of the way in which churches have received the faith —as it is taught or explained by the Church of England in its historic formularies (Melanesia, New Zealand, Nigeria, West Africa, South Africa, Sudan, Tanzania, Uganda, Wales, and West Indies).

The relevant paragraph in the Melanesian constitution is perhaps illustrative of this two-fold method of reference (although in most respects the Melanesian document is also the most idiosyncratic of all the constitutions). It states: "We accept and teach the faith of our Lord Jesus Christ and the teachings, sacraments and discipline of the One, Holy, Catholic and Apostolic Church as the Anglican Communion has received them." It goes on to list the sources from which this faith has been received.

The same pattern can be perceived in most constitutions. The universal faith is repeatedly identified as being scriptural and credal in its content, catholic in its interpretation, and sacramental and episcopal in its out-working. Each term deserves attention.

1   *Scriptural*   With impressive unanimity the Anglican constitutions describe the Catholic faith as biblical at its core. The faith is "revealed in Holy Writ" (Canada) or "commanded by the Lord in His Holy Word" (New Zealand, Nigeria, and West Africa). Scripture is frequently specified as comprising "the canonical writings of the Old and New Testaments" and spoken of as the "revelation of God" (Japan), or the principal authority by which the faith is "taught" (Central Africa, South Africa, Sudan, and West Indies). It is received typically as the "ultimate rule and/or standard" (Australia, China,

Indian Ocean, Ireland, Jerusalem, Kenya, Melanesia, and Uganda) of "faith" or "faith and life." Some constitutions describe scripture as "inspired" (Australia, Indian Ocean, Ireland, Jerusalem, Kenya, Melanesia, Tanzania, and Uganda). In a characteristic phrase, however, scripture is most often spoken of as "containing all things necessary for salvation" (Australia, Canada, China, Indian Ocean, Ireland, Japan, Jerusalem, Kenya, Melanesia, Tanzania, Uganda, and the United States of America).

The mere recitation of these phrases does not convey much. After all it is not just the existence of scripture but its function that is significant to any doctrine of the church. Some provinces do indeed outline their doctrinal standards by means of a series of separate propositions which seem to establish scripture as authoritative simply by definition (Australia, Indian Ocean, Ireland, Japan, Jerusalem, Kenya, Melanesia, Nigeria, Tanzania, and Uganda). Others, however, provide more of a scheme of revelation within which the function of scripture is included incidentally (Canada, New Zealand, and South Africa). This utilizes some distinctive terminology whereby scripture is seen to *teach* the faith, which is in turn *preached* by the apostles and *held* by the primitive church, *summed up* in the creeds, and *confirmed*, *affirmed*, or *confessed* by the General Councils (Canada, Central Africa, Indian Ocean, Jerusalem, Kenya, South Africa, Sudan, Tanzania, Uganda, and West Indies).[11] The differences of approach should not be pressed too far. The distinction is not drawn in the constitutions and some provinces (Jerusalem, Tanzania, and Uganda) adopt both methods. Even so, given the problems surrounding such phrases as "the command of the Lord" or "the faith of the primitive Church," it is interesting to see how Anglicans have sought to give attention both to the importance of scripture and to the difficulty of its application to their corporate life. By and large Anglican theology has not attempted to proceed from dogmatic standards which are presumed to guarantee authoritative teaching. More typical is the attempt to see religious authority as an organic process which incorporates a number of sources and the life of the whole church in the course of its doctrinal development.

Other standards of faith are caught up in this ambiguity too, but they can be treated more briefly.

2   *Credal*   The constitutions which lean towards more organic views of revelation refer to the creeds as "summing up" the content of the apostolic faith (Canada, Central Africa, Indian Ocean, Jerusalem, Kenya, South Africa, Sudan, Tanzania, Uganda, and West Indies). Canada also speaks of the way creeds "define" faith; Japan "holds" the faith of the creeds; while Melanesia "adopts" the creeds with scripture as the formal standards of the province. The Irish church simply set itself to "profess the Faith of Christ which was professed by the Primitive Church." In other constitutions, especially where the definitions of faith are more closely linked to the history of the Church of England's standards (New Zealand, Nigeria, Scotland, South America, United States of America, Wales, and West Africa) the creeds are adopted within the English formularies even when they are not explicitly mentioned. Indeed the liturgical use of the creeds, and the influence of the Book of Common Prayer, quite apart from more formal considerations, ensure the central importance of the creeds to the Anglican tradition.

3   *Catholic*   Mention of the creeds usually leads to the further qualification that they have been "confirmed" or "affirmed" by the General Councils of the church. Not surprisingly, the constitutions face some difficulty in stipulating what this process involved. Most references are to "the undisputed Councils of the Holy Catholic Church," although Jerusalem delimits the procedure to the "dogmatic discussions of the first four Councils," Canada to the undisputed Councils of "the undivided Primitive Church," while Melanesia seeks to resolve the dilemma by giving "special honour to the teachings of the early Church, especially the decisions of those General Councils of the Church as are accepted by the Eastern and Western Church." The influence of patristic studies on Anglican consciousness is unmistakable.

4   *Sacramental and Episcopal*   Administration of the sacraments is generally listed along with a church's general commitment

to the faith, doctrine, and discipline of Christ (Australia, China, Central Africa, Indian Ocean, Ireland, Jerusalem, Kenya, Melanesia, New Zealand, Nigeria, South Africa, South America, Sudan, Tanzania, Uganda, Wales, West Africa, and West Indies). Faith must find a tangible form, and it is usually in the matter of sacraments and ministry that the constitutions link the faith of the church to the more specific tradition of the Church of England or the Anglican communion. Interestingly there is little attempt to define which sacraments are referred to in the general constitutional provisions, although Canada and Japan do refer to their respective participation in "the divinely ordained Sacraments" and "the two Sacraments which [Christ] instituted" as marks of their authentic catholicity. The Episcopal Church in Scotland treats questions of sacramental discipline at some length although no mention of the sacraments occurs among its fundamental articles. A similar situation is found in ECUSA's constitution.

Standards for ministry are treated more variously. Any church committed to the use of an Anglican ordinal is presumably thereby committed to the notion of episcopacy, but as may be expected, no single explanation of what this involves can be found. Several provinces state their intention simply to maintain the principles of the Church of England's Book of Common Prayer and Ordinal (Central Africa, Indian Ocean, Jerusalem, Kenya, New Zealand, South Africa, Sudan, United States of America, and Wales). A few state separately their adherance to the three-fold order of ministry as a matter of principle (Australia, Central Africa, and Japan). Others offer a brief rationale for their form of ministry and government: Canada refers to "the ministry of . . . Apostolic Orders"; China to maintaining orders "which have been in Christ's Church from the time of the Apostles"; Tanzania and Uganda hold and teach "that from the Apostles' time there have been these orders in Christ's Church: bishops, priests, and deacons." The Tanzanian constitution goes on to exclude from ministerial office anyone who has not been admitted by episcopal ordination. The

Episcopal Church of the United States of America has a detailed canon regarding the proper qualifications of episcopal ministry and the provision of a "conditional ordination" for cases where doubt exists. Melanesia, in rather different vein, contends that while the three-fold order is agreeable to Holy Scripture and the teaching and practice of the catholic church, and while lawful ministry in the province is founded upon ordination in the historic succession, yet, "this article does not mean that other forms of ministry in other Communions are not real, nor does it mean that only those who are ordained share in the ministry of the Church. The whole People of God, clergy and laity, shares in that ministry." ECUSA's canon also recognizes the validity of other ministries, and explains that the ordination of ministers from other communions who wish to function as Episcopalians does not deny the significance of their previous ministry but is for the purpose of "adding to that commission the grace and authority of Holy Orders as understood and required by this Church for the exercise of the ministry."

Legal documents are not the most appropriate places in which to expose theological controversies, but references like those just noted clearly reflect wider issues. It has sometimes been charged that in ecumenical discussions Anglicans have used the Lambeth Quadrilateral to impose stricter obligations on other churches than they are used to observing themselves. Whatever the validity of that claim in specific instances, it is clear from the examination of Anglican constitutions that the tenets of the Quadrilateral — scripture, creeds, the adminstration of sacraments, and the historic episcopate — do provide elements for a normative description of Anglican faith and order. It is equally clear though that there is no general agreement as to how these elements are to be understood or used in Anglican theological analysis. Despite internal disputes, however, it can be asserted that the churches of the Anglican communion, formally at least, describe their doctrinal stance in ways that are quite compatible with each other. At a fundamental level Anglicans share a common faith. This is a necessary if not a sufficient condition of Anglican "cohesiveness."

The Common History of the Anglican Communion

For the faith of scripture, creed, and tradition to be received or maintained, it must also be embodied within a concrete historical and liturgical framework. It is to this framework that attention must now turn. If it is granted that a study of their constitutions suggests that the Anglican provinces share a family likeness in their standards of doctrine, then the reality of their communion will be tested by the way in which those standards are expressed at the level of worship, ministry, and mission. What is it that makes the family "Anglican"? This question has assumed critical proportions because of the manifest cultural diversity which exists within the Anglican fellowship. Is the affection which holds the family together really grounded in a common history, or is it simply an attraction to things English and nostalgia for the quaint ways of the "C of E"? The distinctive markers of Anglicanism must be reviewed again: not only must they be linked with the general and universal standards of world Christianity, they must also prove adaptable to the local and particular demands of each individual province. What light is thrown by the provincial constitutions on this second requirement?

1   *An Anglican Inheritance*   The double reference to the universal and particular dimensions of the church in constitutional terms has already been noted. It can be further underlined in the foundation documents of the Provinces of South Africa or the West Indies. Their constitutions insist that they adopt the faith of the holy catholic church "according as the Church of England received (and set forth) the same." Virtually every province makes a similar declaration, usually ascribing normative authority to the English formularies or at least accepting them as "agreeable to the Word of God."

  The earlier constitutions (United States of America, New Zealand, Canada, Ireland, and in this respect too, Wales) take over the English standards of Prayer Book and Ordinal, and, less directly, the Thirty-nine Articles, claiming them as their own possession by virtue of historical origins and a shared liturgical tradition. Even the provinces which have been founded comparatively recently and which have only indirect connections with English ecclesiastical history, repeatedly refer to the Prayer Book and Ordinal as crucial authorities (Central Africa, Indian Ocean, Jerusalem, Kenya, Nigeria, South America, Sudan, Tanzania, and West Indies). In virtually every case, vernacular liturgy is an established fact and distinct liturgical traditions are highly developed, but this is always seen to follow "the principles of worship" of the Prayer Book and the work of liturgical revision is held to be consistent with its "spirit and teaching." A second variation on this pattern is provided by Japan and China which follow ECUSA's historical liturgical model, and ECUSA in turn had drawn inspiration from the Scottish tradition. Scottish canon law is riven with the competing claims of English and Scottish precedents. Melanesia declares its resolve to follow a single liturgical pattern while allowing liberty for local adaptation, but gives no indication of what the pattern should be. In fact, in every case the living liturgy of the churches has moved on quite independent lines, but the historical evidence of liturgical dependence and independence are still to be found in the constitutional record.

The use made of the Book of Common Prayer as a liturgical model raises important issues concerning mutual accountability within the Anglican communion. Plainly the liturgical diversity of the provinces makes the use of the model remote, and this is accentuated by the independent liturgical developments of the Church of England. The problem has been widely recognized for some time, and it is clearly argued throughout the communion that the churches share a common liturgical structure not a common liturgical form.[12] But while the Prayer Book represents part of Anglicanism's shared history, it is by and large not part of its current liturgical life. Appeals to the "spirit and teaching" of the book are less and less credible, yet while there is no alternative standard of worship, Anglican liturgies remain recognizably similar: this in itself is evidence of the non-coercive power of history in the Anglican communion, as distinct from the more efficient but potentially divisive effects of legislation or centralized control.

Another aspect of the Church of England's heritage, the Thirty-nine Articles, holds only a marginal place in provincial documents. Even when the Anglican communion began to take shape, the Articles were seen as a doubtful asset by many churchmen, and they passed into the legal consciousness of the new churches mainly as an appendage to the Prayer Book. In the more recent constitutions, the Articles are rarely mentioned — only Australia and Uganda give them any prominence. Kenya and Tanganyika indicate that although the Articles are not mentioned among their fundamental clauses, this does not "preclude their use" at a diocesan level. West Africa and Nigeria refer to the Articles as expressing the faith of the Church of England which contributed much to their own development, but they do not see them as authoritative in their own life. The Episcopal Church in Scotland, which reluctantly adopted the Articles at the turn of the nineteeth century, has recently removed reference to them from its canons, and abolished the forms of assent associated with them. ECUSA still includes the Articles among a collection of historical documents that illustrate the history and development of its doctrinal character, but they do not function directly in the life of the province. The Church of England made the practice of "reading in" clergy with the Articles a voluntary matter in 1975.

In any fully developed discussion of Anglican ecclesiology, the Articles would still hold an important if by no means decisive place. However, for a variety of reasons, it must be admitted that this is not reflected very clearly in the constitutions of the Anglican provinces. This fact throws further weight on the liturgical resources of the communion to provide the theological undergirding for its fellowship, with all the attendant problems which have already been noted.

2   *The Indigenous Achievement*   Mention of liturgical revision and development has introduced the second level at which Anglican standards must be judged. Anglicanism as a worldwide phenomenon is required not just to appropriate the details of the English religious tradition which gave it birth, but to incorporate elements of that tradition in an authentic response to the needs of a local church's circumstances. A number of provincial constitutions, especially the newer ones, specifically acknowledge the need for this process of adaptation. Even when this is not so, the existence of the provinces,

and in particular the older ones, indicates ways in which it has effectively been done.

Adaption is not innovation. Most constitutional documents state, for instance, that changes of worship must remain consistent with fundamental articles (Australia, Nigeria, and West Africa); the principles of the Book of Common Prayer (Central Africa, Indian Ocean, Jerusalem, Kenya, South Africa, South America, Sudan, Tanzania, and Uganda); scripture (Melanesia); or the creeds (Tanzania). Others (Canada, Ireland, New Zealand, which draws a clear distinction between changes in doctrine and changes of worship, South America, Uganda, Wales, and West Indies) add that liturgical changes can only be made by carefully regulated constitutional procedure which is in turn governed by other fundamental requirements.

Ireland asserts a "constant witness against all innovations in doctrine and worship, whereby the Primitive Faith hath been from time to time overlaid, and which at the Reformation this Church did disown and reject." The constitutions of West Africa and Nigeria provide for their synods "power to order [their] discipline to banish and drive out all erroneous and strange doctrines which are contrary to God's word as understood and interpreted [by their formularies]" — an interesting application of familiar words from the English Ordinal.

Quite apart from these formal stipulations, a number of constitutions give more direct evidence of a Christian sensitivity to their cultural environment. Most of the African provinces include reference to the non-racial and non-tribal implications of the biblical doctrine of humanity. In a number of instances there are signs of the difficulties of maintaining a sense of provincial unity across sharply divisive national frontiers, or provisions for the continued administration of a province if its synod should be prevented from meeting or find themselves declared illegal. For the Church of England, the idea of a national church has become identified with the machinery of establishment. No other province is established, but the validity of the Anglican communion as "a fellowship of national churches"(as it has often so described itself) is partly to be demonstrated by the way in which its members identify with and minister to the social and national aspirations of the countries in which they are set. Historically Anglicanism has sought to set the demands of state and society against those of the kingdom of God. A survey of their constitutions suggests that, in principle at least, the Anglican provinces recognize both dimensions of their responsibility.

The Personal Quality of the Anglican Communion

When John Howe referred to affection and love giving cohesion to the Anglican fellowship, he was undoubtedly reflecting upon the warmth of regard which he had himself found within the communion. It was no coincidence, however, that in his address to the ACC, Howe should go on to speak of the way in which the personal character of the Anglican family had a focus in the person of the archbishop of Canterbury.

To speak in this way is not to suggest that the archbishop is located at the epicentre of episcopal life, from which the ripples of Anglican authority are generated. One of Howe's enduring convictions was that in the Anglican communion authority moves *towards* not from the centre.[13] But Anglicans do participate in a communion not just a federation of churches, and the inter-relatedness or indeed the unity of ministry between those churches is a further sign and realization of their cohesiveness.

At one level the importance of the See of Canterbury for the historical origins of the Anglican communion is self-evident, but more than this is involved in referring to the archbishop as a focus of Anglican unity. While the constitutions of the Anglican churches do not provide enough material for a theory of primacy as such, they do indicate some of the ways in which personal factors complement more theological and historical ones to safeguard their fellowship.

From the beginning the episcopal and constitutional development of the Anglican communion has sought to protect bishops from having to act on their own.[14] Anglican bishops exercise their authority in concord with their synods, and in concert with one another. When the provincial constitutions turn from dogmatic to more structural considerations, these two poles of episcopal activity become apparent. In questions of ecclesiastical discipline for instance, it is apparent that church courts function only within the voluntary sphere of the synodal compact and therefore deal essentially with disputes concerning doctrine or ministry. The discipinary powers of the courts are drawn directly from the constitutional standards by which the province exists. At the same time discipline is exercised under a graduated series of authorities. Thus the decision of a diocesan court is subject on appeal to a provincial body, and beyond that various forms of ultimate appeal are available. At each level of judgement the bishops hold an increasingly important, though rarely exclusive, balance of power.

Such procedures illustrate how Anglican constitutions seek to balance the claims of synodical government with the collegial responsibilities of the episcopate. The colonial churches purchased their independence with the currency of synodical authorization. By the system of voting by separate houses with the requirement that all three houses concur, episcopacy was rendered constitutional, while at the same time retaining to the bishops a power of veto over proceedings. This form of polity, which is exemplified by the disciplinary courts of the provinces, is also demonstrated by the way constitutional powers are balanced by them at different points. Several provincial structures began as bishops' conferences, and this is evident in churches (e.g., West Indies and East Asia) where the house of bishops is retained as a kind of upper chamber, independent of synodical action. So Tanzania and China give the bishops the right to approve candidates for episcopal office prior to the convening of an electoral synod, although they do not normally have the right to decide the final appointment. By contrast, the Australian church stipulates that its senior appeal court must be chaired by a layman, and one qualified in law, such is the constitutional power of its organization.

The same episcopal-synodical tensions can be seen in the way that, while some constitutions define the role of archbishops by their formal functions, others (notably Central Africa, West Africa, Nigeria, and Tanzania) outline duties which are not only administrative but also include the right to visit and the responsibility of supervising the dioceses of the province. Melanesia, following tribal customs, goes so far as to require a vow of obedience from diocesan bishops to their archbishop. The Scottish church on the other hand stresses the fact that primacy is a responsibility shared by all bishops; the primus is an episcopal chairman. In America, this view is accentuated by the way the presiding bishop holds office for an elected period.

This difference of emphasis is parallelled by different attitudes to the relationship of diocese to province: where does ultimate responsibility lie? Such a question is to some extent inevitable for a church which seeks to uphold both authority and freedom, but it is also an outcome of the differing circumstances in which provinces were formed. Where a province has come into being by a process of subdivision from a larger unit, its authority will tend to be more centralized: if it is an amalgamation of local churches, then its organization will be more federal in character. Nevertheless, as has been indicated previously the provincial system was intended to provide a pattern of consistent metropolitical oversight. Bishops should not be left to act on their own. Churches may be autonomous, but they were not meant to be isolated. So from the beginning, provincial constitutions spelt out the line of accountability between dioceses and province, and potentially at least, between one province and another. At the very time in which it became clear that, for practical as well as legal reasons, the archbishop of Canterbury could no longer exclusively function as metropolitan, it became essential for churches to stand on their own feet. Gradually provinces established their own system of primacy. Of special interest are cases where metropolitical authority is exercised not by an individual but jointly through a council (e.g., South America, the South Pacific and East Asia). In the last mentioned, the council preserves, for the meantime, not only the canons of the church in Hong Kong but also the church on the Chinese mainland.

All this, however, merely postpones the essential question of How, if at all, a province is subject to any controls beyond those of its provincial constitution? A positive answer to that question has been suggested by some of the more recent constitutions. For them the need to have recourse to authority beyond their own boundaries may seem more pressing, even when there is no consensus as to who or what that authority should be. For example, changes to the fundamental provisions of the constitutions of Central Africa or Nigeria must be referred to the archbishop of Canterbury, and in the case of Nigeria, to all other metropolitans too, to ensure that terms of inter-communion are not threatened. For several other churches, a final court of appeal is exercised by the archbishop of Canterbury (West Africa); the archbishop and two other bishops of his choosing (Central Africa, South Africa); the archbishop and the Anglican Consultative Council (Jerusalem); or the general secretary of the ACC (Sudan). Others nominate the ACC or the Lambeth Conference as their "higher authority" should the need arise.

While the older province did not and could not raise the question of metropolitical responsibility in quite this way, their practical course of action was remarkably similar. The archbishop of Canterbury was both the primate of a province of the Anglican communion and also the source of authority within their own. The existence of the Lambeth Conferences indicates the way in which autonomous churches chose to act in concert wherever that was possible, and more recently, the creation of the Primates' Meeting is further evidence of the way in which primacy is conceived of as a corporate and consultative activity. It is in that setting that the archbishop of Canterbury provides a focus of unity for the Anglican communion, as (in Randall Davidson's words) "a pivot . . . a point of common touch, common information, common life." When the archbishop visits an Anglican province he goes as an honoured guest in order to learn, not to exercise jurisdiction, however shadowy.[15]

The Cohesion of the Anglican Communion

Until recently at least, the constitutions of Anglican provinces were not drawn up against any particular pattern. For all that, a comparison of their provisions indicates a significant measure of agreement between them in the ways they define fundamental commitments in doctrine, and the manner in which those commitments are worked out in church life. The provinces are not identical but they do share a family likeness and differences between them are resolved, actually or potentially, by the mutual respect and deference that family feeling creates and which the role played by the archbishop of Canterbury has come to symbolize. The constitutions do not provide a legalistic proof of Anglican unity, but they do indicate a consistent basis upon which the relationship of autonomous national churches can be expressed in terms of an Anglican fellowship.

It goes without saying that constitutional documents represent a very small part of what comprises Anglicanism today. The constitutions do not set out to address problems concerning doctrinal development or liturgical continuity, leave alone proposals about the nature of a universal primacy for the church. More importantly, they leave aside matters to do with the experience of faith and worship, mission and ministry, which might make the Anglican family one which it is worth belonging to. But they do provide evidence of the way Anglican churches have demonstrated what they hold to be essential to their life, and a comparison of them has served at least to confirm John Howe's contention that there is a legitimate line of succession running through the Anglican communion and that its members bear a family resemblance moulded by faith, history, and personal recognition.

One question remains: How does the Church of England relate to this pattern? At face value the answer seems obvious. It is the faith and history and line of ministry of the English church in which the rest of the communion's life coheres. This intuitive answer can be given a more convincing and realistic demonstration, however. While the established character of the Church of England makes it difficult to find a strict basis of comparison with the constitutions of other provinces, a study of the laws by which the Church of England is governed — such as that undertaken by the Archbishops' Commission on the Relationship of Church and State in England — indicates that it is bound by a variety of constitutional measures as to standards of doctrine and worship which centre on the historic formularies and provide a system of reference for departures from those standards. Such measures are quite consistent with the other provincial standards, and make it perfectly feasible to speak of a family of Anglican churches.

The Anglican communion is of course not the only family of Christendom, and it is not always conspicuously successful in resolving the challenges which it faces. Those very facts, however, make it important to recognize that there is a theological basis upon which Anglicans can respond to the demands of both unity and mission, and when this basis is typified in the ministry of someone like Bishop John Howe it makes that response eminently worth working for.

Notes

1. *ACC-4: Anglican Consultative Council, Fourth Meeting* (1979), 72.
2. *ACC-5: Anglican Consultative Council, Fifth Meeting* (1981), 7. Howe's repeated use of the family metaphor can be traced through the prefaces of successive ACC reports.
3. *ACC-3: Anglican Consultative Council, Third Meeting* (1976), 46.
4. *The Report of the Lambeth Conference, 1978* (London, 1978), 41 and 122ff.
5. There is no official depository of provincial documents for the Anglican communion. The ACC archive collects material it receives in black document containers, and this represents the nearest thing to a complete record of provincial constitutions. Material available for reference at the time of writing was:

Church of England in Australia, latest revisions	1978
Church of the Province of Burma, (draft)	1970
Church of the Province of Burundi, Rwanda, and Zaire	1979
Anglican Church of Canada	1962
Church of the Province of Central Africa	1977
Church of England	1985
Church of the Province of the Indian Ocean	1973
Church of Ireland	1978
Japan Holy Catholic Church	1971
Episcopal Church in Jerusalem and the Middle East	1978
Church of the Province of Kenya	1970
Church of Melanesia	1973
Church of the Province of New Zealand	1978
Church of the Province of Nigeria, (draft)	1977
Anglican Church of Papua New Guinea	1977
Episcopal Church of Scotland, (draft)	1979
Church of the Province of South Africa (changed to Southern Africa in 1982)	1970
Anglican Council for South America, (draft)	1980
Province of the Episcopal Church of the Sudan	1976

Church of the Province of Tanzania   1970
Church of Uganda (originally Uganda, Burundi, Rwanda,
and Zaire)   1972
Episcopal Church of the United States of America   1979
Church of Wales   1980
Church of the Province of West Africa   1970
Church of the Province of West Indies   1959

This list also gives the official titles of the churches whose constitutions are reviewed. Where geographical contractions are used in this essay it is hoped that the meaning is clear, and that the usage is not offensive to the bodies concerned.

6. The dramatic realization of this fact and its implications for the Anglican communion is described by A.M.G. Stephenson, *The First Lambeth Conference, 1867* (London, 1967), 66ff.

7. H.L. Clarke, *Constitutional Church Government in the Dominions beyond the seas and in other parts of the Anglican Communion* (London, 1924); G.W.O. Addleshaw, "The Law and Constitutions of the Church Overseas," in *The Mission of the Anglican Communion*, ed. E.R. Morgan and R. Lloyd (London, 1948), 74-98; S. Ervin, *Some Deficiencies in the Canon Law of the American Episcopal Church* (New York, 1961); *An Introduction to Anglican Polity* (Ambler, Pennsylvania, 1964); *The Polity of the Church of Ireland* (Ambler, Pennsylvania, 1965); *The Polity of the Church of the Province of South Africa* (Ambler, Pennsylvania, 1965); *The Political and Ecclesiastical History of the Anglican Church in Canada* (Ambler, Pennsylvania, 1967); *The Development of the Synodical System in the Anglican Church of Canada* (Ambler, Pennsylvania, 1969).

8. *The Report of the Lambeth Conference 1978* (London, 1978), 98.

9. Stephenson, *The First Lambeth Conference 1867*, 66.

10. "Guidelines for Provincial Constitutions and Metropolitical Authority" in *ACC-4: Anglican Consultative Council, Fourth Meeting* (1979), 47-50.

11. This formula was also incorporated in the Preamble to the Resolutions of the first Lambeth Conference.

12. E.g., *The Lambeth Conference, 1958* (London, 1958), Part II, 80-81. The 1978 Conference did not refer to the Prayer Book at all in its discussion of the distinctive marks of Anglicanism, but noted that "ordered wordship" in a variety of forms was "a witness to the apostolic

Gospel in word and sacrament, (which) patterns and limits the diversity which characterized Anglicanism from the first.'' *The Report of the Lambeth Conference, 1978,* 99.

13. *ACC-5: Anglican Consultative Council, Fifth Meeting* (1981), 17.
14. *The Six Lambeth Conferences, 1867-1920* (London, 1920), 187 and Appendix, 37-38.
15. G.K.A. Bell, *Randall Davidson, Archbishop of Canterbury* (London, 1935), I, 444.

Towards a Theology and Practice of the Bishop-in-Synod
K.S. Chittleborough

Introduction

It is one of the mysteries of Anglicanism that we can have both bishops and synods with overlapping authority working effectively in the government of the church.

In Australia in the mid-nineteen-seventies, in the course of the Anglican-Uniting Church conversations, on the question of mutual recognition of ministries, it became necessary for Anglicans to try to explain to our Uniting Church brethren our theology of the bishop-in-synod. This essay on synodical government springs from the context of that debate, although its conclusions clearly bear upon other bi-lateral conversations, notably the work of the Anglican-Roman Catholic International Commission on Authority.

The original research undertaken in this enterprise began from an examination of the constitutional documents and the actual operations of synods in Australian dioceses. The attempt to thus elucidate a theology of bishop-in-synod revealed, rather surprisingly, a coherent ecclesiology and a rich and yet coherent view of authority in the church behind the variety of legal documents and constitutional history. It is only the conclusions of that research which are offered here. Those conclusions call for critical testing against the constitutional documents and experience of dioceses throughout the Anglican communion, as well as the testimony of scriptures and the doctrinal traditions of the church.

The Historical Context — Synodical Government

Synodical government, like other church institutions, grew out of the necessities of corporate life. It assumes a variety of forms down through history — depending upon response to the gospel in particular historical contexts, the personal style of the bishop, the constitutional procedures taken over from the political societies within which churches were set, and the missionary task confronting them.

In apostolic times, councils were held at Jerusalem to define with a common authority the teaching of the church in disputed matters.[1] In the first century we know of two synods summoned in Asia for the reformation of the church and the consecration of bishops.[2] In the following centuries everything points to the fact that bishops acted in those days according to their temperament. No body of fixed laws limited the bishops' power to act *proprio motu*. There were arbitrary bishops as well as constitutional ones and yet the ideal of common action and consultation was never lost, and in course of time these were incorporated in the rules and canons of national, provincial, and diocesan synods. Cyprian of Carthage, for example, declares that he decided at the beginning of his episcopate to do nothing without the advice *(concilium)* of his clergy and the consent *(consensus)* of his laity.[3]

When in the eighteenth and nineteenth centuries the colonial churches first gained their independence from the Crown, they found their seat of authority in synodical government. The system of voting by houses — bishop, clergy, and laity — which this embodied, and the requirement that these houses concur, rendered episcopacy constitutional while leaving bishops with the power of veto over proceedings. Authority was thus shared between the episcopate and synod, and the bishop had certain powers and responsibilities proper to his episcopal office which he could not delegate to his synod. The reason for this was not simply a pragmatic one which allowed the bishop to take personal initiatives which synod could not or would not take. It enshrined theological principles which it is the purpose of this essay to try to make clear.

The Anglican experience of synodical government in Australia rests upon a long tradition which thus goes back beyond the sixteenth-century Reformation in England. Modern synodical government, in the form revealed by the constitutions, canons, and rules in the various Australian dioceses, with lay representation going back over a hundred years, is typical of the whole Anglican communion outside England.[4]

It is important to keep in mind that in important respects the Church of England is *not* typical, being an "established" church, and because lay people were given constitutional rights in synods only in 1965.

The Centrality of the Diocesan Synod

The formal principles and practical operations of authority in the Anglican church are contained in the constitutional documents of the various dioceses, and these reveal a common pattern amidst their variety — namely that legislative authority resides neither in the "house" of bishops, nor in the various committees and bureaus of the church, but in *diocesan synods*, and to a lesser degree in provincial and national synods.[5]

Other structures of authority within Anglicanism, such as the National Bishops' Meeting, the Lambeth Conference, and the Anglican Consultative Council, are advisory, relational, and collegial but not legislative. The conscious decisions to give them no legislative power have led to a repudiation of centralized government and a refusal to have a legal basis of union. "The positive nature of authority which binds the Anglican Communion together is therefore seen to be moral and spiritual, resting upon the truth of the Gospel, and on a charity which is patient and willing to defer to the common mind" (*Report* to the Lambeth Conference 1948, see the Appendix).

The focus then in this essay is primarily on the *diocesan* synod, that is, a duly constituted body of three houses of bishop, clergy (priests and deacons), and laity, who together share in different ways in directing the life and growth, the good order and government of a diocese as the key to the way in which the lordship of Christ and the guidance of the Holy Spirit are made concrete and empirical. The constitution of the Anglican Church of Australia makes quite clear the centrality of the diocese: "A diocese shall in accordance with the historic custom of the One Holy Catholic and Apostolic Church continue to be the unit of organisation of this Church and shall be the see of a bishop" (Constitution, Section 7).

The relationship between the bishop and his synod has no real parallel in parliamentary democracy, autocracy, oligarchy, or bureaucracy — as these are found in the secular world — but is a complex one which springs from a combination of theological principles held in balance.[6] This theology which gives coherence to the not infrequently chaotic appearance of the Anglican experience of authority has come to be called the theology of "dispersed authority."

The Theological Context — A Theology of Dispersed Authority

The Anglican theology of dispersed authority arises from the Anglican experience and forms a common pattern behind the variety of constitutional documents of synods. A section of the Lambeth Conference of 1948 produced a statement of this theology which has not been bettered. Some parts of it might be phrased differently now: for example, the analogy between scientific method and the way in which the various factors in authority are ordered could be modified today, although the analogy still stands; there are traces of sexist language which, however, do not affect the points made; and so on. More serious work on the theology of dispersed authority needs to be done to update and clarify it, and this process of theological criticism would be in line with the statement itself.

The reader is referred to the text of the statement quoted in full in the Appendix. The implications of this statement for our subject will be drawn out in the sections which follow.

The Theology of the Bishop-in-Synod

Against the background of this view of dispersed authority Anglicans see embodied in the synodical government of their church the following theological principles:

1   *The Lordship of Christ.* The Anglican church accepts the traditional episcopal, presbyterial, and congregational elements inherent in the structure of a synod with its three houses as the means through which the lordship of Christ in his church may be "realized," that is, discerned and responded to.[7]

   The *personal oversight* of a diocesan bishop must go hand in hand with the *corporate responsibility* shared by bishop, presbyters, deacons, and lay people acting together. The overlapping authority of the bishop and the bishop-in-synod ensures this. What is said in the Lima Document about personal, collegial, and communal dimensions of oversight exactly describes the Anglican experience.[8]

2   *The Holy Spirit Is Given to the Whole Church.* The power of the Holy Spirit, which may also be called the power of the gospel of Christ, is the dynamic (*dynamis*) from which all exercise of authority proceeds. The Spirit is not given to a privileged few, a hierarchy or intellectual or spiritual elite, but to the whole church.

Every Christian therefore exercises the authority bestowed upon him or her by his or her reception (by word and sacrament) of the gospel. The *consensus fidelium* — the consent of the faithful — is therefore a reality, and the house of the laity acting in constitutional conjunction with the clergy and the bishop make it so. (See further in section 5 below.)

The risk to bishop, clergy, or laity of misusing their authority is merely concealed if it is pretended that power is not distributed in the church. This would amount to a massive self-deception. Anglicans relate lay and clerical authority by *simultaneously* assigning a presidential role to the ordained person and by giving open access to all the criteria for all decisions in the church. These criteria centre on the scriptures and the Book(s) of Common Prayer which are thus "in a language understood of the people." Anglicans remain true to their tradition when they *simultaneously* insist on the exercise of real power by those entitled to claim it and on the necessity of open criticism of the quality of the exercise of the power. Both of these principles are derived from scripture, are consistent with the traditions of the early church and the Reformation, and are enshrined in the structure of a synod.

3   *Episcope — The Bishop. Episcope* — oversight — although exercised by the bishop, is best understood as a function of the body of Christ — the whole church. This has various practical outcomes:

(i)   The bishop of a diocese is elected by the clergy and laity through the synod; and he is consecrated (if not already a bishop) by at least three other bishops.

(ii) The synod of a diocese is not the diocese but the organ of it which exercises *episcope.*

(iii) Episcopacy (as a distinct office) is "the source and centre of our order." The bishop wields his authority "by virtue of his divine commission and in synodical association with his clergy and laity, exercising it in humble submission as himself under authority." Anglicans therefore have not regarded episcopacy as a purely administrative appendage.

(iv) *Episcope,* if it truly reflects the lordship of Christ and the gift of the Holy Spirit to his whole church, involves the practice of "collegiality" at various levels. Not only does the bishop share *episcope* with his synod, but with his fellow Anglican bishops and beyond that. "The episcopate is one, each individual bishop exercising his *episcope* as joint tenant of the whole" (*Episcopatus unus est, cuius a singulis in solidum pars tenetur* — St. Cyprian, *De Unitate Ecclesia,* 5).

(v) The problem of *episcope* in a disunited church then arises. The Anglican episcopate shares its peculiar responsibilities with those called and chosen to execise *episcope* in the totality of Christ's church, and acknowledges that it has a special obligation to consult with leaders of other churches.[9] Professor Stephen Sykes puts it thus:

> Since no Anglican bishop believes that he alone exercises the fullness of *episcope* in any region in which other bishops or church leaders are active, he is bound to consult. If an Anglican bishop claims to be a bishop in the *church of God* as he does, he may not restrict the exercise of his *episcope* to his own denomination. Uncoordinated oversight of the church of God is simply not oversight. There is very good reason to believe that Anglican bishops ought to feel this problem with special acuteness. Their use of the concept of "collegiality" cannot therefore be borrowed unmodified from its use in Roman Catholicism.[10]

No diocesan synod in Australia, to my knowledge, has written this obligation of its bishop to consult ecumenically into its canons and constitution, but it is to be strongly recommended that they do. In any case, many bishops do in fact consult over a very wide range of issues.

The bishop therefore has, in the Anglican view, a particular responsibility for teaching the faith, for encouraging, promoting, and maintaining the proclamation, in word and sacrament, of the apostolic gospel by and in the whole church, for the pastoral care of his own flock, and for making visible the unity of "the one, holy, catholic, and apostolic church" of the creeds.

4   *The Bishop and the Sacramentality of His Order.* The question of ordination and apostolic succession has, in the past, often been debated as an isolated issue, as though "apostolic succession" was guaranteed by tactile succession of a hierarchy alone (the "pipeline theory"). Anglican experience and tradition does not support this, though Anglo-Catholics have argued that way.

Whatever the various "theologies" of episcopacy put forward, the essential theological point concerns the notion of *sacramentality*. The *Report* to the 1948 Lambeth Conference describes this when it says that in our experience the authority of God is "mediated in the Ministry of Word and Sacraments, by persons who are called and commissioned by God through the Church *to represent both the transcendent and the immanent elements of Christ's authority*" (italics mine).

Just as the pattern of Christ's authority and power is that it operates simultaneously as immanent in and transcendent of the structures and limitations of human life, so this is represented by the bishop who is, for example, both a *part* of his synod, and yet his episcopal authority *transcends* it. He is a "sacramental man," and by virtue of his consecration has reponsibilities which do not derive from his synod, nor can these inherent episcopal powers be delegated to his synod. Cases in point are the power to ordain others, the licensing of ministers to their place or cure, and the resolution of certain cases of conscience which he may "reserve" such as the remarriage in church of divorced couples.

The Anglican system of having bishop and bishop-in-synod with overlapping powers is not just "messy and inefficient management" — it rests upon one outcome of the sacramentality of order. What is "sacramental" is not simply the act of ordination, but the subsequent life and work of the person admitted to holy orders.[11]

> *For* you I am a bishop, but *with* you I am a Christian. . . .
> As then I am gladder to be redeemed with you than I
> am to be set over you, I shall, as the Lord commanded,
> be more completely your servant. (St. Augustine)[12]

Much more could be said about the sacramentality of orders, but I hope enough has been said to indicate that the tension between the bishop and his synod is, when Anglicans are true to their tradition, experienced as a sacramental reality which lies close to the heart of the gospel of the Incarnation.

5   *The Sensus Fidelium*. The authority of Christ, described in the scriptures, ordered in the creeds and continuing theological reflection, mediated by the ministry of word and sacraments is "verified in the witness of the saints and in the *consensus fidelium*." The *Report* to the 1948 Lambeth Conference goes on to say that "the Christ-like life carries its own authority, and the authority of doctrinal formulations, by General Councils or otherwise, rests in part on their acceptance by the whole body of the faithful."

The *sensus fidelium* in Anglicanism should not be understood as unanimity in the sense of everyone being exactly of the same opinion, nor is it shown by majority vote in Synod. Synods are not parliamentary democracies, although many parliamentary rules of business procedure have been adopted. Rather than truth or wisdom being "democratically" determined by majority vote, consensus government emerges with time, patience, and often costly love which is willing to defer to the common mind even when it has not yet emerged, and when it is "genuinely free."

Synods can be manipulated by bishops, theologians, lawyers, priests, or lay people; and Anglicans are not blind to the realities of partisan politics invading the church. But this is a declension from the ideal of true consensus. The safeguards against manipulation are, first, the example of Jesus Christ, his service and humble obedience unto death; second, the constraint of the appeal of the gospel to the human moral will; thirdly, openness to theological criticism; and fourthly, time for people to reflect and reconsider.[13]

Tyrannous or psychologically manipulative uses of power are to be identified, criticized, and abandoned. It must also be noted that their very recognition depends upon fallible human judgement.

Thus a dispersed, non-centralized structure such as synodical government gives the laity as well as the clergy constitutional opportunity for the kinds of consultation, criticism, and comment which promote genuinely free consensus. Our Anglican experience is that the Christian church requires *both* the discriminating exercise of authority *and* the discriminating exercise of criticism if Christ's work is to be done in the world. The tensions, conflict, and debate as well as the time required to make the *consensus fidelium* an essential part of keeping the church in the truth of Christ, spring from the theology of dispersed authority, and are part of a "charity which is patient and willing to defer to the common mind."

There is reason to believe that "the bishop-in-synod," especially in the provision for lay representatives to be *elected* by their local congregations and for them with their clergy to go back and consult them, may in practice give more weight to the *consensus fidelium* than the concept of the bishop-in-presbytery where the synod *appoints* the lay representation. It is at least arguable.

Oversight in the Uniting Church

By contrast with the Anglican system of bishop-in-synod, oversight in the Uniting Church is exercised *corporately* by the presbytery and other councils or assemblies. This corporate *episcope* is, however, modified in various ways by pressures and needs leading to more personal oversight being exercised by various officers. Of the three traditions which entered into union in 1973 — Presbyterian, Methodist, and Congregational — only one had been presbyterian in its polity. The Methodist church though connexional in polity, had had the experience of semi-episcopal officials in its district chairmen, and especially those in rural areas who had been "separated" from parish responsibilities.

The framers of the first Proposed Basis of Union (1964),[14] no doubt with an eye to facilitating wider union, envisaged a form of episcopacy through "bishops-in-presbytery" through a concordat with the Church of South India. The *Basis of Union*[15] which was finally adopted in 1973, however, omitted all reference to bishops, although it left room for the development of personal as well as corporate elements in the *episcope* of the presbytery and other councils. According to the present *Basis of Union*:

> *The Presbytery* (the district council) . . . consists of such ministers (elders), leaders and other church members who are appointed thereto. . . . Its function is to perform all the acts of oversight necessary to the life and mission of the Church in the area for which it is responsible, except over those agencies which are directly responsible to the (regional/State) Synod or (national) Assembly. Paragraph 15 (c)

Some personal oversight is, however, exercised by the presbyter officer or presbytery-chairman whose duties are "to constitute, preside over and generally direct the business of the meetings of the Presbytery, to exercise pastoral oversight, and to perform such other duties as may be prescribed" (Regulation 3.4.24).

Stuart Murray reflecting on Uniting Church experience since the union, in a paper presented to the Joint Anglican-Uniting Church Committee, has said:

> Neither the role of chairman nor the role of presbyter officer has more than very muted episcopal overtones. What is missing is an effective means for maintaining the purity of the faith. The Regulations locate this responsibility at the level of the Assembly, but that is rather remote from the lives of the presbyteries where issues of doctrine and adequate teaching may and do emerge. There is no person within the structure of the presbytery who is given authority to "speak for the Church." The result is that too often the Church is silent when it should speak, and that sometimes it is perceived as speak-

ing when it should be silent. This is what happens when publicity is given to the views of a churchman or woman who seems to be speaking for the Church, but has no authority to do so. There is no authentically prophetic voice speaking out of the heart of the body.

But the *episcope* of the presbytery has great strengths. Its greatest strength is its ability to discern the body. The presbytery will seldom move at a pace which is insensitive to the ability of the whole body to follow. This may mean that it will often move far too slowly or sluggishly, but there is no doubt concerning its sensitivity to the needs of the whole Church . . . and also to the wider community.[16]

The dynamics of authority operating here are fascinating; and, transposed into different keys and different levels of association, will be familiar to all who reflect on authority in the church in whatever denomination. The pressures to centralize, to provide for officials with personal authority to speak and act for the whole body, the type of authority to be accorded them, and where to draw the line between legislative/judicial authority and moral authority can be seen, according to one's point of view, as the promptings of the Spirit or the very devil.

The re-opening of official conversations between Anglican and Uniting churches in Australia in 1979 again raised the question of bishops in the context of the mutual recognition of ministries. The Steering Committee drew up a statement in 1980 for approval by the two churches recommending recognition "of each other's ministries of Word and Sacraments, while acknowledging that they show distinctive marks, emphases and differences exercised within different structures and disciplines." The proposal was treated with extreme caution by the Anglican Bishops' Meeting and the Standing Committee of General Synod, who asked for more theological argumentation to support the proposal for immediate mutual recognition of ministries. Nonetheless, the General Synod of August 1981 passed a resolution (22) on conversations with other churches, which reads in part, "That this Synod . . . . (b) adopts an immediate policy of working towards unity in diversity rather than organic union and strives for a mutual recognition of ministry and sacraments which will enable a free interchange between traditions" (Proceedings, p.31). The

Uniting Church General Assembly of May 1982 accepted the 1980 Statement and acknowledged the Anglican General Synod Resolution as a step along the way to organic union. It is again considering the question of personal episcopal oversight in its General Assembly of May 1985.

A survey of this ongoing debate clearly shows that many of the theological principles already referred to are held in common, although in a different balance. One of the pivotal issues is that many Uniting Church members are not able to grasp the "sacramentality of order," and Anglican woolly thinking as well as our "confusion of threefold orders" has not helped them. Much more theological work needs to be done to clarify the notion of sacramentality along the lines of the *Report* to the 1948 Lambeth Conference.

Centralized Authority: Primacy

Analagous to the dynamics operating at the level of the Uniting church presbyteries and the Anglican dioceses in Australia are those behind the development of papal "primacy" in the church. As Christian communities respond to the demands of the gospel in a variety of historical, political, and cultural contexts, many different types of personal as well as conciliatory primacy have developed. The ARCIC Statements on Authority have traced the development of papal primacy very clearly,[17] and they raise the question, Is it possible to *add* centralized to dispersed authority and yet leave the theology of the bishop-in-synod intact? The short answer to this question is: Only if it leaves intact the *balance of theological principles* inherent in the bishop-in-synod.

It is clearly possible to "add" centralized authority to dispersed authority, and the church has in fact done so in response to its mission. In Australia, where we are blessed with the "tyranny of distance," there are at present strong forces towards centralism. But the questions to ask are, Is this or that primacy *necessary* for all time and in all places and for all people? Upon what theological principles is it accepted, and what sort of constitutional authority, i.e., canonical jurisdiction, is a particular primacy to be given?

In its third statement, Authority I, ARCIC claimed to have reached, or very nearly reached a consensus. It arrived at what "amounts to a consensus on authority in the Church, and in par-

ticular, on the basic principles of primacy."[18] All that is left to
do is to pass from these "basic principles" to settle some of the
"particular claims of papal primacy and its exercise." This claim
to have discovered an existing consensus between our two churches on the principles of primacy is highly questionable. Fr.
Adrian Hastings, a member of the Preparatory Commission which
produced the Malta Report, comments on this claim:

> As a matter of fact there is not today a consensus within either
> of our two Churches, let alone between them, and a statement
> of this sort cannot provide what does not exist. As a conse-
> quence it simply does not ring true, appearing instead — to
> put it unkindly — as a bad amalgam of Anglican woolliness and
> Roman double talk.[19]

Has the theology and practice of bishop-in-synod as the basic pattern any light to shed? The following pointers may be worthy of
consideration.

1. *The Doctrine of the Church: Organic or Hierarchical?* It is clear
    from the theology of dispersed authority already outlined that
    an organic or systemic doctrine of the church and its total
    ministry undergirds it: "This authority possesses a sup-
    pleness and elasticity in that the emphasis of one element over
    the others may and does change with the changing condi-
    tions of the Church. . . . The elements of authority are
    moreover in *organic* relation to each other . . . so Catholic
    Christianity presents us with an *organic* process of life and
    thought. . . ." The *Lambeth Report* then goes on to refer to
    the scriptures, the creeds and continuous theological study,
    the ministry of the word and sacraments, the witness of the
    lives of the saints, and the *consensus fidelium* as the elements
    in this organic whole. It is this organic view of the church
    and its whole ministry which is inherent in the constitution
    of bishops-in-synd for here not only the bishop and clergy
    but the laity as well are given canonical authority and jurisdic-
    tion in matters of faith and discipline.
      On this matter there are two basic ways to think of the
    church's nature and function. First, the church can be seen
    as an institution governed and directed by clergy who shape
    the policy and make plans for implementing it, and then enlist

recruits, the laity, to assist them in carrying out these plans. This is the hierarchical view, and Anglicans are familiar enough with it to be sensitive to its operation in the structures of the Roman communion. With this view goes a concept of the ordained ministry which thinks of the bishop as having the "fullness of ministry" while priests, deacons, and the laity derive their ministries in descending ranks and functions from him.[20] It cannot be stated too strongly that this hierarchical mode of operation is *not* inherent in the structures of bishop-in-synod when it is true to its own theological principles, although there are people who, consciously or unconsciously, try to impose it in practice. Secondly, the church can be viewed as the people of God, the body of Christ, in which every member by virtue of baptism has a common though differentiated responsibility for the church and its service of the word and sacraments. In this organic or systemic model there is no place for a *cursus honorum* by which one rises from lower to higher rank, status, and responsibility. Each minstry in the church has its own integrity, function, and type of authority which is not "derived" from the bishop.

Now while the ARCIC statements repudiate the word "hierarchical authority" (Elucidation 1981 paragraph 5), and claim to be "dealing with a form of authority which is *inherent in the visible structures of the Church,*" the whole argument regarding the principles of primacy is conducted on the hierarchical model. Nor is it reassuring to examen *Lumen Gentium*, the Constitution and the Church of Vatican II, in which the hierarchical model is clearly paramount. When we look at the partial recovery of the organic view of the church as a result of Vatican II, and the way in which different popes have exercised their papal primacy, we see a struggle going on between the organic and hierarchical models of the church. Furthermore, the Preface to the *Final Report*, where ARCIC tackles the question of the ecclesiology undergirding their statements, we find no answer, in its treatment of the church as *koinonia*, to this quite crucial question of which basic view of the church and its ministry should be primary on biblical and doctrinal grounds.

The two doctrines of the church are to be found warring within Anglicanism itself in each of our parties, catholic, evangelical, and liberal. We, too, in common with the West from the fourth century, have inherited a fundamental change in church and ministry from the principle of organism in which the whole is greater than the sum of its parts, to the principle of hierarchy in which the "greatest" is the sum of its parts. There is with us, too, no consensus. But the point to be made is that the Anglican communion has resisted, so far, giving legislative authority (*jus*), as distinct from moral authority (*auctoritas*), to its primates alone — or even its bishops or priests *alone*, because it would change the basic character of the church itself.[21]

The organic nature of the church has been safeguarded by giving legislative power to bishops-in-synods, which includes giving legislative authority to duly elected and representative lay "ministers" of the gospel. So, from a church in whose constitutional structures for more than a century the laity have been given collegial, canonical authority and juridical powers in matters of faith and morals comes the question: In a united church, is the Church of Rome prepared to grant rightful canonical standing to the legislative "collegiality" of not on-ly bishops and priests but to duly elected, representative, lay persons? If this is not the case, it is difficult to see how cen-tralized authority can be *added* to dispersed authority.

2   *Universal Immediate Episcopal Jurisdiction.* ARCIC, in *Elucida-tion* 6, says, "We understand jurisdiction as the authority or power (*potestas*) necessary for the effective fulfillment of an office. Its exercise and limits are determined by what that office involves (cf. Authority II, paragraphs 16-22)," and in Authority I, 24, "The First Vatican Council intended that the papal primacy should be exercised only to maintain and never erode the structures of the local Churches. The Roman Catholic Church is today seeking to replace the juridical outlook of the nineteenth century by a more pastoral under-standing of authority in the Church." While we may applaud the intention of the First Vatican Council and the pastoral understanding of twentieth-century Roman Catholics, the problem is that what ARCIC understands by jurisdiction is not what is usually meant by it. Jurisdiction (*jus*) is the authority and power given by *law*, in the case of the church by canon law, contained in constitutional documents — while

moral authority (*auctoritas*) is not — it carries weight by its own intrinsic truth or wisdom. Anglicans are (usually) quite clear about the difference between a primate (or a synod) having jurisdiction and one who has moral authority. The archbishop of Canterbury, for example, has no jurisdiction in Australia, though he has considerable moral authority. The ARCIC treatment of jurisdiction, if it is really intent on exploring "what is inherent in the structures of the Church" is confusing the real issue, to say the least.

Defending the Commission's statements, Dr. Chadwick and Fr. Yarnold have written: "the exercise of the Pope's immediate jurisdiction outside Rome is extremely rare, even rarer perhaps than the exercise of his papal infallibility."[22] This assertion is presumably meant to suggest that the Roman claim to universal immediate episcopal jurisdiction has been misinterpreted, and properly understood should not be hard for Anglicans to swallow.

But is it true? Is not the appointment of every bishop of the Latin rite an example today of the pope's immediate jurisdiction, and is that rare or unimportant? To add *this* sort of centralized jurisdiction to the Anglican church would certainly be incompatible with the organic principle of bishop-in-synod where (in most cases) synod elects its bishop, the people generally consent, and three bishops consecrate.

The pope has many roles. The titles of the present one are "Johannes Paulus pp II, Bishop of Rome, Vicar of Jesus Christ, Successor to the Prince of the Apostles, Sovereign Pontiff of the Universal Church, Patriarch of the West, Primate of Italy, Archbishop and Metropolitan of the Roman Province, Sovereign of the Vatican City, Servant of the Servants of God." While Anglicans are prepared to acknowledge the moral authority of the pope according to the truth of what he says and the wisdom of his moral judgements, we are entitled to ask, "In a united church, to which of the pope's particular roles or 'hats' would Anglicans be required to give legal enactment in their diocesan synods?" If the answer is, "None," what becomes of the claim to universal immediate jurisdiction? If the answer is, "One or two, or more," we are entitled to ask *which* ones? It is in the interface between theology and constitutional law that the real questions of authority in the sense of jurisdiction arise — questions which have been glossed over by the ARCIC statements.

There may be historical circumstances in the future in which it may be appropriate for the Anglican communion to give a pope universal jurisdiction. Who can tell? "Synodical government assumes a variety of forms down through history." But response to the gospel, the personal styles of the bishops we see, the constitutional procedures taken over from the political societies surrounding us and the missionary task confronting us — these suggest that it is highly unlikely that Anglicans would agree that that time has come.

It would be wrong to suggest that no growing together, no interchange or mutual learning can take place until all the complex theoretical and practical problems concerning authority are solved. The consensus of ARCIC on the eucharist and ministry more truly reflects the actualities in our two churches, and on that basis we may ask, "Has not the time arrived when we have reached such a measure of agreement on so many of the fundamentals of the gospel that a relationship of shared communion can be encouraged by the leadership of both our churches?" [23]

The Actual Operations of Bishop-in-Synod

In drawing out the theological principles detectable in the constitutional documents of Anglican synods, it would also be wrong to suggest that the actual operations of synods always live up to those principles, or that every individual Anglican always detects them. My point is that the principles are there to be appealed to, even when they are not always articulated, are forgotten, or are acted against. The theology outlined is at once a description of Anglican theology and a criticism of Anglican *praxis*.

The bishop of Bombay, in an article entitled "Christian Ministry and Synodical Government," [24] describing the experience of the Church of North India has some words which should be heeded:

> The main problem facing any Uniting Church is how to combine the three traditional elements in Church polity (the episcopal, the presbyterial and the congregational — and we

might add, the primatial) in such a way that, in fact, the spiritual and not the demonic predominates. In other words, the right combination of different polities can allow Jesus Christ to be Lord. But a wrong or injudicious synthesis might result in the *de facto* rule of his Satanic Majesty! If Synodical government is not to be a stumbling block but a means of grace, considerable thought and experiment will be needed. Perhaps this is also true of Churches not yet united!

Anyone who has sat through sessions of synods can say, "Amen" to that.

Notes

1. Acts 15 and 21.
2. Eusebius, *Eccl. Hist.*, iii, 20.
3. See H. Lowther-Clarke, *Constitutional Church Government* (London, 1924), 1-14. There is no space to go into the constitutional history in detail, and I do not here wish to enter into the question of the difference between ancient synods and modern synodical government.
4. See R.A. Giles, *The Constitutional History of the Australian Church* (1928), and Stephen Sykes, *Authority in the Anglican Communion,* from the Anglican Primates' Meeting, Washington, April 1981, 18-25.
5. See an important article by H. E. Thomas, "Some Principles of Anglican Authority" in the last mentioned work, 18 ff. See also *Canon Law in Australia* (General Synod 1981), 92, which calls dispersed authority "chartered anarchy."
6. Democratic, autocratic, and bureaucratic procedures have, from time to time, influenced the way in which synods operate. For the influence of sociological factors that have shaped episcopacy, see G.M.D. Howat and G.V. Bennett, "Today's Church in Today's World," in the Lambeth Conference 1978 Preparatory Articles, 215-229.
7. See Kennedy's article in *Today's Church in Today's World*, 171 ff.
8. See *Baptism, Eucharist and Ministry* (Geneva, 1982) sections 26 and 27, pp.25 and 26. Compare *The Church: Its Nature Function and Ordering* (Report prefaced to the 1964 Proposed Basis of Union of the Uniting Church in Australia), 45-47.

9. So the Anglican Primates' Meeting in 1981: see *Authority in the Anglican Communion*, 33, section 5.

10. Sykes, *Authority in the Anglican Communion*, 16.

11. See Rayner, *Today's Church in Today's World*, 265.

12. Ibid., 241.

13. See Sykes, *Authority in the Anglican Communion*, 12-13, 17 on this whole section.

14. *The Church: Its Nature Function and Ordering* (Report prefaced to the 1964 Proposed Basis of Union).

15. *Basis of Union* (Melbourne, 1971).

16. Stuart Murray, *Episcope through Presbytery*, 8.

17. *The Final Report* (1982), Authority I, 8-12.

18. Authority I, 24. Compare Authority II, 1.

19. "Malta Ten Years Later," in *One in Christ* (1978), XIV, 1, 28.

20. Compare, for example: "The bishop alone is the direct and immediate sign of Christ to his flock, while the priest is a sign, not directly of Christ the Priest, but of his bishop"! Bishop Guildford Young in his commentary on "Decree on the Ministry and Life of Priests," in W. M. Abbott, S. J. Chapman, *The Documents of Vatican II* (London, 1967).

21. For an interesting treatment of the effect of the hierarchical principle taking over the organic from the fourth century on the decline of the permanent diaconate, see James M. Barnett, *The Diaconate, A Full and Equal Order* (New York, 1981).

22. E.J. Yarnold and Henry Chadwick, *Truth and Authority* (London, 1977), 34.

23. Archbishop Coggan, *The Times*, 29th April 1977.

24. Kennedy, *Today's Church in Today's World*, 176-177.

The material in the first part of this essay originally appeared in *St. Mark's Review*, No. 109, March 1982.

The Making of a Tradition: Provincial Synod in the Church of the Province of Southern Africa[1]

Michael Nuttall

1870 has been described as a watershed in English history;[2] it was not less so for Europe. It saw the completion of Italian unification. It saw the outbreak of the Franco-Prussian war. It saw the meeting of the First Vatican Council, with its declaration on papal infallibility, that thunderclap which reverberates still in the life of the church. Some thought that Robert Gray[3] was aspiring to a kind of papal claim, with himself as the infallible head of an independent Anglican church in South Africa. The notion was ludicrous, but one can see how it was that the point came to be made; while Pius IX presided over his Council in Rome, Gray presided over his Provincial Synod in Cape Town.

The year 1870 was not the landmark in South Africa that it was in Europe. Nonetheless, events were astir which have made historians look back upon that period as one of decisive change in the history of the country. Diamonds had been discovered, the first one in 1867, and this, together with the discovery of gold in the 1880s, was to revolutionize the social, economic, and political history of southern Africa. The age of railways was to begin. The clash between British imperialism and Boer republicanism reached a climax in the war of 1899 – 1902, and out of the ashes of that war there arose, on the one hand, a nationalism quickened and increased by conflict and adversity, and, on the other hand, a political union in 1910 of the Cape, Natal, Orange Free State, and Transvaal contrived by a mixture of common sense, goodwill, and a fear of fresh perils. There were those like the young M.K. Gandhi, who had in this very period applied for the first time the searching principles of Satyagraha in resistance to unjust laws, and John Dube and Sol Plaatje, leaders of an emerging articulate black voice, together with white liberals such as W.P. Schreiner and his more famous sister and author, Olive, who said that the union was no true union because it was essentially confined to those of British and Dutch origin.

The newly elected Anglican archbishop, William Carter,[4] added his voice to this critique. The Union of South Africa took as its motto the phrase "unity is strength," which has always meant different things to different South Africans.

It was in this formative period that the first sessions of Provincial Synod took place. One is tempted to reflect that, before the turn of the century, the great issues of the day seemed to pass Synod by. One does not find in its decisions a mirror of South African history. Not until 1904 were there any resolutions which could bear the epithet "political," unless one were to include the mild resolutions of 1891, one expressing concern about religious education in state schools, the other respectfully seeking legislation from the various governments in the subcontinent "for the protection of young persons exposed to the peril of immorality."[5] The major social concern in this period was temperance. The 1870 Synod resolved "that in order to assist persons seeking deliverance from the sin of intemperance, a Committee be formed. . . ."[6] Even in those days the first thing people thought of was a committee. Earnest efforts were made at all seven sessions of Synod from 1870 to 1909 to set up an adequate organization to further the aims of temperance. The notorious "tot system" was condemned,[7] and members of Synod were quaintly urged "to witness against intemperance . . . by abstaining from the practice of using intoxicating liquor, except at meal times. . . ."[8] This characteristic Anglican compromise would hardly have satisfied seasoned temperance campaigners of the time such as William Booth of the Salvation Army.

If, as appears to be true, social and political interests were minimal during the early period of synodical government in southern Africa, there is one obvious reason close to hand. Synod's concern was of necessity primarily ecclesiastical. It would be wrong to judge the early sessions of Synod by the standards and considerations of the present time. Some would in fact argue that recently Synod has veered too much in the direction of the great issues of the day, and that the chief purpose of a synod is still to legislate, not to make moral pronouncements. Others would say with equal vehemence that particularly with the advent of *apartheid* since 1948 and, moreover, with the increase in the number of black representatives in Synod in recent years, it was not only inevitable but also right that political issues should receive attention. Indeed, it could be said that in earlier times those attending Synod were allied far more closely than at present to the political establishments of the day, and were therefore less likely to be critical of them. Nevertheless it remains clear that the first duty and task of the earliest sessions of Synod was to legislate for the constitutional life of the Church of the Province. This was done with a skill and determination which are extraordinarily impressive. Nowhere is this more clear than in the famous debate over the Third Proviso. The subject is highly technical, but that increases rather than reduces its significance.

The Constitution of the Church of the Province begins with a clear acceptance of the standards of faith and the formularies of the Church of England, but subject to three provisos. The third of these provisos lays down that in the interpretation of the standards of faith and the formularies, the Church of the Province is bound by the decisions only of its own recognized tribunals. Here was the constitutional fruit of the Colenso controversy, in which Bishop Colenso[9] had been upheld by the Judicial Committee of the Privy Council in England against the decision of Gray's metropolitical court in Cape Town. Synod wished the Church of the Province to maintain the closest possible ties with the Church of England as the mother church, but without the subjection to a secular court which in England was the price paid by an established church. The Third Proviso reflected a running controversy over the spiritual jurisdiction of the Privy Council, which had gripped England since the 1830s and which had created deep cleavage in the life of the church in southern Africa. In spite of the deposition of Colenso by Gray in 1863, when the first Provincial Synod met in 1870, Colenso was still bishop of Natal in full legal possession of all the property and jurisdiction of the diocese. Mrs. Colenso wrote in scathing terms about the Provincial Synod, referring to Gray as "the pope of South Africa" who "would . . . like to have the regulation of everyone's affairs in his own hands."[10] Colenso's diary makes no reference to the Synod; with an almost studied indifference, it records the purchase of a bag of mealies and a new plough.[11]

Synod's response to this state of affairs was the firm though unspectacular language of the Third Proviso; the church in South Africa would interpret its standards of faith and discipline in its own courts. The Proviso was a cry, born of experience, for the church's independence in the government of its affairs; no matter whose side one chooses to take in the great battle between Colenso and Gray, it is evident that an important constitutional principle in the life of the church was at stake. More broadly, the Third Proviso was a reflection of pressures for the creation of local legislatures — "responsible government" — in the Cape and Natal, and of the trend towards the establishment of constitutionally independent "Colonial Churches" in Australia, New Zealand, and Canada.[12]

Then suddenly, after being formally ratified at the 1876 Synod, the Third Proviso, in the Synod of 1883, became the subject of sharp debate. The case of *Merriman v. Williams*[13] had occurred in the interval, in which both Chief Justice de Villiers in the Cape Supreme Court and the Judicial Committee of the Privy Council had declared that because of the Third Proviso the Church of the Province was constitutionally a different church from the Church of England, and that it therefore had no legal claim to property which had been granted to the Church of England in South Africa. Panic ensued, and those who had participated in the first two synods began to reflect that they had entrenched the independence of the Church of the Province more radically than they had intended. It is ironical that in the year of Colenso's death (1883), a man who had been one of Gray's most enthusiastic supporters and had been one of those to delate Colenso for heresy, should now take the leading part in an attempt to expunge the Third Proviso from the constitution. Such was the turn in events.

Hopkins Badnall, archdeacon of the Cape, was a person learned in the canon law. In moving the expunction of the Third Proviso, he expressed his conviction that it had been included in the constitution "without any idea of the results now assigned to it,"[14] and that it had thrust the Church of the Province into a premature independence which "would tend to isolation."[15] Throughout the afternoon session of Wednesday, 31 January and for most of the morning session next day, Badnall argued his case. It was a speech lasting five hours. His main opponent was the metropolitan himself, Gray's successor, William West Jones,[16] who spoke on the subject for only three hours. The debate continued for three and a half days, with both clergy and laity participating; it was stated at the time that at this Synod the influence of the laity was more distinctly felt than before.[17] Learned comparisons were made with the Episcopal Church in America. Henry VIII's Statute of Appeals was intricately debated. A comparison was made between the church in South Africa and the Anglo-Saxon church of the seventh century. It is clear that at times feelings were as high as learning was deep. Dr. A.T. Wirgman, from Port Elizabeth, claimed that the question before Synod raised the whole issue of the rights of Christ and Caesar,[18] while the Revd. W.M. Cameron, from the diocese of St. John's, "pointed to the open Bible in the midst of the Synod and said that we must close that Bible if we remove the Proviso."[19] Lay representatives participated on both sides of the debate, without the melodrama shown by Cameron. Eventually, Badnall's motion was lost in the house of the laity, by three votes to eight, and it is certain that if it had been put in the houses of clergy and bishops it would have been defeated there as well.[20]

But if the motion was lost in 1883, the issue was kept alive. Badnall brought it up again in the Cape Town diocesan synod, and it was not finally laid low until the Provincial Synod of 1904. This was the Synod which *The Cape Argus* unwittingly described in a headline as the "Provisional Synod": an early instance, no doubt, of the perplexity created in the secular mind by the ecclesiastical term *Provincial*.[21] It was no provisional synod, but it was another "Proviso" synod. This time it was a layman, Col. E.M. Greene, K.C., who moved that the Third Proviso be deleted from the constitution. These were the days when some members of Provincial Synod happened also to be members of colonial parliaments. John X. Merriman, son of Bishop Merriman, was the most famous. E.M. Greene was a member of the Natal legislature, as well as being king's counsel; though he spelt his name differently, he was also the son of Dean James Green of Pietermaritzburg, who had been Colenso's arch-oppenent. For two hours Greene spoke to his motion; it was a high-water mark of lay initiative in the history of Provincial Synod. Once again West Jones took a strong line against the repeal, and once again the motion was lost in the house of the laity. If clerical argument predominated in the issue of the Third Proviso, the history of the voting shows that the responsibility for the retention of the Proviso lies with the lay members of Synod. What the prolonged discussion, from 1870 to 1904, strongly suggests is that the early synods were of necessity concerned mainly with the creation of a clear, acceptable, and dependable constitutional structure for the Church of the Province.

It could, of course, be argued that much of the work had been done before Provincial Synod ever began to meet. Robert Gray, for instance, circulated in December 1869 a draft set of canons, prepared (as he put it) "under a great pressure of other work,"[22] and Henry Cotterill, bishop of Grahamstown, produced a draft constitution. Cotterill, even more than Gray, was the master builder in the creation of the synodical and constitutional life of the church in southern Africa. At the Lambeth Conference in 1867 he had been secretary of the Committee on Synodical Government, and there is a close connection between the decisions reached there and the clauses of the CPSA Constitution.[23] If Cotterill was the builder, Gray was the architect. Soon after his arrival at the Cape in 1848, he had become convinced of the need for some kind of synodical structure for the Anglican church in this subcontinent, and after the division of his vast diocese in 1853,[24] he was sure that this should include a provincial synod as well as diocesan synods. Indeed, he was in correspondence with at least twenty-five bishops in other parts of the Anglican communion about the possible creation of what he called a National Synod, which would represent the whole Anglican church and be its ultimate legislative authority.[25] Gray's ideal in this respect was perhaps far-fetched. Yet today there are those who are asking all over again where the ultimate source of authority is for the Anglican communion as a whole, and whether there should not be some accepted decision-making machinery to give the official Anglican response to fundamental ecumenical matters and to questions of faith and order in the church.[26] The Lambeth Conference, which was in part Gray's inspiration, falls short of being a decision-making body, but at least it draws together the Anglican bishops for consultation from all over the world.[27] While Gray failed to achieve the creation of a "National Synod" for the whole Anglican communion, synodical developments in southern Africa itself took place precisely as he had envisaged. He had a vision of what might be, matched by a capacity for relentless planning. "I have looked forward these many years to this day," he said with a simple ardour in his opening address to the first Provincial Synod.[28] It was an understatement. He had not simply looked forward; he had worked for his ideal with an enthusiasm near to passion.

Yet if much of the work had been done before Synod first met, this does not mean that Synod acted as a mere rubber stamp. All the issues were keenly debated, and Gray's draft canons were extensively amended. Cotterill's draft of the Third Proviso was itself amended in 1870. The Synod of 1870 lasted for four weeks, right through the dusty heat of February, when Gray's hope had been that its work would be completed in half that time.[29] Dean Williams of Grahamstown seems to have prolonged the proceedings by an iconoclasm which must have amused the members even if it didn't help much to forward the work. He "is a fluent Irishman," wrote the bishop of Maritzburg at the time, "who will speak by the hour about anything or nothing very cleverly indeed, often contradicting at the end of his speech that with which he started, and sometimes voting against himself." Macrorie went on to say that this nonetheless had the useful effect of "picking holes in other men's work."[30] These men talked. They also worked, and with a meticulous care prompted by a strong grasp of principle, they laid the constitutional foundations of the church's life in this subcontinent. It was a task that persisted for more than a generation, and West Jones in his powerful adherence to the Third Proviso was the heir to Gray and Cotterill.

A question now arises which will underpin most of what I aim to say in the remainder of this chapter. The question is this: What were the principles governing representation in synod, and how did these work in practice? Peter Hinchliff, in his history of the Anglican church in South Africa, has argued that "the list of members of the first synod reveals a weakness the Province has not as yet entirely managed to remedy."[31] He is trenchantly critical of the absence from that first Provincial Synod of any African clergyman or, indeed, of *any* clergyman born in this land. "The English Church in this country," he writes, "after nearly three-quarters of a century's existence, was still unable to find any priest born and bred in South Africa, of any race or colour, who could represent it at what was probably the most important synod in its history."[32] It is a pungent comment suggesting that Bishop Gray and others had relied too heavily on England for resources in men and money. In 1883 the bias towards England was still strong; out of a total of 218 clergy in the Church of the Province, only fifteen were colonial-born whites and fourteen were black.[33] Yet it is also true that the early leaders wanted to advance the interests of a South African-based church life.

Pastoral and organizational problems were such that developments were bound to be slow. Perhaps it was too soon in 1870 for indigenous clergy to be present in a body such as the Provincial Synod which included only a very few representatives from each diocese.

In the context of 1870 there is something more important to notice than the absence of colonial-born clergy, black or white, and that was the presence in the first and subsequent sessions of Provincial Synod of laity as well as clergy. In its time this was an almost revolutionary feature. The church in England had no body in which clergy and laity together governed the affairs of the church. Parliament was supposedly the lay body, and Convocation, which was an entirely clerical body, had only begun to function again in 1855 after an enforced hibernation of nearly 150 years. The Church Assembly, designed specifically to represent the laity in England, was not set up until 1919. Even the Wesleyan Methodists in Britain, who had done so much to encourage lay initiative at a local level, were notoriously slow about admitting lay members to the governing bodies of their church. This caused a major split in nineteenth-century Methodism, and it was not until 1877 that laymen first became members of Conference, almost a hundred years after its foundation. Lay representation in Anglican synods was pioneered in Australia and New Zealand in the 1850s, and subsequently taken over in Canada and South Africa. It was something that Gray had long striven for, not so much out of theological conviction as on the practical ground that if the church in South Africa was to stand on its own feet and grow into maturity, it would have to have the unstinting support of its laity.[34] In some circles, there was shocked surprise at the presence of lay people in Synod. The main concern seems to have been that they might be involved in deciding doctrinal questions: that having tossed the Judicial Committee of the Privy Council out of the door, a fresh lay peril was being allowed in at the window. What was allowed in was a breath of fresh air, and if it threatened to become a hurricane there was after all the provision for a vote by houses.

We have already noticed the prominent role played by the laity in the debate on the Third Proviso. They formed no *bloc,* for they were as divided among themselves as were the clergy; their vote on the issue was crucial. Perhaps even more striking than the debates on the Third Proviso was a speech made at the 1898 Synod by P.W. Tracey, a lay representative from Johannesburg. He spoke of the duty of every member of the church to take his share, by personal labour, almsgiving, and prayer in the missionary work of the church, and he indicated the missionary opportunity awaiting the church in the great mining district on the Reef. It was one of the earliest summonses to what we today call "industrial mission," and it came from the lips of a layman. Tracey's speech left such an impression that Archbishop West Jones referred to it specifically in his Charge to Provincial Synod six years later, in 1904.[35]

To speak of lay representation in the earlier synods includes an assumption about which everyone without exception must have been agreed: namely, that it should be confined to men. There was one woman, interestingly enough, at the first Provincial Synod, and that was Sophy Gray, the metropolitan's wife. As at all previous synods in Cape Town, she faithfully kept the minutes. She was already a sick woman, and the demands of this Synod, including the protracted hospitality that went with it at Bishopscourt, almost certainly helped to shorten her life. She was present at the Synod, but as its voluntary employee. Had she been able to enter the debates, there is no doubt that she could have shown to bishops, clergy, and laymen that she had a strong mind and judgement of her own.[36] The wheels of change move slowly. It was not until 1970, the centenary year of Provincial Synod, that the first woman took her seat as a lay representative. Now such participation is accepted as natural and normal. The focus has shifted to the question of the ordination of women. Already approval has been given for the admission of women to the diaconate. This in itself opens the possibility that women will before long take their place among clerical representatives at Synod; if they are to be ordained as priests (a decision not yet taken), the possibility becomes a likelihood.   There was another feature of the representation in the early synods which was striking and important. Members of Synod were drawn from a very wide political spectrum, as indeed they still are. In 1870, as one historian has put it, "Southern Africa probably contained as many contrasting forms of government as have ever been juxtaposed within a single sub-continent."[37] Basically, so far as European colonization was concerned and not taking into account the independent African chieftaincies that still existed, the dividing line was between the Afrikaner republican tradition of the north and the British pattern to the south and east where there was a mixture of protectorate, crown colony, and representative government. It was a kaleidoscope. Provincial Synod quite naturally cut across these differences of government and political life, and gave to South Africa a foretaste of the unity that was to be achieved in 1910. Members of Synod were aware of this. For example, in 1883, Dean James Green of Pietermaritzburg insisted that the Third Proviso happily freed the Church of the Province from an undesirable political tie with England. How could the Privy Council in England, he asked, have jurisdiction in a diocese like the Orange Free State beyond the bounds of the British Empire? It was a good question. "It is the office of the Church," said Green, "to be the healer of the nations, and to unite all in one. . . . The heart of every Colonist must rejoice in seeing Bishops, Clergy and Lay Representatives from the various states and governments of South Africa gathered in the unity represented by this Synod. This Provincial Synod will, in time, be the foundation stone on which will be built that political unity which the hearts of many fervently desire to see accomplished. In short, the Church of South Africa is the one true 'South African Bond.'"[38] Green had a flair for rhetoric, and his vision was no doubt limited by the white colonial assumptions of his time. Yet his words contained within them an important kernel of truth which persists today in that the Church of the Province includes the countries of Mozambique, Swaziland, Lesotho, Namibia, and St. Helena within its boundaries, as well as South Africa. For this reason its title was changed in 1982 to The Church of the Province of *Southern* Africa, reflecting today what the title "South Africa" expressed in 1870.

There was, in fact, a further aspect to what was occurring. In other parts of the British Empire — Australia, New Zealand, Canada — similar developments in synodical government were taking place and independent branches of the Anglican church being created. This was a period, too, of the disestablishment of the church in Ireland. Yet in no instance did this process weaken the bonds of communion with the mother church in England. Instead, the Lambeth Conference of bishops from different parts of the Anglican communion became a focus of unity for the independent provinces of the church. There was a commonwealth of churches before the British Empire had transformed itself into the Commonwealth of Nations. In every case the churches have led the way, because the process which was begun in the nineteenth century has continued in the twentieth.[39] It was easier for the churches; their numbers were smaller, and there were not the political implications. But it is worth remembering that as late as 1840 there were no more than ten bishops at work outside the British Isles. What was achieved was a fine piece of ecclesiastical statecraft, which has stood the test of time and remains in the world today at a time when the political Commonwealth has been shaken by new and challenging tensions. Robert Gray wrote as follows to the Cape governor, Sir Philip Wodehouse, in April 1870:

> You intimate that we have established a new Church. We say that the Church is the same that it ever was; but that. . . we are now through the labours of our Provincial Synod, organized like other Colonial Churches . . . on the basis of voluntary contract. . . . And . . . we have before any desire for separation has sprung up, united ourselves to the Mother Church in the only way left open to us, mutual compact and engagement. [40]

Gray's language was legal. What the Church of the Province was trying to do was to give a lead both as liberator and as reconciler. Its Synod stood for the principle of unity-in-diversity, both on the local South African scene and in the wider world.

To sum up, then, so far: as a representative body, Provincial Synod drew into a common task not only the bishops and clergy but also the laity, for the government of the province. In addition, it drew together people who lived under a variety of secular governments, transcending that variety in the pursuit of a common purpose, showing that the church is not bound, even if it is influenced, by political frontiers. At the same time the Church of the Province transcended its own ecclesiastical frontier by uniting itself with the rest of the Anglican communion throughout the world.

But other frontiers remained. Those whom Synod drew together, whether clerical or lay, were English-speaking to a man.

Where were the Dutch? Robert Gray used to say with a smile that he knew nothing of the Dutch language, while his chaplain knew less.[41] But he strongly welcomed the publication of a Dutch-English Prayer Book in 1853, saying that it was highly appreciated by the Dutch population at the Cape and would be useful for services among the church's growing coloured congregations. Especially in the early days of his episcopate, Gray was deeply indebted to Dutch Reformed ministers who made their churches available for his confirmations, and to many a Dutch family who provided hospitality during his visitations.

In 1870-71 there occurred a fascinating episode in ecumenical history in this country. It arose directly out of the very first resolution passed by Provincial Synod, a resolution which deplored the divided condition of Christ's flock and opened the way for the bishops to enter into discussions with other Christian leaders. It is at once chastening and encouraging to realize that the first resolution Synod passed a hundred years ago was related to the quest for Christian unity, a quest which still continues. In June, 1870 Gray sent the resolution to Dr. P.E. Faure, Moderator of the Nederduitse Gereformeerde Kerk. Correspondence ensued between Gray and Dutch Reformed leaders, together with a day's meeting at Bishopscourt in 1871. It would do Anglicans and Dutch Reformed Christians good to read the published correspondence.[42] There is no doubt about the earnestness and cordiality of the negotiations, even though they were so brief. But cordiality and goodwill are not enough. The Dutch found no place for themselves in the English church any more than the English found themselves a place in the Dutch. There was some interflow between the two, but on the whole they faced each other as equals. As late as 1909, Provincial Synod sent "brotherly greetings" to the Synod of the Dutch Reformed church meeting at the same time in Cape Town.[43] In ways such as this the frontier was crossed, but always, one senses, with a fairly quick return to home base. In the 1870 negotiations, though both sides agreed upon the supreme authority of scripture, the home base for Anglicans was episcopacy, ordained of God and impossible to abandon, while for the Dutch Reformed the parity of ministers was a scriptural principle which could not be sacrificed. Pulpits, argued Gray, could not be exchanged while there was still so much that kept the two churches apart. Anyway, he wrote that he was not prepared to have "liberals" in Anglican pulpits.[44] It was *theological* liberals he was afraid of: Colensos preaching in Dutch.

Here, then, was a frontier. Provincial Synod cannot claim to have been representative of Dutch- or Afrikaans-speaking South Africa, except for those whom the state calls "coloured," many of whom prefer anyway to use English in church even if their home language is Afrikaans. An Afrikaans speech in Synod would provide a salutary shock and would certainly need to be translated. As the heirs of Robert Gray we are still very English. On the other hand, in a province where ten languages other than English are officially used, the *lingua franca* of English is an undoubtedly binding factor.

This brings us to another feature of much significance about representation at Synod. We have already noted the point made by Hinchliff that there were no indigenous clergy among the representatives at the first Provincial Synod. It was not until 1898 that the first black representative was elected. This was the Revd. John Xaba from the diocese of St. John's in the Transkei. Other churches were ahead of the Anglican church in producing African leaders of distinction, such as the Revd. Tiyo Soga in the Free Church of Scotland. In 1883 the Conference of the Methodist Church in South Africa included as one of its delegates the layman Tengo Jabavu, who kept his seat in Conference without a break for thirty years, developing a reputation as a fine debater.[45]

There was no flourish or fanfare accompanying Xaba's participation in the 1898 Synod. No special resolutions were passed; he was accepted like any other member. He also made his influence felt, modestly yet candidly. For on the sixth day of Synod he gave notice of a question: Had the bishops taken into consideration the movement known as the Ethiopian or Native Episcopal Methodist schism?[46] The archbishop replied that the bishops had not considered the matter, but would do so; he asked for fuller information from Xaba.[47] Xaba's question was timely, for in the very next year (1899) the bishops were approached by J.M. Dwane, and the agreement of 1900 between the Church of the Province and the Order of Ethiopia[48] was the result.

In the 1904 Synod there were two Africans present. The Revd. J.M. Dwane, leader of the Order of Ethiopia, was one of them, brought as a deacon by the bishop of Grahamstown. The other was the Revd. Jacob Manelle, an elected member from the diocese of St. John's. At the next Synod, in 1909, Manelle was again present, together with two African deacons, Dwane and the Revd. W. Mochochoko from the diocese of Bloemfontein. In 1915 there were four elected black clergymen from three dioceses, and from the diocese of St. John's came the first black *lay* representatives.[49] It was all very natural and unpretentious. Yet these developments in our synodical life occurred in a historical context which gives them a profound significance.

The liberal view of nineteenth-century South African history sees two distinct traditions of government and representation coming into being. There was the so-called northern tradition of the two republics which allowed for what Eric Walker once called "one white man, one vote,"[50] and there was the Cape liberal tradition which conferred the franchise on men who fulfilled certain basic qualifications, regardless of race, language, or colour. In the making of Union in 1908-9, these two traditions came into head-on collision, and it was only by virtue of compromise on both sides that deadlock was broken. Subsequent history has seen the liberal tradition of the Cape overtaken by the tradition of the north, particularly in the removal from the common voters' roll first of African then of coloured voters in the Cape.[51] In this historical perspective, there have been two traditional ways of doing things in South Africa, not one; what has happened in that one tradition has been swallowed up by the other.

Natal, at the turn of the century, was in an ambivalent position. In theory she belonged to the Cape tradition; in practice she adhered more and more to the tradition of the north. In 1896 the Natal legislature abolished the Indian parliamentary franchise, and at the National Convention in 1908-9, Natal delegates, who were English-speaking, played a leading role in opposing the Cape system. It was E.M. Greene, the same person who as a lay representative at the 1904 Provincial Synod had proposed the deletion of the Third Proviso, who at the National Convention in 1908 moved that "non-Europeans" should be excluded from membership of both houses of the South African Parliament.[52] Louis Botha, from the Transvaal, was quick to agree[53] and the proposition went through. Even John X. Merriman supported Greene, though he fought hard for the entrenchment of the Cape franchise.[54] True, no black person had ever sat in the Cape Parlia-

ment, but ever since the introduction of representative government in 1854 the right had existed. Significantly, in 1910, just as
the National Convention's decision came into operation for the
new South African Parliament, Walter Rubusana, a minister of
the Congregational church, was elected to the Cape Provincial
Council. But any developing pattern of inter-racial government
was forestalled by the makers of Union.

As against the liberal view of South African history, a more recent and more radical view sees the coming together of white
economic and political interests to the detriment of legitimate
black aspirations as being of far greater significance than the
relatively minor differences of opinion within white political traditions. Very soon after the Union came into being legislation was
passed which gives substance to this point of view. The 1911
Mines and Works Act laid a legislative basis for racial job reser-
vation in South African industry, and the 1913 Natives Land Act
limited African land ownership to the so-called "reserves" con-
sisting of seven per cent of South African territory.[55] Mining and
large-scale agriculture, which were the dominant economic
interests of the new Union government, exerted an overriding
influence. In this situation the South African Native National Congress, direct forbear of the African National Congress of today,
was founded in 1912. Its essential aim was to resist the explicit
exclusion of black people from political and economic power.
Interestingly enough, another political grouping crystallized two
years later: the Afrikaner National Party, the eventual architect
of *apartheid* in 1948. This was the group which felt that fellow-
Afrikaners had compromised themselves by joining politically
with English-speaking South Africans. All these events, taken
together, set the stage for the political and economic history of
South Africa in the twentieth century.[56]

Is it not significant that at this crossroads in South African
history, the Church of the Province began moving towards a
representative pattern which was the very opposite to that
adopted by the secular government of the land? This was a time
when a marked articulation of black opinion was occurring, in
journalism, in political organizations, in farmers' associations, in
church life — including the growth of Ethiopianism which was
essentially a striving for ecclesiastical autonomy and self-control,
and including the inauguration in 1906 of interdenominational

missionary conferences in which African Christian leaders, lay and clerical, soon played a prominent part. It was entirely appropriate that in the Church of the Province at that time, black representatives should begin to participate in its highest legislative body. It could be said that it happened just in time.

It is true that this happened naturally, without flourish or fanfare, but in another sense it was accompanied by a minor ferment in the life of the church. Different ideas about representation were jostling in the minds of churchmen as well as statesmen. For example, the Synod of 1904 passed a resolution on what it called the "organization of the Native Church."[57] The archbishop was asked to appoint a commission on the subject, and among those consulted, three-quarters supported the appointment of assistant bishops for "native" work, and just over a quarter favoured the establishment of "native" synods.[58]. The church did not escape the influence of segregationist thinking at that time. The whole question as to whether African and European work should be separately organized came up again for prolonged discussion at the Provincial Missionary Conference in 1906, at a time when this conference was probably the best sounding-board of African opinion in the church. The bishops present were sympathetic towards the idea of assistant bishops for African work, but Bishop Carter of Pretoria declared that diocesan bishops had no desire to cease being fathers in God to black and white alike. African delegates saw the cogency of such arguments, and yet on practical grounds they argued for specialization. One of them also asked ominously and pertinently: "How can we think we are welcome in white men's synods when we are unwelcome in their railway carriages?"[59]

Here is a problem that has continued to vex the minds and pierce the hearts of churchmen, especially black churchmen, in South Africa. Here is one illustration. In 1941, two African members of the Provincial Board of Missions — the Revd. H.M. Maimane of Pretoria and the Revd. J.A. Calata of Cradock — produced a document entitled *African Branch of the Catholic Church.*[60] It said:

> In view of the South African political and social situation . . . the CPSA should now inaugurate her African branch of the Catholic church. This should be done in order to enhance, and

use to the full, the African spiritual gifts and powers, as well as African ability and intelligence where it may be found. . . . It is all very well to talk of "no racialism" in the CPSA, but this is only "talk". . . . The CPSA is already in two camps. Why not then make the two camps definite, and be true to the situation?

That document reveals a tension that exists in the Church of the Province because it is a tension that exists in the whole of South African society. Some in more recent times have spoken of the need for a black confessing church. Yet the document contains also a paradox; while its language is radical, the remedy asked for is relatively mild. The writers asked for the appointment of assistant bishops who should be Africans. They did not want to create a new African church; they specifically said that each diocese should continue to have *one* synod. It was as if, in the midst of their radicalism, they saw that a vital principle was at stake: the principle that, no matter what the practical difficulties or tensions may be, Christians should go on learning to do *together* what others choose to do separately.[61]

From this principle the Church of the Province has not budged in its synodical life. What we have done, together with other churches that practise the same principle, is to offer a living alternative to the kind of representation that operates in the secular sphere. It is true that this affects a relatively small area of South African life, but it is a reminder to South African society as a whole that there is another way. Few would assert that it is a way we have learnt to work perfectly yet. Our procedural methods can be complicated, especially for the uninitiated. Canonical legislation follows the parliamentary procedure of three "readings," which wisely prevents rushed decisions. Increasingly in recent years representatives have taken care to master and participate freely in this procedure; but some are still left baffled and confused. Much depends on clarity and patience from the chair! To help members, a booklet has been produced with the optimistic title *How to succeed at Synod*.

There is also the important question of language. Care is normally taken at diocesan level to elect to Provincial Synod those who can understand and debate in English. Nevertheless, those whose mother tongue is not English must sometimes find themselves at a disadvantage. Some have envisaged the day when simultaneous translation will be used. With up to ten major languages represented at Provincial Synod, this would be complicated as well as a costly operation. Meanwhile, any Synod member is free to address Synod in his or her own language, provided an interpreter is also available.

If it *is* true that our church offers in its system of government a workable alternative for South African society, no effort should be spared to make it an instrument which is efficient and effective. It is not enough to have a system which is sound in principle. It needs to work so well that all who participate in it will feel that they really belong to it and can give expression to their ideas and aspirations through it. For here is a system which holds out a constructive message of hope in our fractured society. This is even more apposite under the new constitutional dispensation, introduced after the referendum of 1983, whereby South Africa came to possess the extraordinary phenomenon of a tricameral legislature, one for whites, one for Indians and one for so-called coloured people, while the black majority is excluded altogether. Those who support the new arrangement see it as an improvement on the all-white parliament of 1910, but it nevertheless entrenches racial difference and racial exclusion in a way which is perilous for the future of South Africa. We can be thankful that the Church of the Province resisted, eighty years ago, the notion of separate synods for black Anglicans.

Since Union, Provincial Synod has concerned itself more and more with the social, economic, and political issues of the day. In the Synod of 1919, for example, there was quite a spate of resolutions on these subjects.[62] Was this development due in any way to the changing composition of Provincial Synod? It is not easy to say. No doubt the presence of African members made Synod more aware of issues affecting black people. But the minutes of the Synod of Bishops, where there was no black member until 1960, also show a growing awareness of such issues over the same period. Part of the truth, I think, is that the issues were themselves becoming more real and more pressing; so it was that the church's concern increased. Moreover, the basic task of laying sound constitutional foundations for the church had been performed. This does not mean that Synod's legislative role ceased. Major questions came up, such as the question of Prayer-

Book revision which persisted for over thirty years, and is now upon us again. In the Synod of 1945 substantial amendments were made to the canons on discipline. In the Synod of 1976 the same thing happened to the canon on marriage, when divorced people, whose previous spouse is still living, were allowed under certain conditions to be re-married in church. The legislative task has remained. But there has at the same time been scope for Synod to involve itself in other questions vitally affecting the life and witness of the church in Southern Africa. In this way Synod has provided a forum for the expression of opinion on important issues, in some instances by people who have little chance in the secular sphere to make their views known.

Sometimes canonical legislation and socio-political concern coincide. There was an apt example of this at the most recent session of Provincial Synod in July 1985. One of the canons lays down that no clergyman may officiate for more than one Sunday in a diocese other than his own without the permission of the bishop of that diocese. This is based on the good principle that ministry in the church is to be exercised under due authority represented in the person of the bishop. The exception made in the canon is the ministry of "a Chaplain to the Forces."[63] This is also based on a good principle, namely that a military chaplain, if he is to minister adequately to soldiers in his care, must be free to go wherever a particular war may take him. The proposal before Synod was that the exception in the canon should be removed. The particular effect of such a change would mean that in the conflict in which the South African Defence Force is engaged, chaplains would need the permission of the bishop of Namibia to minister to troops in that diocese.

What happened in the debate was that at the first "reading" the proposed change was accepted, while at the third "reading" some days later it was rejected. How is one to explain this strange turn in events? There was an interplay in Synod between the prophetic and pastoral roles of the church. On the one hand, an attempt was being made to distance the chaplaincy from the state at a time of increased militarization in defence of an unjust political and social order. This was the prophetic voice. On the other hand, there was pastoral concern for ministry to those caught up in the conflict, usually through no choice of their own. This was enhanced when the bishop of Namibia let it be known that he would not be willing to authorize chaplains to minister to what he regarded as a foreign army of occupation in his country. Both the pastoral and the prophetic voice was evident in Synod as it changed its mind in the course of an agonizing debate.

Inevitably the tendency over the years has been to concentrate on South African issues in spite of the fact that, in its representation, Synod embraces almost the entire subcontinent.[64] There are two main reasons for this. One is the preponderance of members from the larger South African dioceses. Representation at Synod is caluculated on the number of licensed clergy serving in a particular diocese; on this basis the dioceses of Johannesburg, Cape Town and Natal have the largest representation. Traditionally it has been mainly representatives from the South African dioceses who have placed items on the Synod agenda; it is sometimes forgotten that Synod attends only to those matters which are specifically brought before it. The other reason for the preponderance of South African issues has been the affront to human dignity contained in the policy known worldwide as *apartheid*, together with its ancestry of racial discrimination prior to the advent of the present government in 1948. As time passes and *apartheid* is finally dismantled, as it must be, the balance will hopefully be redressed and other matters of importance will be brought to Synod's attention. It is not to be thought that those parts of the Church of the Province other than South Africa are without problems that deserve the church's attention. Broad issues of justice, peace, and reconciliation affect us all, and the perspectives of the diocese of Lebombo or Niassa (both in Mozambique) or the dioceses of Lesotho and Swaziland on such matters are of as much value as the insights gained from within the South African context. Ethical concern for the fabric of society is not likely to cease as the years go by, for it is founded on the belief, sustained by the scriptures and tradition, that the Lord of the church is also the Lord and Father of all.

1870 may seem a far cry from today. Yet there is an unmistakable link between the two. The Church of the Province has in different ways been engaged in working out the implications of being a free church. In 1870 it was a question of freedom to make domestic decisions unimpeded by external appeals; this freedom was enshrined in the paper-work of a constitution and a set of canons. Today it is a question of the freedom to offer an alternative way in government and representation; this freedom is to be found in the people who constitute our synods. "We are a multi-racial Church," said Archbishop Clayton in his Charge to the 1950 Provincial Synod. "The very aspect of this Synod shows that we draw men of diverse races into the one Church and give them their voice in its administration and government."[65]

Clayton's words may seem smug in a church which in many ways falls short, especially in its everyday life, of the ideal he sets forth. It has been slow to indigenize itself. To take but one symbolic example of this: the first South African-born archbishop took office as late as 1974,[66] and the election of a black archbishop first occurred only in 1986. In the daily circumstances of its membership the church too often reflects rather than contradicts the society in which it is placed. There is no room for a complacent self-congratulation. Yet, as this essay has attempted to show, a significant development in the church's synodical life has taken place over the years. This stands as a sign and token of hope, for it is an indication to a society where the conflicting aspirations and assumptions of black and white have free course, that stumbling blocks can be turned into stepping-stones.

Note on Sources

The main repository of primary material on the history of the Church of the Province of Southern Africa is the CPSA Record Library, University of the Witwatersrand, Johannesburg.

Notes

1. The substance of this chapter first appeared in a lecture to mark the centenary of Provincial Synod in the Church of the Province of Southern Africa in 1970. Various amendments and additions have been made. Copyright permission has been granted for the lecture to be re-published in this revised form.
2. R.C.K. Ensor, *England, 1870-1914* (Oxford, 1936), 136.

Authority in the Anglican Communion

3. Robert Gray, born near Durham in 1809, was the first bishop of Cape Town, 1847-1872. See C.N. Gray, ed., *Life of Robert Gray*, I and II (London, 1876). Unfortunately there is no more recent biography.
4. William Carter was archbishop of Cape Town from 1909-1930. Before that he was successively bishop of Zululand and bishop of Pretoria.
5. Resolutions 15 and 17 of 1891. These can be found in *Constitution and Canons, 1904-1915* (Cape Town, 1915).
6. Ibid., Resolution 17 of 1870.
7. Ibid., Resolution 26 of 1904. The "tot system" was the practice whereby wine farmers in the Cape paid wages partly in alcohol. A similar practice was adopted by mine managers on the Witwatersrand to attract African labour. See C. van Onselen, *Studies in the Social and Economic History of the Witwatersrand, 1886-1914* (Johannesburg, 1982), I, 60.
8. Ibid., Resolution 11 of 1876.
9. John William Colenso, born in Cornwall in 1814, was the first bishop of Natal, 1853-1883. He was deposed by Bishop Gray in 1863 for erroneous teaching, but he retained legal occupation of his see until his death. For two contrasting studies of Colenso, see P. Hinchliff, *John William Colenso — Bishop of Natal* (London, 1964) and J.J. Guy, *The Heretic — a Study of the Life of John William Colenso, 1814-1883* (Pietermaritzburg, 1983).
10. W. Rees, ed.,*Colenso Letters from Natal* (Pietermaritzburg, 1958), 211.
11. See P. Hinchliff, *The Anglican Church in South Africa* (London, 1963), 113-114.
12. The Cape obtained responsible government in 1872 and Natal in 1893 after two decades of local agitation. See below for further comments on ecclesiastical developments in other parts of the world.
13. Nathanael James Merriman was bishop of Grahamstown, 1871-1882. Williams, his arch-opponent, was dean of the cathedral in Grahamstown. See M. Goedhals, "Nathanael James Merriman, Archdeacon and Bishop, 1849-1882 — a study in church life and government" (Ph.D, Rhodes University, Grahamstown, 1983).
14. *The Church Chronicle*, IV (1883), 74.
15. Ibid., 75.
16. William West Jones was bishop of Cape Town, 1874-1908. The title of "archbishop" was used from 1897. The archbishop of Cape Town is also metropolitan of the Province. See M.H.M. Wood, *A Father in God — the Episcopate of William West Jones, D.D.* (London, 1913).
17. *The Church Chronicle*, IV (1883), 55.

18. Ibid., 100.
19. Ibid., 90.
20. Normally in synod matters are decided with everyone voting together. Any member can, however, ask for a vote by "houses." In such a case the laity vote first, and only if they pass the motion does it go to the clergy, and so finally to the bishops. In this way each house has a veto.
21. See *Cape Church Monthly and Parish Record* (Feb. 1904), 17. The term *provincial*, like the word *diocese*, comes from the description of units of administration in the Roman Empire. It was simply taken over by the church at that time. A province consists of a number of dioceses in a given area. *The Cape Argus* is a South African newspaper.
22. See the preface to Gray's draft canons (Provincial Records, I, Grahamstown Diocesan Library).
23. See A.M.G. Stephenson, *The First Lambeth Conference, 1867* (London, 1967).
24. In that year the two dioceses of Natal and Grahamstown were created.
25. See, for examples, *Gray's Letter Books*, IX, 372-373, in the CPSA Record Library, University of the Witwatersrand, Johannesburg.
26. Two examples of such issues are the *Final Report* of the Anglican/Roman Catholic International Commission and the question of the ordination of women.
27. See A.M.G. Stephenson, *Anglicanism and the Lambeth Conferences* (London, 1978).
28. *The Church News*, 43, (March 1870), 1.
29. Gray to W.K. Macrorie, bishop of Maritzburg, 4 December 1869 (in Macrorie Papers, USPG Archives, London).
30. Ibid., Macrorie to F. Pott, 1 March 1870. William Kenneth Macrorie was bishop of Maritzburg, 1869-1892. He was consecrated by Gray to replace Bishop Colenso in Natal. Since Colenso still legally occupied the see, the fictitious title "Maritzburg" (a shortened version of the name of the capital city) was used.
31. P. Hinchliff, *The Anglican Church in South Africa* (London, 1963), 116.
32. Ibid.
33. "Report on the Supply and Training of Candidates for Holy Orders," Schedule A in *Acts and Resolutions of Provincial Synod, 1883*, 19-24. When Gray arrived at the Cape in 1848 there was a total of only fourteen Anglican clergy in the colony.

34. See P. Hinchliff; "Laymen in Synod — an aspect of the beginnings of synodical government in South Africa," in G.J. Cuming and D. Baker, ed., *Studies in Church History* (Cambridge, 1971), VII, 321-327.

35. W. West Jones, "Charge to Provincial Synod, 1904," in *S.A. Sermons and Addresses, II, 1851-1909* (CPSA Record Library, University of the Witwatersrand, Johannesburg), 9.

36. See T. Gutsche, *The Bishop's Lady* (Cape Town, 1970), *passim* and especially 210.

37. C.F. Goodfellow, *Great Britain and South African Confederation, 1870-1881* (Cape Town, 1966), 10.

38. The reference to the "South African Bond" was no doubt an allusion to the Cape-based Afrikaner Bond which in the 1880s and 1890s acted as the dominant political vehicle of both Dutch and British Cape farmers and merchants, seeking to further their interests through the formation of a South African Customs Union and more generally through the creation of a united South Africa under its own flag. See T.R.H. Davenport, *The Afrikaner Bond — the history of a South African political party, 1880-1911* (Cape Town, 1966).

39. See, for example, C. Smyth, "In Duty's Path — Fisher of Lambeth," *Theology* (Feb. 1970), 70.

40. *Gray's Letter Books*, X, 327-328.

41. J. Eedes, "Notes on Some Recollections of the Life and Church Work of Bishop Gray in South Africa," in *The Cape Church Monthly and Parish Record* (Dec. 1892), 6.

42. *The Unity of Christendom. A Correspondence Relative to Proposals for Union between the English and Dutch Reformed Churches in South Africa* (Cape Town, 1871). No. 45 in *Robert Gray: Charges, Sermons, Speeches, III* (CPSA Record Library, University of the Witwatersrand, Johannesburg). *Union of Churches. A Reply to the Letter of the Rev. P.E. Faure, D.D., Moderator, Rev. Andrew Murray, Actuarius, and Rev. William Robertson, D.D., Scriba of the Synod of the Dutch Reformed Church in South Africa. By Robert, Bishop of Cape Town* (Cape Town, 1871). No. 46 in ibid. See also P. le Feuvre, "Cultural and Theological Factors Affecting Relationships between the Nederduitse Gereformeerde Kerk and the Anglican Church (of the Province of South Africa) in the Cape Colony, 1806-1910" (Ph.D, University of Cape Town, 1980).

43. *Acts and Resolutions of the Seventh Provincial Synod*, 28.

44. *Union of Churches*, 35.

45. See D.D.T. Jabavu, *The Life of John Tengo Jabavu, Editor of Imvo Zabant-sundu, 1884-1921* (Lovedale, Cape, 1922), 114-116.
46. *Journal of the Fifth Synod of the CPSA., 1898*, 35.
47. Ibid., 39.
48. The Order of Ethiopia is integrally linked to the Church of the Province, while retaining a measure of autonomy. Since 1983 it has had its own bishop who is recognized as a bishop of the CPSA. He is Dr. Sigqibo Dwane, grandson of the founder.
49. The names of the two laymen were Josiah Guma and John Mahali.
50. E.A. Walker, *The Great Trek* (London, 1934), 208.
51. This was in 1936 and 1956 respectively.
52. F.S. Malan, *Die Konvensie – dagboek van sy edelagbare Francois Stephanus Malan, 1908-1909*, English translation by A.J. de Villiers (Cape Town, 1951), 49.
53. See L.M. Thompson, *The Unification of South Africa* (Oxford, 1960), 219.
54. Ibid., 219-220.
55. This was increased to 13% in 1936.
56. For a useful recent study, see T.R.H. Davenport, *South Africa — a Modern History* (Johannesburg, 1978).
57. Resolution 24. See *Constitution and Canons, 1904-1915*.
58. *Official Report of the Provincial Missionary Conference, October 1906*, 7. Interestingly, the 1904 session of Synod took place during the sitting of the South African Native Affairs Commission, 1903-1905. The Commission was chaired by Sir Godfrey Lagden and consisted mostly of English-speakers. The Lagden Report provided the framework for the political and territorial separation of black and white people which was to be given legislative expression in subsequent years. For details, see Davenport, *South Africa — a Modern History*,332.
59. C. Lewis and G.E. Edwards, *Historical Records of the Church of the Province of South Africa* (London, 1934), 213.
60. "Provincial Board of Missions: Occasional Papers," No. 4.
61. It took almost twenty years for the recommendation made by Maimane and Calata to be implemented. In 1960 the Revd. Alphaeus H. Zulu was appointed bishop suffragan of St. John's Diocese. Six years later he became the first black diocesan bishop as bishop of Zululand. In 1985 there are fourteen black bishops out of a total of

twenty-four, nine of them diocesan bishops in a total of seventeen dioceses. In those dioceses which are in the Republic of South Africa, three out of ten diocesan bishops are black.

62. *Acts and Resolutions of the Ninth Provincial Synod (1919)*, Resolutions 13, 14, 19 and 23.

63. *Constitution and Canons of the Church of the Province of Southern Africa*, Canon 32, Section 2.

64. The exception is Botswana, which belongs to the Province of Central Africa.

65. C.T. Wood ed., *Where We Stand — Archbishop Clayton's Charges, 1948-57, Chiefly Relating to Church and State in South Africa* (Cape Town, 1960). Geoffrey Clayton was archbishop of Cape Town from 1948-1957, and before that bishop of Johannesburg. See also Alan Paton, *Apartheid and the Archbishop — the life and times of Geoffrey Clayton, Archbishop of Cape Town* (Cape Town, 1973).

66. He was Bill Burnett, born in Koffiefontein in the Orange Free State. He was archbishop of Cape Town from 1974-1981, and before that he was successively bishop of Bloemfontein, secretary of the Christian Council of South Africa, and bishop of Grahamstown.

Take Thou Authority:
An African Perspective
John S. Pobee

This essay is written for a symposium honouring the retirement of Bishop John Howe, the first secretary general of the Anglican Consultative Council. My association with John Howe goes back to the period 1946-1950 when he was chaplain of my *alma mater*, Adisadel College, a secondary school of Anglican foundation in the Gold Coast, now Ghana. He was there a teacher and missionary. In both capacities he was an authority figure. He was a representative of a church which in its history was closely identified with the Crown of England, so much so that although that English Church Mission, as it was then known, was not officially established as in England, it was known as *aban mu asor*, literally the church inside the government castle. Thus in one sense John Howe did represent another face of the colonial authority of the Gold Coast. With hindsight we can see that something of the Gold Coast's cultures rubbed off on him; he drank, so to speak, of the well and stream of African culture. And so, in celebrating that retirement, it is fitting that something of that culture should be recalled.

The word, *authority*, and its cognate, *power*, are familiar and yet troublesome. For most people the two are synonymous. In every day life we hear of "power to the people," "student power," "political power," "religious power," etc. The press not infrequently carries news of the misuse of power and of *coups d'état* in Africa. In those stories what is at stake is power and authority. People love power, seek power, seize power, and all too soon get overwhelmed by power and become prisoners of power. But what is power?

Power is "that ability of an individual or group to carry out its wishes or policies, and to control, manipulate, or influence the behaviour of others, whether they wish to co-operate or not."[1] In other words, the wielder of power is supposed to have a wish or even a vision, and resources to enforce or prosecute that vision. Such resources are varied: formal authority, manipulations of social norms or morality, exploitation of ignorance, deception, deceit, position, and social relationships. At the end of the day, power is a social relationship whether it be between persons or groups. To that extent even the power-wielder, *ipso facto*, has obligations, commitments, and even some limitations of his or her freedom of action. The Akan, who constitute about forty-four per cent of the population of Ghana, have their wisdom distilled in maxims and proverbs. One such saying reads *Edom anaa nkoa dodow na ekyere ohene tumi*, literally "large numbers and number of servants indicate the power and authority of the ruler." In other words, power and authority to some extent, if not largely, depend on the number of people who so recognize the leader's authority. *Ipso facto* power, like authority, is a social relationship. For that reason, a chief of the Akan, who did not reflect the best interests and wishes of the people, could be removed from office.

The cognate word, *authority*, is only one manifestation and the most effective form of power. It is "power that is legitimized and institutionalized in a society or other social system."[2] With authority goes status and respect. Normally the authority is inherent in the status itself and is normally not exactly dependent on the personal qualities of the holder of authority. That is why, in spite of the foolishness of political leaders and religious leaders, they are still accorded respect — in public at any rate.

Three types of authority may be distinguished. First is the traditional ruler, chief, or king. His or her title to authority derives from sanctity of customs and is located in a family to which you must belong to qualify. Second is the charismatic leader who is the hero of the moment, especially in emergencies, e.g., the Führer Adolf Hitler or the nationalist leader and dictator Kwame Nkrumah of Ghana. The credentials of his authority are derived from other than human source, i.e., his authority is "a gift of grace." To that extent he is like the judge in the Old Testament. Third is the leader who becomes a leader because he or she has certain clear skills, e.g., a head teacher of a school or even some politicians.[3] Where the ordained person comes in to all this we shall see in due course.

The discussion of authority is taking place in the context of the Anglican communion, a communion of Anglican churches or provinces scattered round the globe. If Canterbury is its spiritual home, today the majority of Anglican dioceses of the Anglican community is outside the British Commonwealth.[4] For that reason, there is need for clarity on ecclesiology, especially an Anglican account of the nature of Christian community itself. The discussion of authority is to be set in the context of Anglican ecclesiology, if such there is. There is a sense then that the discussion of authority, even the African perspective on it, should be at three levels: the international level, i.e., the communion; the provincial level or the national level; and finally the local level. To the communion level we proceed presently.

As mentioned earlier, the spiritual home of Anglicanism is Canterbury. Anglicans are a communion because they are in communion with each other and especially with Canterbury. But Canterbury, respected as it is, has no juridical authority over any province. Unlike Rome, the Anglican communion has no centralized authority. And, of course, Africans, who have struggled to rid themselves of colonial domination with which rightly or wrongly the Church of England was associated, are not about to have another master. On the Anglican calendar stands the Lambeth Conference which is the ten-yearly assembly of bishops of the Anglican world, which meets at the invitation of the archbishop of Canterbury. But the Lambeth Conference, representative of the communion as it may look, has no legislative authority; it can only advise.

The Lambeth Conference of 1958 created the post of the Anglican Executive Officer for the Advisory Council on Missionary Strategy set up in 1948. That metamorphized in 1968 into the Anglican Consultative Council, with the aim of helping Anglicans "to fulfil their common inter-Anglicanism and ecumenical responsibilities in promoting the renewal and mission of Christ's Church."[5] But ACC too has no juridical authority. It "can debate, explore, clarify and propose. But each member Church must respond itself if anything is to be implemented."[6] As its very name suggests, ACC's role is consultative.

From the foregoing then, it can be said that at the communion level there is no centralized authority. Any authority that there is, is at the provincial or even diocesan level. Or at the best, it is a binding force flowing out of a sense of belonging to a community. It is that dispersed authority to which Sykes has drawn renewed attention. There is an implied ecclesiology. The church is the people of God in a diocese, gathered round its bishop in worship. Authority belongs to that people of God.

But what is it that each diocese recognizes as of a binding authority? First is the word of God, the normative form of which is located in the scriptures. But the baptismal rule of faith of the early church, the Apostles' Creed and the Nicene Creed, are also believed to attest to the same central truth of scripture. Through these, faith is evoked and enlivened. Scripture then is one canon of authority of the communion and for that matter, of Christians as a whole.

However, the Anglican ethos insists that scriptures never speak apart from a context. Scriptures like the creeds are always received as interpreted tradition, a text already in interaction with a context. In that context, receiving scriptures in the vernacular is an important principle. Reading scripture through African spectacles bearing the marks of poverty, degradation, and other cultural traits enables the African diocese to bring to the communion fresh insights which will engage and be engaged by other interpretations in mutual affirmation and correction. For the communion, authority lives in the word of God engaging respective contexts and in mutual engagement.

Second is sacramental life, be it Baptism, Confirmation, Penance, Holy Communion, Marriage, Extreme Unction, or Holy Orders. The sacraments are seen as organs in the living body of the church, with special functions to perform for the good of the whole. There is power and authority to a sacrament, though with Anglicanism it needs to be said that "power of the sacrament is not the same as the sacrament itself" (St. Augustine, *Commentary on St. John*. 26, 11). They produce grace in virtue of their own inherent power (cf. St. Augustine, *Contra Donat*. 4, 16). It only needs to be stated that since African societies represent a very iconic, sacramental culture, the sacraments have special force as instruments of authority and power.

Third is the Book of Common Prayer (BCP). It is not without significance that BCP is common to Anglicans all over the world. Despite the heavy marks of English culture on the BCP and despite numerous attempts at local prayer books, the shape, principles, and ethos of Cranmer's prayer book continue to be the paradigm, in short, authoritative. The liturgy has become "the power base for the Christian community as a whole."[7]

We need to mention the Thirty-nine Articles, the domestic creed of *ecclesia Anglicana* which, so to speak, sets the authorized standard of doctrine for the English church. In an illuminating study by Philip H.E. Thomas on *The Status and Function of the Thirty-nine Articles on the Anglican Communion Today,* Thomas concludes, "the Thirty-nine Articles, although not completely mislaid are treated quite differently by different provinces of that Communion. Some of the older churches still give the Articles a formal authority in the interpretation of their doctrine — although it is not at all clear how that authority would or should be exercised. Several others give its Articles some prominence as an indicator of their historical origin and development; but more than half the Provinces identify their Anglican heritage without reference to the Articles at all." So then, authoritative as the Thirty-nine Articles may be, they are not authoritative for all the communion and certainly not for the churches in Africa.

Thus at the communion level there seem to me three authority processes to which all provinces, the African ones included, would agree — scripture, creeds, and sacramental life and BCP. These are applicable to the provinces too. So for the present let us turn to the local level.

Earlier the point was made that there is an implied ecclesiology that the church is the people of God gathered in worship around the bishop. Whatever we may say of the people of God, the bishop is an important authority figure even though he is described as shepherd. The sacrament of Holy Orders is one sacrament, although it has three degrees, namely diaconate, priesthood, and episcopate, which correspond to the measure of the priestly power conferred upon the recipient. In the Anglican tradition as of now, power belongs to the fullness of the priesthood, namely the bishop alone. But how does one define this authority of the *sacerdos*?

First, it is authority "to speak God's Word to his people." This is dramatized in the giving of the New Testament or a Bible to the deacon and priest respectively. "Receive this Book, as a sign of the authority which God has given you this day to preach the gospel of Christ," the bishop says to the priest. Christianity like Judaism is a religion of the book and, therefore, the Bible features prominently as a symbol of authority. To that extent, as at the communion level, the word of God is a manifestation of authority. The Bible is not only a classic piece of literature, but also the charter document of the Christian church, which, besides whatever comfort, hope, and guidance it gives, also gives a real view of human life: good deeds brought about through faith, bad deeds brought about through misunderstanding, distrust, and utter wickedness. The authority of the priest then resides not so much because the bishop had so wished and declared but because he, the priest, symbolizes the church, the people of God as the conscious agent and messenger of the good news of the kingdom of God and the life of the world in which the church lives. Explained thus, the priest's sacral quality and authority are derived from the sociological fact that he symbolizes the whole society. And in so far as the word of God is a powerful instrument for the transformation of the world, the priest holds authority. But it is important not to forget that the *magisterium*, i.e., the teaching authority, belongs to the whole church, the people of God, even if the priest is a special ambassador.

In the history of the church, this *magisterium* has been variously defined: the authority to expound scripture, the authority to banish an erroneous witness, the authority to preach reconciliation in a very divided world. In relation to the first two, the priesthood has become the great defender of truth which is more complex than is realized. One consequence is that a very intellectual component is brought into the priesthood: selection criteria and training programs have a heavy intellectual component. And this intellectual component is expressed in a narrow academic sense and bookishness. Is such a bias really relevant to the African context where the ministry is to a largely non-literate society? There is a danger of authority being based on knowledge or academic attainment. Is that adequate or good enough for the African context? To that we shall return a little later.

The second element of authority according to the Ordinal, is "to minister his Holy Sacraments." This is further defined as "to call his hearers to repentence, and in Christ's name to absolve and to declare the forgiveness of sins. He is to baptize, and to prepare the baptized for Confirmation. He is to preside at the celebration of the Holy Communion. He is to lead his people in prayer and worship, to intercede for them, to bless them in the name of the Lord, and to teach and encourage by word and example. He is to minister to the sick, and prepare the dying for their death." In other words, the authority of a priest consists in faculties to hear confession and offer absolution (cf. John 20:23);

to administer baptism (cf. Matthew 29: 18-20); to celebrate Holy Communion, which is dramatically demonstrated by the giving of the chalice, paten, and chasuble; to administer Holy Unction and marriage. It is authority to be a cult personnel. The authority comes by virtue of the bishop on behalf of the people of God commissioning the priest to be a cult personnel. Africans, precisely because of their background, tend to focus on authority in terms of authority for cult function.

The third element of authority is service. The people of God are called to self-surrender not only in terms of interior emotions and feelings but also in terms of outward obedience. "Worship that is consonant with the truth of the gospel is indeed nothing less than its offering of one's whole self in the course of one's concrete living, in one's inward thoughts, feeling and aspirations, but also in one's words and deeds."[8] Beyond cultic religion and pious attitude, the people of God are called to a daily life of brotherly and sisterly love and moral purity (cf. James 1:27). The priest is expected to incarnate that vocation of service to humanity. The priest's authority comes from service.

Here we must take a look at Mark 9:34 ff. and 10:35 ff. There the sons of Zebedee were desirous of chief seats in the kingdom. But Jesus enunciated the principle that power is for service of God and humanity. The paradox is that one who has authority and power should behave as though he had no legal rights, indeed like a slave. He puts his own dignity and legal rights second to the well-being of those whom he serves. True power and authority comes from selfless and self-sacrificing service and devotion to humanity. Authority has meaning and relevance only in so far as it is rooted in service of humanity.

True greatness is not grandness but caring for people. True greatness is the ability to sacrifice what is most precious to us for the sake of real life and the good of all, in short to take sides for God. True greatness and true authority is not coercing, tyrannizing, and snatching power; rather it is "giving with such royal bounty that in the end one's very life is given."[9]

The three elements of authority — *magisterium* (teaching authority), faculties to be cult personnel, and service — *prima facie* belong to the hierarchy. But it is meaningless to speak of the didactic, cultic, and diaconal authority without reference to the people of God. In other words, how does one speak of the teacher without reference to the taught? Thus the didactic authority, for example, has a complement in the people of God. Authority is not a matter of hierarchy or position; it is functional and a matter of relationships in a community. And a good teacher learns as much from his or her people as he or she gives. So even the didactic authority is a communal authority. As happens in African traditional societies, the community takes part in the education of the priests. Similarly, the function of service is not peculiar to the hierarchy; the faithful are actively there. Thus authority is by definition a social relationship and communitarian. Here we come to the matter of charisma.

Authority in the church is derived from sharing in the power of the Holy Spirit. So it is charism, a concrete way of the Holy Spirit expressing himself in the world. But as Paul insists, a charism, a grace-gift, is given for the enrichment of the community of faith and not of the individual who happens to have been chosen to be the receptacle. Besides, charism is not reserved for the hierarchy. Paul asks ''Are all apostles? Are all prophets? Are all teachers?'' (I Corinthians 12:29). But each member has a charism given for the common good (I Corinthians 12:7) and, therefore, to be brought within the service of the community. And no charism is inferior and it must be recognized as a contribution of a particular ministry. Boff is right that

> charism is the pneumatic force (*dynamis tou theou*) that gives rise to institutions and keeps them alive. The principle of the structure of the Church is not the institution or the hierarchy but rather the charism that is at the root of all institutions and hierarchy. There is not one group of rulers and another group of those who are ruled, there is one group of faith. Those who rule as well as those who are ruled must all believe. Faith, or the charism of faith is the *prius natura* (basic nature) and common factor giving rise to communication and fundamental fraternal equality among all members of the Church.[10]

The rightness of seeing authority in terms of charisms is confirmed by the fact that the Ordinal invokes the Holy Spirit on the priest-to-be. That is the significance of the singing of the *Veni Creator* and the words accompanying the laying on of hands: ''Send down the Holy Spirit upon your servant . . . for the office and work of a priest in your Church." The only word to add is that the Holy Spirit is not the preserve of the ordained, indeed it is believed to be given at baptism to all the faithful so that the priest's charism stands alongside other charisms.

Such a conception of authority accords well with the African world-view; charisms, service, community are very much ideas in the African background. To that we now turn.

Concepts and patterns of authority in the church in Africa today have been inherited from so-called mother churches in the North.[11] But those very Northern concepts and patterns have been accomodated, if not assimilated to respective cultures in the North. There is no doubt that the English bishop has been a religious version of the middle class, if not aristocratic, gentleman of England. Writing of Methodist ministers in Ghana, Dickson has written as follows: "By his training and habits the Methodist minister of today is a fairly accurate copy of the Methodist minister of the time of the first Methodist missionaries in the Gold Coast."[12] This is, by and large, true of all clergy of the historic churches. But even these Northern patterns represent the amalgam of biblical, theological, and cultural insights. None of those insights is ever acultural — even the biblical insights have a large dose of Semitic and Greek culture. Nowhere is this in evidence more than in liturgical vestments and vessels.[13] Therefore, the African churches have no reason to be apologetic for developing an indigenized concept and pattern of authority, negotiating between the non-negotiable insights of the Bible, tradition, and culture sensitively treated.

As one looks at Africa there are two possible paradigms of authority — that of the chief in the traditional political system and that of the priest. To relevant elements of these two let us now proceed.

The political system of traditional Africa, which continues to hold despite the heavy assault of modern political systems,[14] has been variously classified: (a) acephalous societies such as the Dagaaba of Ghana, the Igbo and Tiv of Nigeria; (b) centralized societies, e.g., the Asante of Ghana, the Yoruba of Nigeria, and the Baganda of Bugunda, Uganda; the Swazi, and Zulus; (c) "politics as kingship-writ-large" and (d) age-based society.[15] Authority patterns in each of these are different. Obviously we cannot deal with all the models in one paper. So I wish to take a model of centralized societies, particularly that of the Asante of Ghana with which I am familiar and to which John Howe in conversations tends to refer.

The chief is the zenith of power. The office of a chief is composite: he is at once judge, commander-in-chief, legislator, the executive, and administrative head of the community. But the most important aspect of the chief's office is the religious one.[16] Chieftaincy is a sacred office. The chief then is described as the "double pivot," i.e., he is the political head of the tribe and the centre of the ritual expression. The sacred quality of kingship derives from the sociological fact that he symbolizes the whole society and is for that reason, perhaps, raised to a mystical plane. Further, he derives the title to authority from the sanctity of customs which is located in a family to which he belongs and which entitled him to authority. The only thing to note is that the chief is chosen from royal houses. Eligibility then is determined by belonging to a particular lineage reinforced albeit by election by those to whom custom assigns the right.

The other religious authority is the priesthood which, in fact, is of different classes. There are (a) the *komfo*, i.e., the one who attends to the gods but does not divine; (b) *brafo*, i.e., the special assistant to the priest; (c) *bosomfo*, i.e., the unorthodox priest. But whatever the class, the functions of a priest are multifaceted, involving cultic ministration, prediction, divination, prophecy, and healing the sick.[17] Thus, this one too, like the chiefship, is a composite office, i.e., a priest is as much a ritual specialist as a healer, a powerful person. But he is a holy man who by virtue of being in touch with the spirit–world, is able to divine and prophesy. The priest, like the chief, is also an authority figure in the society. The office is also often located in a family.

I wish to suggest that, in the minds of many Africans, the priesthood in the Christian tradition has been accomodated to the traditional concepts about priesthood and that some of the dissatisfaction with the churches stems from the fact that the Christian priests are not able to live up to expectations. Let us look at some of the elements that will be crucial for evolving a relevant and satisfying religious authority today.

First, authority must be seen as a composite phenomenon and this is to be expected in a society which sees reality in holistic terms, with the sacred and the secular interlocking. The authority is not just to perform a ritual but to make manifest in acts of power the reality of the spirit-world. The very western dichotomy between the sacred and secular, by which the priest belongs primarily to the former, is meaningless in the African context. Religious authority must be visible in the secular life. In other words, a relevant authority of the priest is to some extent derived from his or her ability to achieve results in the activities of the priest as mentioned above. The loss of membership to the African Christian Independency is precisely an issue of credible authority.

Second, authority is community based. The authority is credible and real if it derives from the sociological fact that the priest symbolizes the whole society. Here really is the reason for taking seriously the idea of the church as the people of God. In so many ways in Africa, "the minister of religion (has become) lineage head, the protector and defender of the group both physically and spiritually."[18] The holy man's authority derives from the fact that he is the symbol of the whole society, particularly the Christian community. Even the peculiar African creation called the catechist is a holy man at the grassroots, on whom the rural congregation was focused.

Third, traditionally authority was located in a lineage. A chief was selected from particular lineage; priesthood belongs to a family. Today we live in a world where this is difficult to continue. Here the church cannot but break with African tradition; for in the church God chooses whom he wills and class, colour, race, sex, cannot be a factor.[19] But even in the traditional society it was not any one in the family who would have the authority. Even there, selection criteria for the candidate took particular notice of crisis syndromes such as illness, psychological manifestations, and mystical experience, which is diagnosed as the call of the divinity. In other words, authority derives in part, at any rate, from signs or indications of a call, not just family connections and not just academic attainments.

Fourth, priesthood involved teaching the wishes of the divinity to the people. But such knowledge is not limited to books; knowledge is from the senses, reason, intuition and tradition, experience gained through observation, initiation and participation which presuppose and demand keenness of perception and an alert and adaptive mind. Such qualities make for authoritative teaching.

One last point — contrary to popular ideas, a chief who did not reflect the wishes of his community was removed from office. In other words, the authority was not *ad libitum*: the power was democratized. Where in our churches do we find the right to remove religious authority for misgovernment? A relevant concept of authority in the church must be people-centred and therefore democratized.

Authority is didactic, cultic, diaconal, and democratic. As practised today in Africa these notes are on models from the North. But it is the submission of this paper that from within the African experience there are elements that can be more meaningful interpretations of didactic, cultic, diaconal, and democratic authority in the African context. In any case, authority is a charism which must manifest in every day life the presence of the Holy Spirit, the author of authority.

Over the years, many African church leaders set me tasks. Almost invariably I learnt that it was John Howe who had in a quiet way put them onto this track. We sometimes had informal discussions about church life in Africa. It may be that it was because the years in Cape Coast, Ghana, had rubbed off on him and he had internalized the good elements of African culture, that he believed there could evolve relevant authority concepts and practice *à la Africaine*, which he could promote to the glory of God.

Notes

1. George A. Theodorson and Achilles G. Theodorson, *Modern Dictionary of Sociology* (New York, 1969), 307.
2. Ibid., 21.
3. Max Weber, *The Theory of Social and Economic Organizations*, trans. Parsons and Henderson (London, 1947), 354-360.
4. Tom Tuma, "Direction in Church Growth" in *Today's Church and Today's World. The Lambeth Conference 1978 Preparatory Articles* (London, 1979), 96-102, esp. 96-97.
5. Stephen F. Bayne Jr., *An Anglican Turning Point* (Austin, Texas, 1964).
6. *Anglican Information*, 38 December 1984:2.
7. Stephen W. Sykes, *The Integrity of Anglicanism* (Oxford, 1978), 96.

8. C.E.B. Cranfield, *A Critical and Exegetical Commentary on the Epistle to the Romans*, II (Edinburgh, 1979), 605.

9. C.F.D. Moule, *The Gospel According to Mark* (Cambridge, 1965), 83.

10. Leonardo Boff, *Church, Charism and Power* (London, 1985), 159-160.

11. See M.A.C. Warren, *Social History and Christian Mission* (London, 1967), 33-34; A. Hastings, *A History of African Christianity 1950-1975* (Cambridge, 1979), 19-20; John S. Pobee, "Afro-Anglicanism: Meaning and Movement," paper read at Pan Anglican Conference on Afro-Anglicanism: Present Issues and Future Tasks, Barbados, 17-21 June 1985.

12. K.A. Dickson, "The Minister — Then and Now," in *Religion in a Pluralistic Society*, ed. J.S. Pobee (Leiden, 1976), 179.

13. Rudolf Peil, *A Handbook of the Liturgy* (Edinburgh, 1960), particularly 35-42.

14. K.A. Busia, *The Position of the Chief in the Modern Political System in Ashanti: A Study of the Influence of Contemporary Social Change in Ashanti Political Institutions* (London, 1968). K.A. Busia, *Africa in Search of Democracy* (London, 1967).

15. M. Fortes and E.B. Evans-Pritchard, eds., *African Political Systems* (London, 1940); J. Middleton, *Tribes Without Rulers* (London, 1970); Audrey I. Richards, *East African Chiefs; A Study of Political Development in Some Uganda and Tanzanian Tribes* (New York, 1959); Audrey Richards, "Authority Patterns in Traditional Buganda," in *The King's Men*, ed. L.A. Fatters (London, 1964); M.G. Smith, *Government in Zazzau 1800-1950* (London, 1960); J.M. Assimeng, *Social Structure of Ghana* (Tema, 1981) especially 88-112; B.C. Ray, *African Religions* (Englewood Cliffs, 1976), 119-128; J.S. Pobee, *Studies in Religions and Politics — The Ghana Case. Studies Misionalie Uppsalensia* (London); Rex Collings, *Forthcoming*, Chapter 2.

16. Busia, *Africa in Search*, 26; Busia, *Position of Chief*, 36-37.

17. J.B. Christensen, "The Adaptive Functions of Fanti Priesthood," in *Continuity and Change in African Cultures*, eds. W.R. Bascom and M.J. Herskovits (Chicago, 1959).

18. J.S. Pobee "African Spirituality," in *A Dictionary of Christian Spirituality* (London, 1983), 7.

19. In some of the African Christian Independency such as the *Musama Disco Christo Church* of Ghana and the *Eglise de Jésus Christ sur la terre par prophète Simon Kimbangu* of Zaire, leadership is located in the family of the founder, a son to be precise.

Collegiality and Conciliarity in the Anglican Communion

Gavin White

Resolution 24 of the fifth meeting of the Anglican Consultative Council reads as follows, "The Council requests the Standing Committee to consider, and to report to ACC–6 how, in a Communion which is gaining an increasing awareness of its universality, the practice of collegiality and conciliarity may be further clarified and encouraged." Collegiality was defined as:

> the process by which corporate leadership in the Church is exercised, whether between bishops as chief pastors in a Province, or between a Bishop and his clergy, or between Bishop, the clergy, and the laity in a diocese. In the last case, the more appropriate term may be conciliarity. Within the Anglican Communion, collegiality and conciliarity receive expression in other contexts and relationships. Collegiality may be seen in the Primates' Meetings and in Lambeth Conferences, while conciliarity may be seen in the Anglican Consulatative Council.[1]

Furthermore, collegiality was described as the concept employed by the Second Vatican Council "in which the authority of the Bishop of Rome was seen as being exercised within the context of the whole College of Bishops."[2]

However, the sixth meeting of the Anglican Consultative Council at Badagry, Nigeria, in 1984, concluded:

> We do not find, however, that the interpretation and use of these words within Roman Catholicism are helpful to Anglican self-understanding. It is better, we believe, to speak in terms with which we are more familiar — of a church which is both episcopally led and synodically (or by councils and conventions) governed. The point we wish to stress is that the Church is the whole people of God, and we believe that the best forms of church governance should reflect this, with laity, bishops and other clergy participating together and playing their pro-

per roles according to office, authorization and training. Within the whole body bishops are the personal symbols of continuity and unity for the church and leaders in apostolic ministry and teaching of the faith.[3]

Precisely why this conclusion was reached can only be expressed by those who participated, but certain historical arguments were laid before the sixth meeting of the Anglican Consultative Council and this paper will seek to set them forth in a somewhat different format.

To begin, it is sometimes said that the Second Vatican Council of 1962 until 1965 took the concept of collegiality into Roman Catholic thought from consideration of Eastern Orthodox ideas and specifically of the Russian idea of *sobornost*. This is probably a false assumption. Any survey of Roman Catholic thinking on the subject of collegiality will find some reference to Orthodox teaching and usage, but a much greater reliance on the history of the Western church. And *sobornost* is a much broader concept than that of collegiality. However, it will give some idea of what collegiality is or is not if we study comparable ideas in Orthodoxy. The most quoted writings of Orthodox scholars in this field are those of Khomiakov, Evdokimov, Bulgakov, and Afanassieff, all of whom are Russian.[4] One book by each of the last two named may be taken as representative.

Sergius Bulgakov wrote a book, *The Orthodox Church*, published in English in 1935. He translated *sobornost* to mean "conciliarity"though it might also be taken to mean "catholicity" or "collegiality" in a general sense, and the word *sobor* is commonly used for a synod.[5] In practical terms *sobornost* means government of the church by the *consensus fidelium*, the living voice of all Christians, and Bulgakov argued that the great councils of the church represented all Christians who might have been present were it not for "difficulties of travel."[6] This is not altogether convincing, but he went on to reject "the ecclesiastical fetishism which seeks an oracle speaking in the name of the Holy Spirit and which finds it in the person of a supreme heirarch, or in the episcopal order and its assemblies."[7] This means that he would have rejected the collegiality of the Second Vatican Council, which of course he could not predict, as strongly as he rejected the papacy. If many readers will find it hard to distinguish between councils of Orthodox bishops whom Bulgakov believed to represent the laity, and councils of Roman Catholic bishops whom he believed not to do so, his main point was clear. Orthodox thinking is opposed to too clear an emphasis on the college of bishops on its own, and to too much stress on the universal church at the expense of the local church. Significantly, Roman Catholic use of Orthodox sources in the Second Vatican Council was strongest in the early stages when, as shall be argued, certain thinkers wished to see juridical powers granted to national conferences of bishops.

Nicholas Afanassieff is sometimes mentioned as an influence on the Second Vatican Council, and his thought was expressed in his book, *L'Église du Saint-Esprit*, published after his death in 1975. In this work he argued that the church was based on the eucharist and that "the Eucharistic assembly was the centre of life of each local church."[8] Furthermore, "the church remains always intrinsically universal, each local church containing all the other churches."[9] This rather uncompromising position, which ignored any basis of the church on baptism or the Holy Spirit, was echoed in his view of the ministry, concerning which he asked in rather medieval tones, "Can there exist a ministry superior to that of the person who occupies the place of the apostles in the Eucharistic assembly?"[10] Naturally this required a theory of the bishop as a "first presbyter."[11] Furthermore, he was utterly opposed to Bulgakov's view that all Christians are represented in synods: "The bishop is not a representative of his diocese and cannot act as such. He is the head of his diocese . . . ."[12] Those of us who are not Russian Orthodox may have little concern for rival interpretations of the Synod of Moscow from different bodies in the Russian diaspora, but we may well be troubled by too heavy an emphasis on the eucharist as the basis of the church. Of course there is some truth in this, but it is also true that the eucharist is based on the church, and not just on the local church. Afanassieff is quoted and is significant just because he argues so strongly for the local against the universal church, and because he is so suspicious of the unique position of the bishop. On both subjects he goes to lengths which are unusual in Orthodoxy, but he is very much in the Orthodox tradition in his opposition to collegiality and to any stress on the universal church.

But if the concept of collegiality is not to be found in Eastern Orthodoxy, there is another church which approaches this concept and that is the Presbyterian with its stress on ministerial freedom from lay oversight and on church courts.[13] However, a comparison of Presbyterian and Roman Catholic views is not necessary at this point since nobody has ever suggested that Presbyterians were a serious force in influencing the major development of the Second Vatican Council.

Having concluded that collegiality really is a Roman Catholic idea, we must consider it as defined by its framers, and here the vital words are in *Lumen Gentium* 25:

> Although the individual bishops do not enjoy the prerogative of infallibility, they can nevertheless proclaim Christ's doctrine infallibly. This is so, even when they are dispersed around the world, provided that while maintaining the bond of unity among themselves and with Peter's successor, and while teaching authentically on a matter of faith or morals, they concur in a single viewpoint as the one which must be held conclusively.[14]

However, this definition only makes sense if the episcopate can be clearly distinguished from the presbyterate, and if the local functions of bishops are unimportant compared to their participation in the college of bishops as a universal body. For these views to be held there were some quite labyrinthine preparations made, which preparations made little sense unless they were laying a foundation for the subsequent erection of a concept of collegiality. Thus Karl Rahner, quite the most spirited thinker in this field, twice referred to a speculation that priests could ordain priests without a bishop.[15] The only possible purpose of such a reference was to accustom people to see the episcopate as only necessary for continuing itself, and thus the episcopate must have an essential function in the universal church or it need not exist at all. But, that having been established, the next question is whether the episcopate will collide with the papacy. Rahner says about this, "If it were possible to conceive of two distinct subjects existing in the church both vested with the supreme power . . ." then unity would be lost, so there can only be one supreme body, the college of bishops headed by the pope.[16]

We have now returned to the old argument as to whether a bishop is of a separate order from the presbyterate, or is merely exercising a distinct function within the presbyterate. Roman Catholic teaching on collegiality must have an episcopate which is a distinct order, and in 1965 the future Cardinal Ratzinger dismissed the opposite view by attributing it to the medieval notion, which was stated baldly by Afanassieff, that the power to say mass could not be exceeded by any other power.[17] But it is not quite as simple as that. There is much evidence for the episcopate being a separate order, just as there is much evidence against, and we are probably wise to blur the edges in this debate and to use the episcopate without defining it too closely. We cannot know exactly what happened in the early church. The preface to the Ordinal in the old Prayer Book may have been uncompromising on three orders, but there have been Anglican bishops who were doubtful about whether they could ordain priests without the assistance of priests, and few Anglicans would want an episcopate too far removed from the presbyterate. This is not so much for fear that the bishop should become tyrannical as that the bishop should become remote and ineffective. And yet if we as Anglicans should avoid too much distinction between bishop and priest, this does not mean that Roman Catholics were wrong to move in the direction they did. They needed a separate episcopate because they needed collegiality, and they needed collegiality because they already had an entity which was far removed from the local church, and that was the papacy. They were thus justified in exalting the college of bishops as a form of counterweight, but if Anglicans were to do this they would have to invent something to be a counterweight to the college of bishops.

But that is not the only reason why we should treat the Roman Catholic experience with caution. Whether we put our emphasis on the universal church or on the local church depends very much on our circumstances. These two concepts must always be in balance, leaning first one way and then the other. And in 1962, when the Second Vatican Council began, many Roman Catholic thinkers expected the majority of bishops to oppose change. If that were the case, then the best they could expect was not support from the collegiality of the whole college of bishops in the universal church but only a limited collegiality in national conferences of bishops which would at least allow change in certain countries if not at all. Thus Hans Küng argued in 1962 that the Council must give "juridical status" to bishops' conferences.[18] Yves Congar minimized the importance of the universal church by attributing this idea to medieval developments in social thought,[19] while Afanassieff received notice as a source for the pre-eminence of the local church.[20] In the same vein, Lecuyer asked if local or universal church should be considered first, and Houtart wrote of national episcopal conferences as the modern forms of collegiality.[21] On local conferences and councils Rahner wrote that, "these juridical structures already existed and were put in effect in synods before the universal primacy of the Bishop of Rome became practically evident to any notable effect, in fact, even before the first Ecumenical Council at Nicaea."[22] He went on to ask if "tendencies and energies" did not move the church, not back, but "forward to new structures similar to the old."[23] Yet none of this thinking came to anything. The first session of the Second Vatican Council showed an unexpected majority of bishops favouring change. Thus all "tendencies" moved rapidly away from emphasis on national conferences of bishops and towards the college of bishops of the universal church, which had probably always been the preferred outcome of the debate. But had things gone otherwise we might have found Roman Catholic scholars such as Cardinal Ratzinger expecting to find quite different norms in Anglicanism. In 1983 he wrote in a very frank and friendly article on Anglicanism that it might have been better had the Anglican/Roman Catholic International Commission explained "what sort of teaching authority and jurisdiction" belonged to the Lambeth Conference,[24] but had there been a different alignment at Rome in the early 1960s he might well have expected Anglicanism to be as regional as it really is, and the Lambeth Conference to be without teaching authority.

But that was not all; Ratzinger in the same article virtually rejected the whole idea of the local church:

> This romantic idea of provincial churches which is supposed to restore the structure of the early church, is really contradictory to the historical reality of the early church as well as the concrete experience of history, to which one must not turn a blind eye in considerations of this sort. The early church did

indeed know nothing of Roman primacy in practice, in the sense of Roman Catholic theology of the second millennium, but it was well acquainted with living forms of unity in the universal church which were constitutive of the essence of provincial churches. Understood in this sense, the priority of the universal church always preceded that of the particular churches.[25]

It cannot be denied that much of what is said about provincial churches is merely romantic, but so is much recent writing about the universal church, and Ratzinger's extreme view, while understandable in the context of present day Roman Catholic collegiality, cannot be taken as definitive for all circumstances. If he happens to favour the mainly British and centralist view of the Anglican communion against the outer Anglican and poly-centric view, he is naturally habituated to centralist interpretations for internal Roman Catholic reasons which may well change in the future.

Finally, Ratzinger in the same article praised the noted Ortho-dox scholar Jean Meyendorff who had argued against "ethnic" churches and had said, correctly, that once "central organs of unity" were lost "after the break-up of the old imperial church, this led in fact with compulsive inward logic to state churches springing up everywhere."[26] Of course Meyendorff was writing in the context of an American Orthodoxy plagued by relics of various European ethnic jurisdictions, and even if he wanted an American Orthodox church to replace various American branches of Serbian or Syrian or other jurisdictions, he would still expect Orthodoxy to be polycentric and something like modern Anglicanism. But it is curious, and not solely to be explained by the forces at work in the Second Vatican Council, that Roman Catholics and Orthodox should be looking back in their very different ways to an imagined golden age in the Roman Empire before "state churches" began, while certain Anglicans look back to the imperial church of the Victorian era as a golden age before national Anglican churches began.

Yet Ratzinger must be quoted once more.

Once the universal church had disappeared from view as a concrete reality actually leaving its mark on the local church, and a link had been forged with some political or ethnic reality as a framework for the latter, the whole pattern of ecclesiastical government changed . . . including the evaluation of episcopal office, and so involving alteration in the structure of the church.

Furthermore, "the theological content of primacy" is "offset by the negative legalism which resulted from the tendency to particularize and was in evidence after the break-up of the old empire wherever the link with the unifying function of the papacy had been severed."[27] This is interesting not just because of its heady romanticism about the once universal church, nor because of the intriguing idea that Rome was a guarantee against legalism, but because it is an example of collegiality with papacy being almost unconsciously accepted as the normal way in which churches should be run.

But we must still answer Ratzinger's question about "what sort of teaching authority and jurisdiction" belong to the Lambeth Conference.[28] The report of the fifth meeting of the Anglican Consultative Council mentioned collegiality as something from the Second Vatican Council "in which the authority of the Bishop of Rome was seen as being exercised within the context of the whole College of Bishops."[29] Rightly the reference here is to authority, but the following paragraph avoids the word, "Collegiality is the process by which corporate leadership in the Church is exercised. . . ."[30] There is a jump from a Roman Catholic collegiality concerned with the way in which authority is used to an Anglican collegiality which is without authority, unless collegiality is to be redefined as a means of acquiring authority.

Roman Catholic usage would suggest that collegiality has never been so defined. *Lumen Gentium* 22 is clear on this, "The supreme authority with which this college is empowered over the whole church is exercised in a solemn way through an ecumenical council."[31] In other words, the college already has the power, and there is no reference in *Lumen Gentium* 22 or 25 to authority being conferred through collegiality, but only to the mode of its use. However, authority can be used either through formal councils or in a different fashion outwith the conciliar framework. As Rahner wrote, "This power can be exercised by the college of bishops both in a conciliar way (in an ecumenical council) and in an extra-conciliar way, provided only that a collegial act takes place in co-operation with the pope."[32] Of course the word *con-*

ciliar here is used for a council of bishops; the tentative definition of "conciliarity" by the fifth meeting of the Anglican Consultative Council as a form of collegiality operating between bishops and those of other orders is without precedent. But *Lumen Gentium* does infer that bishops, even when not in council, do have a degree of something which is not quite authority or is an authority not clearly verified. This is seen not only in *Lumen Gentium* 25 but more particularly in *Lumen Gentium* 23, "But each of them, as a member of the episcopal college and a legitimate successor of the apostles, is obliged by Christ's decree and command, to be solicitous for the whole church."[33] Rahner put this a little more strongly when he wrote that any bishop has "a responsibility (not jurisdiction) and a duty towards the whole church."[34] Similarly Houtart distinguished between councils, by which he meant juridical bodies, which define norms in legislative form, and conferences which only determine "common action."[35]

We may now summarize the matter by arguing that if the Anglican Consultative Council was using the word "collegiality" in any conventional sense then it cannot be claimed that there is any collegiality in the Lambeth Conference, since that has no juridical basis or power. Even the term "corporate leadership" is probably not justified with regard to the Lambeth Conference.[36] And the reference to "a Communion which is gaining an increasing awareness of its universality" is unfortunate.[37] Anglicanism has never claimed to be universal, and what is probably meant here is some form of respect for the assumed universal and undivided church of the past, such as has possessed our Roman brethren. Nor can it be claimed that there is "conciliarity" in the Anglican Consultative Council, which has not authority and is not conciliar in any known sense. But if we are to consider all these bodies which meet from time to time then we may attribute to them a solicitude or concern for all the churches, and a responsibility which falls short of jurisdiction while still leading to common action. And that is far from negligible.

But now that the concept of collegiality has been examined in some detail, and has been held to be inapplicable to Anglican use, it might be as well to see what *is* applicable to Anglican use; it would also be as well to consider why there ever has been any suggestion that collegiality or conciliarity should have been held to exist in pan-Anglican institutions.

There has been considerable discussion of the looseness or tightness of the Anglican communion in recent years, and in part this has been because of the ordination of women. Lambeth 1978 agreed that churches should maintain communion whether they ordained women or not, but produced no solution to the problem of some clergy being allowed to function in certain churches but not others. In practical terms this meant England; no one seriously supposed that American or New Zealand priests would be worried if unable to function in Jamaica or Ireland. Probably most American and Canadian women priests were not too worried about what the Church of England thought about them anyway, but some were worried, and in England a good many churchpeople assumed that Anglicans from other lands must regard any ordination not recognized in England as inferior. It was generally forgotten that complete interchangeability of clergy throughout the Anglican communion had never existed anyway, since neither the Colonial Clergy Act nor the oath to the monarch with its effect on American clergy had ever generated much controversy. Furthermore, the Anglican communion has not had complete agreement about communicant status and many who were admitted to Holy Communion in one church were barred in another for reasons of marriage discipline. But it was the ordination of women which generated controversy, both sides claiming that Anglican uniformity was essential though differing in the nature of the uniformity they sought. And this attracted attention to those organs which are intended to facilitate the international activities of the Anglican communion.

There are four such organs: the Lambeth Conference, the Anglican Consultative Council, the Primates' Meetings, and the archbishopric of Canterbury. There have been organs established in this field which have now disappeared, such as Mutual Responsibility and Interdependence, Anglican Congresses, the journal *Anglican World*, and St. Augustine's College in Canterbury. More significantly, there have been unofficial bodies with international functions, and the attempts of the Mothers' Union to enforce Church of England marriage discipline outside England were indicative of the misunderstandings which could arise. But it was the missionary societies which played a major role in the development of world Anglicanism and at the same time found that development threatened their continued authority and independence. It is noteworthy that British Roman Catholic missions broadened their base and sought offshore support as the relative importance of Britain declined, and the same was true of British "faith missions." On the other hand, Church of England societies showed themselves generally indifferent to the need for such a broadened base, sometimes displaying actual hostility to it, the exception being the Church Missionary Society in Australia where the circumstances were fortuitous.[38] But little study of this process has been made.

If we are to study the official organs, we may begin with the Lambeth Conference which was requested by a Canadian synod in the hope that it might be a "national synod" of the Anglican communion, excluding America. This hope came to nothing, and the Conference was limited to advisory functions by the English. If today it is the English or some of them who see it a potential synod, it is the Canadians who are most concerned that it should be no such thing. As for the Anglican Consultative Council, it has administrative duties and sometimes speaks for all of Anglicanism between Lambeth Conferences. It may appear to be more centralist than it actually is, as on the occasion when it suggested a model constitution for churches as provinces of the Anglican communion, which thus gave the churches their identity instead of the churches giving the Anglican communion its identity. Again, the use of the word *province* to mean any Anglican church, whether composed of one province or more, was particularly inappropriate for churches with general, provincial, and diocesan synods, as it implied that if the church was reduced to being a province then there must have been some super-provincial structure above it. But this new nomenclature was probably not intended to have this meaning, and has not been much used outside the Council anyway. Of course some Anglican churches have used the title *province* for many years, but in a quite different sense. As for implicit authority, moral or otherwise, it has not been supposed to rest in the Anglican Consultative Council, even to the extent that it is sometimes supposed to rest in the Lambeth Conference. Primates' Meetings are so new that little need be said of them save that they were at least partly intended to be a counterweight to the Anglican Consultative Council, and in the course of time they may well perform that function.

The archbishopric of Canterbury is more controversial. Its position is never defined, and probably wisely so. Whatever standing the archbishop of Canterbury has in the Anglican communion does not derive from his presidency of the Lambeth Conference, or from any other pan-Anglican body, but it is hard to see how it can derive from his position in the Church of England which sometimes detracts from his usefulness in wider Anglican affairs. The obvious example of this was seen when the archbishop visited New Zealand but was unable to concelebrate with clergy of that church due to the overriding need not to conflict with feeling in the Church of England, though when visiting Canada he could concelebrate with clergy, including women clergy, of other churches. It may be that the archbishop of Canterbury owes much of his status to a history of which he is a living symbol, as does the patriarch of Constantinople in Orthodoxy. The shadows of past empires, whether Roman or Byzantine or British, have lived on in churches, and if the imperial flavour is repugnant to some it is welcome to others. In Anglicanism it probably keeps more people in than it keeps out. Any Anglican or Episcopalian who considers the English dimension a nonsense from the past in unlikely to be troubled by the archbishop of Canterbury, who is no threat to anyone because Britain is no longer a threat. And the fact that the archbishop of Canterbury is not only a British Government appointee but in some senses a state officer, more closely linked to the state than is the Church of England as a whole, strengthens rather than weakens his role as a link with the past.

If these are the four pan-Anglican organs, it cannot be said that any of them has authority or is likely to have authority. Nor can any of them be said to have collegiality, which, so far as any such thing exists in Anglicanism, is severely limited by the work of synods and conventions. These are all mixed bodies of bishops, clergy, and laity, and there is in Anglicanism a distaste for one order trying to do too much on its own. This is seen whenever the clergy in the English General Synod act as a brake on the other orders, and when the Canadian House of Bishops in the 1970s advised against a scheme of church union they rightly felt that they had to show, through an expensive use of modern polling procedures, that they did not speak for themselves alone. If practical experience in Anglicanism is any guide, collegiality in the accepted Roman Catholic sense is distrusted.

Of course it might be argued that pan-Anglican organs have a derived authority. If general synods are sovereign, then they might send ambassadors to act for them on bodies which represent a variety of general synods, and some Anglicans seem to believe that this is what actually happens. But such ambassadors or delegates could only confer power on the wider body in which they sit if empowered to do so, and there would probably be a fairly strong consensus that they are not empowered to do so. Anglican churches have never agreed in advance that they will accept the decisions of any pan-Anglican bodies, though there is a tacit agreement that they will agree to listen to such bodies. Of course it is difficult to prove exactly what people think on the matter which has never much concerned them, but the general impression is that Anglicans are content with the present situation and only occasionally wonder if it should be changed. Even attempts to create more sense of a common Anglican identity, whether by changes of information or of personnel, have usually foundered through apathy.

But it is precisely because there is such a restricted field of agreement between Anglicans on matters of authority and on just what the Anglican communion is, that all such judgements are subject to immediate qualification. It is therefore necessary to venture into the uncertain field of how each Anglican church views the Anglican communion.

The English tend to view the Anglican communion as something which belongs to them rather than as something to which they belong. They believe that the Anglican communion derives its being from the Church of England, and they only differ as to whether this happened in the past or still happens to-day. When they seek closer relations between Anglicans it is on the basis of the "imperial federation" schemes of the early twentieth century, and if they include American Episcopalians in their considerations it is sometimes because they think of them as those who are more British than other Americans in their outlook and culture. It never occurs to them to doubt that the archbishop of Canterbury is in some way a head of the whole Anglican communion. They now seem to have dropped the custom of recognizing other Anglican churches by making selected overseas clerics deans of English cathedrals.

But the English view is best seen in a 1983 report to the English General Synod which correctly referred to:

> a tension between those who prefer to see the Communion as a family of autonomous churches knit together by common bonds of affection, and those who would welcome increasing centralisation. For small provinces in extreme minority situations, a more "centralised" communion would perhaps produce a greater sense of belonging to something with a clear identity. But it is hard to envisage the majority of Provinces agreeing to any increase in centralisation . . . we are left, as so often, with the need to get the balance right — to ensure that each Province exercises its freedom of decision and action only after proper consultation with its sister-churches within the Communion.

And, later, "Over against this desire for coherence lies a fear that if Anglicanism were to fuse more closely into something approaching a World Confessional Family, there would be less incentive for individual Provinces to grow towards their neighbouring non-Anglican churches."[39]

This raises two points. First, it is assumed, and in the subsequent Synod debate it was assumed, that there were only two choices — a centralized Anglican communion, or local church unions, and that national Anglican churches were nothing. They could not stand on their own two feet without a close connection with England. Second, it is not apparently realized that certain Anglican churches have to demonstrate their autonomy by acting *before* meetings of pan-Anglican bodies could advise them. Nonetheless, the mere fact that some English have retreated from demanding common action to demanding common discussion is a sign of increasing comprehension. And the gulf between the English and the others is not really all that dangerous, though it may be inconvenient. The Anglican communion is not vital to the life of the Church of England which can change its views of that communion without undue strain.

The American view is looser. In some ways they see the archbishop of Canterbury as leader of the Anglican communion in a more positive way than do Anglicans who have emerged more recently from English tutelage, but this is because they look upon the Anglican communion in a more negative sense. It is hard to be dogmatic on this matter, but it does seem that American Episcopalians sometimes feel that the Anglican communion is an external body in the sense that no churches are in it. It is merely inter-church machinery, and thus the Canterbury factor is of no great importance. But this goes alongside a feeling that the Anglican communion is more for "Anglicans" than it is for Episcopalians who have been longer out of the empire. Certainly American Episcopalians are quite unmoved by suggestions that the Anglican communion should have more central control, but this may be because they never take such an idea very seriously.

The Canadian view lies, predictably, between the English and the American. Yet Canadian Anglicans probably react more vigorously than anyone else to quite mild proposals for centralization. This may be because they have been in the forefront of the battle to turn an empire into a loose association, it may be because their Church of Ireland heritage has given them a high view of synods, and it may be because they wish to disprove suspicions by non-Anglicans in Canada that they are ultimately ruled from Britain and that the Lambeth Conference is an instrument in that process. But there is also a natural caution lest quite casual British pretentions to primacy should drive a wedge between Canterbury and American Episcopalians whom Canadian Anglicans cannot ignore.

Perhaps only in Australia has there been any sign of a desire for a quasi-imperial Anglicanism, but with Australia at the centre. Only in Australia do we find the suggestion that they have inherited true Anglicanism from an England which has lost or has corrupted it. New Zealand now shares with Australia the distinction of having a primate who is a knight of the British Empire, though in New Zealand there is justification in his being governor-general, but the whole idea must strike Anglicans elsewhere with puzzlement. In fact there is a great deal about Australian religion which merits study, and if Roman Catholic study of that subject has been extraordinary both in its quality and in its quantity, the almost total lack of study of Australian Anglicanism is equally extraordinary — though it must be admitted that the many Roman Catholic scholars have not answered the questions they have asked. But if Australian is perhaps the most unpredictable of all Anglicanisms, it is just possible that it will prove to be the most creative.[40]

Finally, something should be said of new churches, whether formed of a single province covering several nations or whether restricted to one. As noted in the 1983 report to the English General Synod, such churches might well prefer a more structured communion to give them identity and overseas support. Their bishops receive status by attending the Lambeth Conference, and in churches with very little tradition and very large numbers an external point of reference may be more useful than elsewhere. Yet these churches, just because they are new, cannot allow any diminution of their authority. There is a real problem here to which no solution has ever been suggested. And it is also true that these new churches are in desperate need of resources which could be provided by the richer churches, but which are not provided, and will not be provided without some means of identifying the richer churches with the work in the newer churches. The program of Mutual Responsibility and Interdependence sought to meet this need and failed. There is no doubt a lesson to be learned from that failure, but at this point in time nobody knows what it is.

So much for the Anglican communion as it is. There are undoubtedly ways in which it might be better, but the cost of any change is such that it is unlikely to be undertaken. If there is a compelling reason for change it might be supposed to be in favour of a system for supporting growing churches, but in fact the motive for change has been mainly related to the question of the ordination of women. This has undoubtedly imposed strains, but what it would have done to a more rigid structure can only be imagined.

But there is one change which has occurred in the past generation, and that is the way in which Anglicans regard authority. A report to the Lambeth Conference of 1948 observed, "Former Lambeth Conferences have wisely rejected proposals for a formal primacy of Canterbury, for an Appellate Tribunal, and for giving the Conference the status of a legislative synod. The Lambeth Conference remains advisory, and its continuation committee consultative."[41] So it is today, but that 1948 report also saw "dispersed authority" in "Scriptures, Tradition, Creeds, the Ministry of the Word and Sacraments, the witness of saints and the *consensus fidelium* . . . ," while they found "an essentially Anglican authority" in "our adherence to episcopacy as the source and centre of our order, and the Book of Common Prayer as the standard of our worship."[42] Of course the Book of Common Prayer is no longer a common standard, but that is not the major change. In the 1980s "dispersed authority" would be held to refer, not to the remoter standards of Christian life, but to decisions of synods guided by those standards. Even an appeal to the *consensus fidelium* in our own time could only make headway through synodical action.

To conclude, the suggestion that central organs of Anglican life possess an inherent collegiality or conciliarity merited investigation. However, investigation shows that these concepts have not previously been used to describe anything found in Anglican central organs. Nor is there any great likelihood of a change in the situation. If some change were to take place it would not be in terms of collegiality, but the possibility of major change is so remote that it is useless to speculate on what basis it would be undertaken. Solicitude, concern, "the care of all the churches," is enough without jurisdiction, and it will probably continue to be so regarded.

Notes

1. ACC–5, Section 5.
2. Ibid.
3. ACC–6, 84.
4. A.S. Khomiakhov, *L'Église Latine et le Protestantisme au pointe de vue de l'Église d'Orient* (Lausanne, 1872); P. Evdokimov, *L'Orthodoxie* (Neuchatel-Paris, 1960); S. Bulgakov, *The Orthodox Church* (London, 1935); N. Afanassieff, *L'Église du Saint Esprit* (Paris, 1975).
5. Bulgakov, 75.
6. Ibid., 59.
7. Ibid., 89.

8. Afanassieff, 198. Translations are mine.
9. Ibid., 29.
10. Ibid., 31.
11. Ibid., 299.
12. Ibid., 105.
13. W.M. MacPhail, *The Presbyterian Church* (London, 1908), 127-129.
14. *The Documents of Vatican II* (London, 1966), 48.
15. Karl Rahner, *Theological Investigations* (London, 1969), VI, 337n, 343.
16. Ibid., X, 53.
17. J. Ratzinger, "The Pastoral Implications of Episcopal Collegiality," *Concilium*, I, 1, January 1965, 27.
18. H. Küng,*The Living Church* (London, 1963), 362.
19. Y. Congar, et B.D. Dupuy, redacteurs, *L'Épiscopat et l'Église Universelle* (Paris, 1962), 242.
20. Ibid., 251.
21. Ibid., 781, 498.
22. Rahner, VI, 371.
23. Ibid., 372.
24. J. Ratzinger, "Anglican-Catholic Dialogue — Its Problems and Hopes,"*Insight*, I, 3, March 1983, 2.
25. Ibid., 5.
26. Ibid.
27. Ibid.
28. Ibid., 2.
29. ACC — 5, Section 5.
30. Ibid.
31. *The Documents of Vatican II*, 44.
32. Rahner, VI, 362.
33. *The Documents of Vatican II*, 45.
34. Rahner, VI, 362.
35. Congar et Dupuy, 502.
36. ACC-5, Section 5.
37. Ibid.
38. G. Hewitt, *The Problems of Success: A History of the Church Missionary Society 1910-1942* (London, 1977), II, 339-380.
39. Church of England General Synod Paper GS558 "The Anglican Consultative Council with the Anglican Communion" (London, 1983), 8.

40. G. White, "Religious Patterns in the Diaspora of the British," *Collected Seminar Papers* (University of London Institute of Commonwealth Studies, 1982) 31, 205-206.
41. See Appendix.
42. Ibid.

Part Three
The Ecumenical Future
of Authority

Ecumenical Dialogues and Authority

Günther Gassmann

A Special Focus on the Problem of Authority

The issue of authority has been a perennial problem in the framework of Christian thinking, Christian life, and the church. Some aspects of this problem in its contemporary expression are: the crisis of institutional authority and traditional authoritative values in Western church and society and the simultaneous rise of substitute authorities (e.g., in mass media, new religious movements), the new appreciation of authentic personal authority based on competence, commitment and vision, the desire for authoritative norms in a world full of anxiety and confusion, and the growing demand that the churches speak authoritatively to the great issues of our time.

In the midst of this complex *status quaestionis*, the ecumenical movement and dialogue raise additional questions concerning authority. In the encounter between the churches, traditional and often controversial questions are compared and discussed concerning the authoritative sources and norms of faith, doctrine, and church order and the concepts and structures of authority of and within the church. In addition, the ecumenical dialogue itself aiming at better mutual understanding, convergence in formerly dividing doctrinal issues, and agreements in fundamental Christian convictions, raises the question of authority.

I would like to focus my reflections on the issue of authority as it surfaces in this framework of ecumenical dialogue. This approach was chosen because it is part of my own task, but also because it might contribute, in an exemplary way, to the attempt to arrive at a new clarification of our concept of authority.

Authority of Ecumenical Dialogues

The ecumenical dialogue, bilateral as well as multilateral, and on world-wide as well as regional and national levels, raises the question of authority at least in a twofold way. There is, first of all, the authority of these dialogues themselves, of the partners in dialogue and of the results of their endeavours. Official dialogues between individual churches or Christian world communions are obviously more than mere theological conversations between interested individuals. The participants are appointed by their churches in order to represent their doctrine and life as loyally and responsibly as possible. The results of their labours, as a consequence, are again "more" than a theological essay by an individual theologian. The reports of the dialogues are, therefore, a special kind of literary genre. They are not only the product of a corporate dialogue process, but also a reflection of the efforts of people who have received a special responsibility from their churches. They require, accordingly, serious and careful evaluation by those who have authorized such a process.

This formal description indicates that the dialogues — the bilateral certainly more than the multilateral ones — are vested with a certain authority. Yet it is clearly no constitutional, canonical, or automatically effective authority, because the results of the dialogues have, as such, no binding power for the churches. Their authority, i.e., the degree to which they impose themselves on the churches and become acceptable to them, depends finally on the combination between the certain formal authority of dialogue groups and the convincing quality of their work. Here, as in other contexts, form and content of authority belong inseparably together.

Reception as Criterium of Authority

Yet it is a necessary task of the churches which receive the reports to test to what degree the results of ecumenical dialogues carry with them such authority. This leads us to the second aspect of the question of authority in the framework of dialogues. How do the churches undertake this test? What are their structures for evaluation and decision making? How are they teaching with authority because the dialogue results confront them with fundamental matters of faith, doctrine, and order? Most churches can point to their inherited patterns in responding to these questions.

The new phenomenon of the dialogues and their results has, however, challenged many churches to face these questions in a new way. Why?

I believe that the decisive factor which raises and illuminates the question of authority in the church in a new way is the concept of "reception." Of course, the concept and reality of reception is no new theme, nor is it restricted to the church. For a long time reflection has been going on concerning the role and significance of the reception of conciliar decisions by the church. This has led to the conclusion that reception is integral to the conciliar idea itself and is, consequently, also one of the criteria for judging the authority of councils and conciliar decrees. We also notice in the secular realm a wide use of the term "reception" in connection with philosophical systems, literary theories, scientific concepts, and the work of great personalities in the fields of intellectual or artistic creativity. During the last two decades the concept of reception has become very much a present, contemporary issue which is reflected in a multitude of articles and papers. This is a direct result of ecumenical dialogues.

Most of the bilateral dialogues which were initiated after the Second Vatican Council and which are continuously growing in number, have as their goal the manifestation of visible unity between hitherto divided churches and Christian communions. Even dialogues which were initiated with a more modest purpose — to work towards better mutual relations and to stuggle with particular controversial issues — developed a dynamic during the dialogue process which pressed more and more towards that goal and concrete intermediate steps on the way to that goal. The more comprehensive multilateral dialogue within the Commission on Faith and Order of the World Council of Churches, which involves all Christian traditions, also has no other goal than "to call the churches to the goal of visible unity in one faith and one eucharistic fellowship, expressed in worship and in common life in Christ, in order that the world may believe" (By-Laws of the Commission). The results of these dialogues in the form of agreements, convergences, and recommendations are submitted to the churches and Christian world communions in the expectation that they will be discussed, evaluated, "received," and, if possible, acted upon — with authority — so that they become historically effective by changing existing relationships between the churches.

A New Concept of Reception

This constitutes indeed a new challenge for the churches which they did not have to face in the same way in the past. They are assisted in this situation by a new perspective on the understanding of the church which has become very much a part of ecumenical encounter and exchange. It is now often called an "ecclesiology of communion," i.e., an ecclesiology which emphasizes, among other things, the spiritual inter-relation of all levels of church life, the unity and interplay of the personal, collegial, and communal dimensions of life, leadership, and authority. This view of the church led to the awareness that the churches could not deal with the results of ecumenical dialogues only on the level of their traditional instruments for such purposes — specialized advisory committees, ecumenical staff executives, decision-making bodies. Rather the whole community of the church should be involved because steps towards visible unity affect the thinking, life, and mission of all the people of God and require, therefore, their consent and support. Thus a concept of reception which reflects this ecclesiology received a new urgency and meaning.

Reception, in this perspective, is no longer seen as limited to an official acceptance — fully or qualified — of dialogue results. Rather, it is the task of the churches to see to it that these results are communicated and interpreted in such a way that they can be discussed, understood, and evaluated on all levels of church life. Where this happens, reception means that these results have an impact: the understanding of Christian life is broadened by the insights and experiences of other Christian traditions. The spirituality and worship life of one's own church is enriched. The confessional or doctrinal position of each church will be challenged to rediscover forgotten elements in its own history and to transcend narrow or one-sided definitions of that position. Ethnic, cultural, and intellectual provincialisms are, at least partly, overcome. This deepening and transforming process of reception is not an uncritical one. Not every result of a dialogue is by itself acceptable. It has to be examined, tested, evaluated. The result may only be a partial reception, a more or less fully effective, transforming acceptance.

Reception as Integral Element of Authority

It is only in the framework and on the basis of such a broad process of reception that responses, statements, and actions of the decision-making bodies of the churches receive their proper place, weight — and authority — in relation to these dialogue results. They are then seen as the reflection and clarification of a conciliar process in which the people of God are involved. They are not simply the sum total of such a process because decision-making bodies are vested with a "surplus" of responsibility and leadership. But they are, ideally, an expression of the mind of the church, under the guidance of the Holy Spirit. The authority of those exercising individual or corporate leadership and the authority of their actions is not a formal or imposed one, but a supported and accepted one by the involvement of the whole *koinonia*.

The broad, unexpected, and unprecedented process of dealing with the Faith and Order convergence document on *Baptism, Eucharist and Ministry* is for me an impressive illustration and vindication of such a broader, comprehensive concept of reception. In many countries this document is discussed in congregations, ecumenical groups, theological seminaries, ecumenical commissions, local and provincial councils of churches, meetings of pastors, etc. In connection with these discussions the document is used as a resource for liturgical revision, Christian education, and as a means for establishing new ecumenical contacts and relations. It has already had an impact before the decision-making bodies of the respective churches formulated their official response to the document. And in many cases they have done this with explicit reference to the experiences of and reports from these wider discussions. But not only that. There has emerged the general conviction that with these official responses the process of reception has not come to a conclusion. It will continue and, in many cases, make use of the official responses as an additional stimulus for discussion and also as a frame of reference and point of comparison for one's own insights and evaluations.

Conclusions for the Concept of Authority

In the framework of ecumenical dialogues and their results addressed to the churches, we have observed two lines of argument concerning the issue of authority which are directly connected with each other. The first showed us that there are different levels of formal authority, one of which is represented by the official dialogues and the dialogue groups involved. Whether and to what degree such a formal authority becomes an accepted and effective authority, depends on the quality and convincing force of the content of its actions — in this case, the results of its work. This evaluation and judgement — and this is where the second line of argument begins — is implemented in a process of reception. This process involves the whole church. It is not only a process at the level of intellectual judgement concerning the acceptability of the results of the dialogues. In this process effective reception already occurs and this has a transforming impact on the life of the church. This process prepares and leads up to the official acts of reception "on the highest appropriate level of authority"(Preface to *Baptism, Eucharist and Ministry*) in the churches. These are authoritative, because they are representative, binding on the whole church and have, in certain cases, concrete steps in view of the relationship to other churches as a consequence (e.g., the declaration of eucharistic hospitality). Such official, authoritative acts of reception can be the conclusion of a process of reception, but they can also be an intermediate act providing further guidance and stimulus for an ongoing process.

This perspective on authority, which connects the elements of formal pattern, content, and convincing power of authority and reception as an integral element to authority, will not provide an answer to all questions concerning authority in the church, but it may contribute to the clarification of such answers.

Anglicans, Roman Catholics, and Authority

Johannes Cardinal Willebrands

"Reference to the Churches of the statement about common ground on authority and primacy is likely to cause more pondering in both Churches than that on ministry." Bishop John Howe, Review Address at ACC–5, 1981 (*Report*, 20)

On the morning after the death of Pope Paul VI in 1978, Archbishop Coggan spoke to the Lambeth Conference about "the complex and difficult subject of authority in our Anglican Communion," since "we have been searching somewhat uneasily to find out where the centre of that authority is." Negatively, central authority was not located in the person of the archbishop of Canterbury, nor in the Lambeth Conference, nor in the Anglican Consultative Council, nor in the newly formed Doctrinal Commission. The archbishop looked to the influence of increasing consultations in the meetings of primates and their interaction with the ACC. "Without a rigidity which would be foreign to our tradition" he looked to "a liaison between the Churches in the *persons* of the primates and the ACC representing *synodical* government" (cf. *Report of 1978 Lambeth Conference*, 122-4: italics added).

Several factors had contributed to the discussions about authority at the 1978 Lambeth Conference, many of them ably outlined in Stephen Sykes's *The Integrity of Anglicanism* (London, 1978), published just before the Conference met. The most evident question, at least in the eyes of the media, was the diversity of practice and even belief concerning the ordination of women to the priesthood; to what extent could or should autonomous provinces await a consensus of the whole communion, even of the wider ecumenical fellowship, before taking decisive action in so serious a matter? Was this a correct understanding of comprehensiveness or not? Again, a conference of bishops such as is a Lambeth Conference, particularly one with the mission of bishops as a principal theme, was in any case likely to ponder the relationship between their *personal* responsibility and that of *synodical* structures, particularly in the light of rapid developments in the latter in the previous few years. As the archbishop noted, there were plans to make more use of the meetings of primates, and also to set up an inter-Anglican Theological and Doctrinal Commission. To some extent these could resolve some questions about authority; but they raised a few questions as well. There was, moreover, the question of how the Anglican communion was in due course to respond to the work of the Anglican-Roman Catholic International Commission. As ACC-5 was to ask three years later: "How can the Communion speak with a sufficiently united voice to give a measure of authority and coherence to our replies?"(ACC-5, *Report*, 40).

Questions about authority were to the fore in the Roman Catholic church that summer, even if in rather different ways. It was "the year of the three Popes"; so, especially during the conclaves in August and October, the spotlight of world attention was focused on the papacy and its mission in the church. The long pontificate of Pope Paul VI had seen rapid developments in the life of the church as the documents of Vatican II were implemented, but these had brought their difficulties with them; one need only mention the implementation of post-conciliar changes in the liturgical field, debates on moral teaching, and the first meetings of the World Synod of Bishops. Discussion centred particularly on "decentralization" (too often spoken of in pragmatic terms rather than in a properly theological context of the nature and mission of the local church) and on the relationship between the primatial authority of the pope and that supreme authority enjoyed with him by the whole College of Bishops (more recently reaffirmed in the 1983 *Code of Canon Law,* cf. canons 332, 336). In these Roman Catholic discussions of the relationship between the *primatial* and *collegial* aspects of authority we can see a number of points of contact (and some points of contrast also) with the Anglican debate on the *personal* and *synodical* aspects of the episcopal office.

Superficially the two communions might seem to be facing a common problem; but in fact authority was a problem between them. It was not simply a case of Anglicans looking for primacy and Roman Catholics seeking for "dispersed authority." Small wonder, then, that so much of the work of ARCIC I was given to issues of authority. It took the Commission only three years to reach basic agreement on eucharist and ministry (1970-73);

apart from the need to present some *Elucidations* on these in 1979, ARCIC spent the rest of its days in a long and painstaking study of authority in the church (1974-81). The proportions in its *Final Report* speak for themselves; there are more than twice as many paragraphs on authority than on the other two themes put together, and even then ARCIC was aware that further aspects still called for discussion. These proportions were no surprise to anyone with knowledge of the history of Anglican/Roman Catholic division but they clearly emphasize the importance of this discussion if we are to come to that full communion which is the goal of our dialogue.

In fact, it is not simply the content of the *Final Report* that illustrates the questions concerning authority that are to the fore in our two communions. Our common problems and also the particular issues that are of special concern for either communion are illustrated by the very process by which ''the Commission's conclusions'' are now being ''evaluated by the respective authorities through procedures appropriate to each Communion'' (Common Declaration of Pope John Paul II and Archbishop Runcie, Canterbury, May 29th, 1982, 2).

In my address at the opening of the plenary meeting of the Secretariat for Promoting Christian Unity in February 1983, I recalled that:

> our dialogue with the Anglican Communion is the first to submit an overall report to the Church's judgement. The novelty of this fact, which was without precedent, put a delicate question to our Church. Since in fidelity to the Council it has put into action collegiality and episcopal co-responsibility, what method should it use to enable it to form a judgement on the content of such a report and draw the practical conclusions for its relations with the Anglican Communion? There was much discussion about this. In mid-March it was decided that the ARCIC Report should be sent to the episcopal conferences and that the Congregation for the Doctrine of the Faith should send its observations of its experts as a contribution to the dialogue and as a help to Catholics in reading the document with discernment. Like all novel procedures this was not at once understood. It was not immediately perceived what an advance it was in the line of Vatican II. The process is now continuing.

It is a question of finding out whether the Commission, in its effort to say what is the faith of the Church in these aspects of its mystery, and its concern to say this together and today, has really met all the requirements. The process of reaching and announcing decisions must not be hurried.(SPCU *Information Service*, n.51, 1983/I-II, 13)

To say that a process "must not be hurried" is not an invitation to be dilatory! But it is obvious that proportionate care must be taken in arriving at a just evaluation of a document as important as the *Final Report*. In sending out the *Report*, the Secretariat asked episcopal Conferences to "send a considered judgement on the work done"; it takes time to come to a considered judgement, especially in what I have called a new situation. The seriousness with which Conferences have approached this task is most encouraging. During the last three years we have received substantial replies from a number of major Conferences, all of them positive in their general appraisal, and most of them reflecting extremely careful and well-researched work. In some cases the task of drafting a response was entrusted to a group of bishops, theologians, and ecumenists; their reaction was then discussed, amended, and accepted by the Conference. We know that a number of other Conferences are still following a very similar process, and we look forward to receiving their reactions before long.

But what then? Here again we are in a new situation. When all the responses have been received and synthesized it will not be a question of simply counting heads; there will be need to prepare an overall evaluation of these reactions. If, as we hope, these reactions are substantially consonant, this task will not be too difficult, but should there be profound divergences in the responses to the *Report*, further exploration and discussion will be needed. In this whole process, the various Roman offices will have their part to play, as part of their direct service to the pope as head of the episcopal college.

At the end of the process it will be the supreme authority of the Catholic church, the pope in communion with the College of Bishops, whose views he has solicited, that will give the Catholic church's official evaluation of the *Report*. In what form this will be done remains to be seen, as indeed does the content of such an evaluation. But the process has started and is going according to plan.

The processes being followed in the Anglican communion have their similarities and their dissimilarities. Just as the Secretariat has sent the *Final Report* to episcopal conferences throughout the world, so too the Anglican Consultative Council has sent it to all the member churches of the Anglican communion for discussion and decision in their general synods and conventions. This too will not be a speedy process. Not only are there provinces in which the General Synod meets only every two or three years, but synodal discussions on such important matters have to be thoroughly and carefully prepared. Some synods will almost certainly remit the *Report* for discussion in diocesan synods, as the Church of England General Synod did in February 1985, before a more definite decision is reached. And even when all twenty-seven general synods have recorded their votes, even if all these votes were wholly favourable, there will still be the task of transforming all these answers into one answer, the answer of the Anglican communion as such; that was the point of the question about authority in this respect that was raised at ACC-5 in 1981. No doubt similar questions will recur at ACC-7 in 1987 as it surveys the responses of the synods in order to facilitate the task of the 1988 Lambeth Conference voicing the consensus of the Anglican communion.

But for the Anglican communion, as for the Roman Catholic church, "novel procedures" are involved. A Lambeth Conference has, as such, a moral rather than a magisterial or legislative authority for the Anglican communion; member churches need to make Lambeth decisions formally their own before they acquire full authority in each church.

On either side, then, the process of evaluation is one that itself illustrates the present understanding and exercise of authority in each communion. It is encouraging to hear that ARCIC II, as part of its studies on "Growth in Reconciliation," has invited two of its members to reflect on what our procedures for the evaluation of ARCIC I show us about our understanding of the goal of our dialogue and also about our understanding of the nature of authority. For each of us such "new" processes involve areas of uncertainty or unpredictability. As Cardinal Ratzinger stressed in his article in *Insight* (March 1983), it is the very exercise of authority — itself largely expressive of an underlying perception of theological principle — that is one of the questions that still has to be investigated more fully in our dialogue. In ARCIC I's *Final Report* the principles of primatial and synodical authority were relatively easily agreed; but the *Report* also illustrates continuing Anglican "fears" regarding what limits, other than moral ones, would apply to the exercise of jurisdictional or doctrinal authority by a universal primate. In a different way, in his address in Westminster Abbey in Lent 1981, Archbishop Runcie touched on such themes when he asked, for example, what sort of relationship the offices of the Roman Curia would expect to have to the churches of the Anglican communion when that communion was "united but not absorbed" with and in the communion of the Roman Catholic church.

Catholics too have their questions about the exercise of authority in the Anglican communion. Some may apply more particularly to the "established" status of the Church of England and its relationship to the sovereign and to Parliament. Others stem from Catholic observation of divergences in practice and even in principle within and between Anglican churches on such matters as the ordination of women, the remarriage of the divorced, the reconciliation of ministries in union schemes. To the average Roman Catholic some at least of these may seem at first sight to exceed what he understands to be the limits of "comprehensiveness" or "legitimate pluralism." And Catholics can also be puzzled by the way in which bishops, although "teachers and judges of the faith," do not always carry the day in synodical debates. But this is an Anglican debate too, as was seen at ACC-6, 1984, in the report on the evaluation of the life and work of the ACC (cf. *Bonds of Affection, Proceedings of ACC-6*, Badagry, Nigeria, 1984, 35-6). After listing the structural aspects expressive of "dispersed authority," the report remarked:

> But the way in which authority is derived and expressed is not settled simply by stating these realities. It is necessary to clarify "operational implications" and "guidelines of accountability" if the nature of "dispersed authority" is to be understood. These . . . cannot be achieved easily, nor will they remain static because of the many historical, cultural, power and economic differences which exist both within and between provinces.

All to often in the past we have raised such questions about one another in too polemical and aggressive a way. We are inclined to look at one another's practice in the most unfavourable light and to draw drastic conclusions about one another's beliefs. Now, I hope, we raise these questions in a new and constructive spirit. Precisely because we have found such a measure of agreement on doctrinal principle concerning the nature and basis of authority in the church, we are determined to dispel misunderstandings and resolve differences concerning its exercise in practice where these constitute a barrier to our growth together. After all, in the long run our goal is not simply to recognize abstract principles in each other. We hope, through God's grace, to come together in the reality of a full communion that will allow for differences in practice, but can do so only if such differences are properly understood as rooted in one faith.

Without prejudging our official responses to ARCIC, we can already see in its *Final Report* a measure of agreement about authority in the church, a measure that would have startled us two decades ago if we could have foreseen it. It is precisely because of this measure of agreement that we are anxious to resolve remaining problems about authority and its exercise. Indeed, this measure of agreement in principle is the basis for a real confidence about the outcome of what still has to be done. And it is because of this measure of agreement that we watch with very involved interest, and certainly in no spirit of Olympian detachment, the development of the processes by which the authorities of our two communions, each in accordance with their own procedures, are now coming to judgement on the work of ARCIC I and fostering the new tasks entrusted to ARCIC II.

An Anglican Comment on Papal Authority in the Light of Recent Developments
J. Robert Wright

At least from the time of the Reformation there have been three major Christian answers to the question of "authority," all of which have had some following within the Anglican tradition. The first approach has been to locate authority within the Holy Scripture, as if the truth contained therein were univocally obvious to anyone who reads it. A second approach has been to find the source of authority within the individual testimony of the Holy Spirit as perceived by each true believer in prayer, who would in this way be enabled by private guidance to distinguish among contradictory interpretations. And a third approach has resorted to the calm certainty afforded by the institutional church, which offers a collective wisdom that is presumably more objective. Variations on each of these approaches have been numerous, and the one most commonly cited as "Anglican" is most frequently labelled by the triad of scripture, tradition, and reason. Even if this triad, as such, cannot be proven to originate with Richard Hooker, it does have the advantage of attempting to combine, in a way, all three of the answers to the problem cited above, locating the individual testimony in reason and the collective wisdom in tradition. But it still does not solve the matter of contradictory interpretations, it does not provide a *magisterium* that can deal with the complexity of doctrinal development, and for this reason it is sometimes contrasted with what is claimed to be the more typically Roman Catholic triad of scripture, tradition, and authority, the last term being understood as the papacy itself in both its primatial and infallible roles. Sometimes this contrast is even colloquially caricatured by the assertion that to Roman Catholics it seems Anglicans can believe anything they like and that to Anglicans it seems Roman Catholics are not allowed to think: when asked for an authoritative answer to a direct question the Anglican may reply that the Bible says so-and-so, Christian thinkers in various periods have said such-and-such, and he or she now believes thus and so, whereas the Roman Catholic may merely reply that the church teaches — or that the pope has spoken. We come, therefore, to the subject of this essay, ''An Anglican Comment on Papal Authority in the Light of Recent Developments.''

In a previous essay related to this subject (in *A Pope for All Christians?*, ed. Peter J. McCord, New York, 1976), I gave evidence to suggest that the Anglican view of papal authority has evolved historically from the consciously ''anti-papal'' polemic of the sixteenth century to a more neutral ''non-papal'' attitude by the mid-twentieth century which today is even expressed in a positive interest to explore the possibilities that some form of papal leadership may offer to the one church of the future. For Anglicans, the question is whether *any* sort of papal primacy, of a single personal focus of unity and authority in the bishop of Rome, can be accepted and acknowledged as desirable. Such an acknowledgement would of necessity involve, as the Anglican-Roman Catholic International Commission (ARCIC) has perceptively observed in its *Final Report* (London and Cincinnati, 1982), an Anglican-Roman Catholic agreement about the meaning and binding nature of such terms and topics as the Petrine texts, divine right, universal ordinary jurisdiction, and infallibility, as they relate to the papal office. The *Final Report* is the most recent development for Anglicans on the question of papal authority, and the comments that follow will perforce make frequent reference to it. Because the *Final Report* has focused on the four terms and topics just mentioned, I shall do the same within the limitations of this essay, although still other aspects of papal authority — especially of its use and/or abuse, its sources and its exercise — would need to be treated at length in any comprehensive account. (Further see the two other articles on the *Final Report* which I have published, in *Ecumenical Trends* 11:10, Nov. 1982, 149-157, and in *Anglican Theological Review* 66:2, April 1984, 177-187, both of which are drawn upon in this present essay.) Note will also be taken in passing of some of the major responses to the *Final Report* that have appeared thus far, as well as of other statements and writings where pertinent. The Roman Catholic church ''is convinced that in the ministry of the bishop of Rome it has preserved the visible pole and guarantee of unity in full fidelity to the apostolic tradition and to the faith of the fathers,'' claimed Pope John Paul II openly before the World Council of Churches at Geneva on 12 June 1984 (*Origins* 14:7, 28 June 1984, 99), and as we enter this Anglican consideration of papal authority we must be asking whether this is really what the Roman church believes, whether there is any way in which we can believe it, and no matter which way we answer the first two questions — whether such a belief is necessary for the restoration of full communion between our two churches. If the following remarks seem somewhat critical of papal authority, it must be said here that the author would be equally critical (in another direction) had he been asked to write about *Anglican* authority, and would be much more complimentary had he been asked to write about the ecumenical potential of other aspects of the Roman Catholic church as a whole.

Questions for Anglicans

First, however, we must note from these three sources some of the broader questions about papal authority that the *Final Report* has posed to Anglicans. The first place must be given, in courtesy, to some of the questions of Joseph Cardinal Ratzinger, prefect of the Sacred Congregation for the Doctrine of the Faith (SCDF, as it was then called; recently the adjective *Sacred* has been officially dropped):

> If there was surprise afterwards at the fact that the Roman Catholic Church can give an authoritative answer more immediately than Anglican structures allow for, this is surely an indication that too little attention had been paid to the actual functioning of authority. It was probably not made clear enough that the Pope — especially since Vatican II — has a special authentic teaching function for the whole Church: it is not indeed infallible but does make authoritative decisions. On the other hand the text left one completely in the dark as to the concrete structure of authority in the Anglican community. Those well acquainted with Anglicanism know that the Lambeth Conference, originally instituted in 1867, was not due to meet for several years, according to its regular timing, and that no authoritative pronouncement could be made before that date. But ought not the text to have mentioned this structure in order to give a true explanation of the problem of authority

without stopping short of the concrete reality? Would not the right and indeed necessary thing have been to explain what sort of teaching authority and jurisdiction belongs or does not belong to this assembly of bishops? Should one not also have gone into the question of the relation between political and ecclesiastical authority in the Church which first touches the nerve-point of the question of the Catholicity of the Church or the relation between local and universal Church? In 1640 Parliament decided as follows: "Convocation has no power to enact canons or constitutions concerning matters of doctrine or discipline, or in any other way to bind clergy or religious without the consent of Parliament." That may be obsolete, but it came to mind again in 1927 when on two occasions a version of the Book of Common Prayer was rejected by Parliament. However that may be, these concrete questions should have been clarified and answered, if a viable agreement about "Authority in the Church" was the aim in view. For it is of the essence of authority to be concrete, consequently one can only do justice to the theme by naming the actual authorities and clarifying their relative position on both sides instead of just theorizing about authority. . . .

How is Scripture recognized in the Church? Who decides whether what you say is in accord with Scripture or not? It is rather ambiguous when ARCIC says: "Neither general councils nor universal primates are invariably preserved from error even in official declarations. . . ."

The phrase "manifestly a legitimate interpretation of biblical faith" catches one's attention. The dogmas of the pre-Reformation Church are quite certainly not "manifestly legitimate" in the sense in which "manifest" is used in modern exegesis. If there were such a thing as the "manifestly legitimate," obvious enough to stand in its own right out of range of reasonable discussion, there would be no need at all for councils and ecclesiastical teaching authority. ("Anglican-Catholic Dialogue: Its Problems and Hopes,"*Insight* 1:3, March 1983, pp.2 and 4)

The Church of England Response (London, 1985) has had this to say:

The most pressing question put by ARCIC to Anglicans, who confess their faith in "one, holy, catholic and apostolic

Church" is, how is the unity and catholicity of the Church to be manifested? And if, as we maintain, the exercise of authority and discipline is a necessary part of the Church's existence, what form or forms of authority should serve the manifestation of this unity and catholicity? We cannot be concerned only with the deposits left behind by the exercise of authority in times past, the Scripture, the first ancient General Councils. The question is, through what persons or institutions is Christ's authority now mediated in the universal Church?

The question of universal authority raised by ARCIC faces us inescapably with the question of authority in the Anglican Communion. We ought not to take refuge behind the "legal" autonomy of each national church or province in order to evade the theological question of our coherence as a Communion. The work of ARCIC as well as Anglican practice suggests that the coherence is to be manifested both in personal (episcopal and primatial) and in conciliar forms. It is not a matter of creating some new "central" authority, by delegation or transference of power from national churches conceived as "sovereign," but of recognizing the authority inherent by virtue of ordination in the bishops and primates, whereby they can act together, in consultation with the laity, on behalf of their churches. Having recognized that inherent authority it is our task to discover structures through which the authority can be most adequately expressed and acknowledged.

Finally, Anglicans need to give critical attention to the role played in the Church of England, both past and present, by state authority. The Co-Chairmen of ARCIC refer to the problem of papal authority as lying at the source of our divisions. They might also have raised the matter of royal authority. Ought we not to think carefully about the nature of the authority attaching to the General Synod? There is need to distinguish between the authority that it derives from Parliament through the Enabling Act and subsequent Measures, and the inherent authority that it has as a combined meeting of the two Provincial synods of Canterbury and York (which are older than Parliament) together with representatives of the laity of the two provinces. There is need to consider the relation between decisions of a representative church body and reception by the Church in this context. There is need also to consider the limitations of decisions taken by parts, smaller or greater, of the universal Church. Further, the control exercised by royal authority over appointments and canonical legislation in the Church of England should be examined in comparison with similar forms of state control over churches in other lands. (97)

This last question, of establishment, is also raised by the *Response* of the English Roman Catholic hierarchy (London, 1985): "Legislative action will be necessary before the state of communion between the two churches is established" (15, para. 43).

And the *Response* of the Episcopal church in the U.S.A. (hereafter ECUSA; published in *Ecumenical Bulletin*, no. 71, May-June, 1985) has put similar questions in this way:

> From the statement of our 1979 General Convention on "The Visible Unity We Seek," the Episcopal Church is already on record as affirming that some form of collegiality, conciliarity, authority, and primacy will need to be "present and active in the diocese with its parishes as well as nationally, regionally, and universally." The statement also said, "We do not yet see the shape" of those structures at the present time. We therefore believe the ARCIC *Final Report* now calls us to look carefully at two urgent questions: 1) the limits of doctrinal diversity or comprehensiveness that are compatible with an authentic and credible ecclesial unity, and 2) the process of authority by which decisions about faith and action should be taken for the sake of the Church's mission.
>
> Anglicans have of course been discussing these questions among themselves for many years, even centuries, but they confront us now with new urgency for two reasons: our old answers to them seem even less clear or compelling than before, and our current ecumenical dialogues (especially the *Final Report*) demand that we now proceed to discuss and answer these questions no longer in the abstract but in the hope, even in the distinct possibility, that our Church may be visibly one, in full communion, with other churches in the foreseeable future. For these reasons, therefore, the traditional Anglican concept of "dispersed authority"(Lambeth 1948) needs further elucidation. We are now being asked to give a direct answer to the questions: How are decisions reached,

what people finally decide for the Anglican Communion, and how should this be done in the coming great church of the future that we believe to be God's will? Which interpretations of Scripture and tradition are faithful and acceptable and which are not? The *Final Report*, as well as the reports coming from many other of our ecumenical dialogues today, ask that we specify how we as Anglicans decide what we believe and what we should do, and that we describe our position in relation to other churches facing the same problem and with whom we hope to reach a common mind about God's will for the Church's mission and a common strategy for effecting it. (27-28)

To the above, I would add that the notion that Anglicans believe in some theory of "dispersed authority" needs to be questioned, and this concept at least elucidated, in the light of the *Final Report* as well as recent Anglican developments. Modern Anglican appreciation of a theory of "dispersed authority" seems to stem from the collection of papers and documents in a booklet entitled *Authority in the Anglican Communion,* prepared at the request of the primates of the Anglican communion in response to Resolution 11 of the 1978 Lambeth Conference and published in 1981 under the sponsorship of Bishop John Howe, whom this present essay is intended to honour, when he was secretary general of the Anglican Consultative Council. This theory, whose roots are helpfully traced in that booklet (13) but incorrectly ascribed to the 1948 Lambeth Conference itself (25), was expounded in a report prepared for the 1948 Lambeth and printed with its proceedings (Part II, 84 ff.) but never adopted by the Conference itself. More recently, this theory was endorsed by the 1981 meeting of Anglican primates in Washington, D.C., for which the papers published by Bishop Howe formed the background, and the statement to come from that meeting boldly claimed as its very first point of agreement, "The Anglican Communion accepts and endeavours to practice the theology of dispersed authority as set out in the 1948 Lambeth Conference document." The thrust of the Lambeth *Report,* however, was to say that authority "is distributed among Scripture, Tradition, Creeds, the Ministry of the Word and Sacraments, the witness of saints, and the *consensus fidelium,*" that is, authority is found within many dispersed *sources;* but what the Lambeth document did *not* say is that the *exercise* of authority is dispersed among many different *persons* or *institutions*. Thus, the contrast that the Lambeth *Report* made is not really one of "a dispersed rather than a centralized authority," in spite of its use once of this phrase, but instead a contrast between the one source of authority (God) and the many sources where authority is found. Presumably a papalist, as well as an Anglican, could agree with this point, and so it is not surprising to find the *Final Report* concluding, "We can now together affirm that the Church needs both a multiple, dispersed authority, with which all God's people are actively involved, and also a universal primate as servant and focus of visible unity in truth and love" (97-98). It would be a mistake, therefore, to conclude that the theory of "dispersed authority" *as it is explained in the Report prepared for Lambeth 1948* is somehow incompatible with the sort of authority that Roman Catholics know as being centralized in the papal primacy. Both churches would in a general way agree that the *sources* of authority are dispersed, although Anglicans (and some Roman Catholics) would want to add that its *exercise* is and should be more widely distributed throughout the church. (The 1964 General Convention of ECUSA, in fact, adopted a statement of "Levels of Authority within the Church" which describes very well such a distribution of the exercise of authority: *Journal, 312.*)

The possible compatibility of a universal primacy with the active involvement of "all God's people" in the exercise of authority, for which the ARCIC *Final Report,* calls, is certainly a question that Anglicans need to face directly, both as regards the role of bishops in the church as well as lay persons. That bishops have a particular responsibility for teaching the faith and promoting the church's unity is agreed both in the 1981 Primates' Statement (point 4) as well as in the Church of England's *Response* to the *Final Report,* (87), but the comparatively small place given in the *Final Report* to the role of the laity in the exercise of church authority is a problem of note. This is remarked in the Response of ECUSA:

> The development of the role of the laity in the councils of the Church, however, involving the sharing by lay men and women in the governance of the Church, has become one of the hallmarks and glories of Anglicanism. The practice of the

Episcopal Church in the United States from the beginning has included laity with a decisive voice and vote in diocesan, provincial, and General Conventions. This synodical structure has gradually commended itself throughout Anglicanism, and should not be lost. The role of the laity which has developed in our communion seems to involve considerably more than that envisioned in the *Final Report* for the place of the laity, even in the elucidations: ". . . that all the members of the Church share in the discovery of God's will, that the *sensus fidelium* is a vital element in the comprehension of God's truth . . ., and that all bear witness to God's compassion for mankind and his concern for justice in the world" (*Final Report* 73). Particularly in view of the increased attention currently being given to the ministry and vocation of the laity in both our Churches by reason of their Baptism, we urge careful consideration of this matter in future conversations. (26)

Thus the question remains for Anglicans: Beyond the dispersed *sources* of authority cited in the *Report* to Lambeth 1948, can the modern Anglican concept of a dispersed *exercise* of authority, especially as regards bishops and laity, be compatible with the kind of centralized papal authority that the *Final Report* proposes as an ideal? Or, from the Roman Catholic side, the question of a centralized authority in this context is put well by Fr. Cuthbert Rand: "Perhaps Anglicans need to be involved more fully in the process of stabilizing doctrine. For centuries they have been able to enjoy the fruits of the achievements of the early centuries and to criticize the errors and immobile uniformity of Rome while having its confident stability as a point of reference" (*One in Christ*, 1977, 194).

Petrine Texts

We turn now to the question of papal authority in the Petrine texts (The *Final Report*, paras. 2-9, which expand upon para. 24a and other references in Authority 1). The tenuous nature of these texts today is underlined by the comment of Heinrich Fries and Karl Rahner upon this section of the *Report:* "The unanimous view of today's Catholic exegetes is that on the basis of historical

criteria, the so-called Petrine passages of the New Testament cannot be understood in the sense of the institution of a universal
primacy for the post-apostolic Church and its equipment with
universal jurisdictional plenitude of power'' (*The Tablet*, 6 Nov.
1982, 1124; cf. Avery Dulles, S.J., in *The Resilient Church*, New
York, 1977, 117: there is ''no direct biblical proof for the institution of the papacy as a continuing office in the Church'').
However, in the commission's agreement that ''the New Testament attributes to Peter a special position among the Twelve,''
a ministry or leadership of service, the commission is in line with
what many other scriptural scholars and ecumenical commissions
are now saying (cf. *Peter in the New Testament*, ed. Raymond E.
Brown et al., Minneapolis, 1973). I too agree, and must add here
my own opinion that the failure to say this about the ''Petrine
ministry'' is one of the few shortcomings of the recent Lima Statement of the Faith and Order Commission of the World Council
of Churches in its own discussion of the ministry of the Twelve
(Ministry, paras. 9 and 10).

The *Final Report* goes on to reason, on grounds of analogy,
history, and theology, that the association of Peter's ministry with
Rome, taken together with the authoritative responsibility of the
Roman see in the early church and need for *koinonia* in the church
today, calls for the universal primacy of the Roman bishop in a
reunited church, modeled on the role of Peter, as a sign and
safeguard of such unity (cf. 64). In my opinion, such a conclusion should be acceptable to most Anglicans, so long as they are
not bound to regard it as dogmatically necessary in the wording
of Vatican Council I (*Pastor Aeternus* 1, DS 3055). I think, however,
that greater attention could have been given here to the history
of the exercise of papal primatial authority in the past: what went
wrong with it, when, and how, as well as to a case for a universal primacy in the church today based on pastoral and administrative grounds (for example, in a vigorous social critique of
society, such as John Paul II does give). When the English Roman
Catholic hierarchy's *Response*, for example, states that a universal primacy is ''intrinsic to the nature of the Church'' and ''of
necessity to the Church'' (14, para. 40), it would help to know
whether they discern this need upon the basis of an exegesis of
scriptural texts, a doctrine of divine providence, pragmatic

usefulness, or something else. The argument pursued in the *Final Report*, paragraph 7, that "it is possible to think that a primacy of the bishop of Rome is not contrary to the New Testament and is part of God's purpose . . . while admitting that the New Testament texts offer no sufficient basis for this," while quite weak as it is put in the *Report*, can be strengthened by the *Church of England Response's* observation "that the church of Rome was exercising leadership long before anyone is known to have sought to justify this authority by quoting Petrine texts from the New Testament. (The First Epistle of Clement shows this in operation already)"(91).

Divine Right

The next section of the *Final Report* (85-88; cf. 65; paras. 10-15) discusses *jus divinum,* or the language of "divine right" as applied to the authority of the bishop of Rome. It interprets this phrase as merely one way of describing the Roman primacy as being part of God's plan or design or purpose for the unity and *koinonia* of the church, under the guidance of the Holy Spirit and as more or less equivalent to the term *divine providence* (para. 13). Again there is the question of whether the commission is basing its argument solely on history, although in its own elucidation it claims its commendation of the Roman primacy "is a doctrinal statement" (76). The reservations in the *Church of England Response* to this point are noteworthy:

> Appeals to the working of the divine providence in history are open to more than one interpretation. . . . There would be a difficulty here if the argument were to be that the empirical history of the papacy is so remarkable that an unprejudiced mind would be bound to regard it as a sign of providence . . . . Moreover, some would feel that if the argument is to proceed on the basis of historical providence, more evidence must be provided that this development is in accordance with the inner and essential character of the Christian faith. . . . Such arguments appear more readily compelling to those who already possess the ministry in question, be it episcopacy or papacy, than to those who do not. (92-93)

Why, one may also ask, is not the historical *rejection* of the Roman primacy by so many churches itself an act of "divine providence"?

The difficulty of asserting that whatever happens in the church happens by God's design or providence, and thus by divine right, can be illustrated from the recent *New York Times*/CBS News Poll conducted on the eve of the 1985 Roman Catholic Synod of Bishops. This study, which had a margin of error plus or minus six percentage points, indicated that "68 percent of American Catholics now favor the use of artificial means of contraception, 52 percent favour the ordination of women as priests, 63 percent favor marriage for priests and 73 percent favor remarriage for divorced people" (25 November 1985 A7). On the critical question of women's ordination, Roman Catholic men were as supportive as Roman Catholic women, Roman Catholics in the 18-39 age range favoured it by sixty-eight per cent, and overall the development of support for it among American Roman Catholics has risen from twenty-nine per cent in 1974 to thirty-four per cent in 1979 to the present fifty-two per cent. Does such an historical development possess the authority of divine providence, or is divine right on this question possessed exclusively by the recent papal pronouncements against it? If the latter, then in what sense can papal authority here be said to be "expressing the mind of the church"? How does the pope consult and learn what is really the church's mind, or is it all — as one party at the 1985 Synod of Bishops asserted — essentially a "mystery"? And in spite of the overwhelming popular preferences indicated by this recent poll, at least for American Roman Catholics, the reason for the comparative silence of the Synod report on all these issues is estimated by the *New York Times* to be "a simple reason. Pope John Paul II has effectively ruled out change on any of them. Even bishops who disagree with the Pope privately are often reluctant to do so publicly, especially in Rome" (E. J. Dionne, Jr., 15 Dec. 1985, 24E). If this kind of authority is what we are asked to accept as papal divine right, I must reply that Anglicans cannot accept it and that we are amazed that so many wonderful Roman Catholic bishops and priests and laity are willing to tolerate it. But the same survey indicated that almost four out of every five Roman Catholics felt it possible to disagree with the present pope on such issues "and still be a good Catholic," so it may be simply that Roman Catholics — like Anglicans — are willing to live with the ambiguities they already have!

Such points notwithstanding, I do believe the overall thrust of this section of the *Final Report* can in principle be generally accepted by Anglicans (cf. the spectrum of present Roman Catholic opinion outlined in J. Michael Miller, *The Divine Right of the Papacy in Recent Ecumenical Theology*, Rome, 1980), so long as it is not interpreted as meaning that canonical communion with the Roman bishop is at present necessary in order to be recognized as a church, or that acceptance of all recent papal pronouncements *expressis verbis* is necessary for the restoration of communion between separated churches. The *Final Report* is unclear, however, when it observes (at the end of para. 12), ''The Second Vatican Council allows it to be said that a church out of communion with the Roman see may lack nothing from the viewpoint of the Roman Catholic Church except that it does not belong to the visible manifestation of full Christian communion which is maintained in the Roman Catholic Church.'' Did the Commission, especially its Roman Catholic members, believe this is the case with the Anglican communion? Is this all we ''lack''? If so, why have they not said this directly? If not, then why make the observation at all? Or, if the Commission was divided in its opinion about this, why give the impression of a false unanimity?

Jurisdiction

Jurisdiction is the subject of the next section (88-91, paras. 16-22), and it is defined as ''the authority or power necessary for the exercise of an office.'' Here the Anglican members of the Commission agree to the traditional Roman Catholic terms of ''universal, ordinary, and immediate'' to describe the jurisdiction of the bishop of Rome, the reasons given being that this jurisdiction ''is inherent in his office'' and must be such as to ''enable him to serve the unity and harmony of the *koinonia* as a whole and in each of its parts.'' To an explanation this simple I think there could be general Anglican assent. However, the term we would be more ready to use is *primus inter pares,* which is even described in the *Response* of the ECUSA as ''a concept which we know and accept,'' and I wonder why the Anglican members of the Commission were unable to gain its inclusion in the report, even if only to explain its apparent inadequacy? This latter term, though, is usually taken by us, as by the Orthodox, to imply a primacy more of honour than of jurisdiction, and, given the Roman Catholic church's apparent preference (under the present pope) in seeking an accord with the Orthodox East, I think we as Anglicans will watch closely to see whether the Orthodox are willing to accord any jurisdictional primacy at all to the Roman bishop. Certainly this was denied to him by the Orthodox in the international Anglican-Orthodox "Dublin" Agreed Statement of 1984 (para; 27; cf. 28). Perhaps, though, we should say that "honour" is not so important in the church, that something more than a nominal figurehead is needed, and that — especially today and for the foreseeable future — some limited kind of jurisdictional primacy is really necessary, i.e., something *more* than a *primus inter pares*. Nevertheless, I wonder whether the *Final Report*'s interpretation of "universal, ordinary, and immediate" in its ideal sort of papal jurisdiction will really be acceptable to the Roman Catholic church, especially to a pope such as John Paul II, and exactly what kind of restraints or safeguards could be introduced to ensure that this ideal would not be exceeded or reduced? One excess that would certainly need restriction is the papal provision of bishops to vacant sees, all but invariable in the western, Roman-controlled church only since the mid-fourteenth century, which prevents Roman Catholic bishops from being understood as "leaders" or "representatives" of their local churches in the full sense but rather unfortunately all too often casts them in popular eyes as mere puppets or clones or mouthpieces for the particular pope or apostolic delegate through whom their appointment has come. Even though local choice of bishops, by contrast, usually prevents the Anglican episcopate from appearing to have a "united front," and even though the method of episcopal appointment in the Church of England is seriously questioned elsewhere in the Anglican communion, still it seems certain that Anglicans would not be willing to accord to the pope the power to appoint their bishops nor reserve to him the right to sanction or withhold their consecrations.

The first sentence of the *Final Report*, paragraph 20, claims that "the scope of universal jurisdiction cannot be precisely defined canonically," but I suggest that some such limiting definition is precisely what most of the intelligent Catholic world wants. In fact, it is striking that ARCIC would make such a claim when, in a way not congenial to Anglicans, the tradition of Roman Catholic canon law codes on papal authority is one of rather precise definition with virtually no jurisdictional limits. In the new (1983) *Code*, for example, canons 338-341 specify that the Roman pontiff alone may convoke an ecumenical council, decide its business, preside over it in person or deputy, suspend or dissolve it, and promulgate its decrees, and these canons merely repeat with little change the provisions of canons 222, 227, and 228 of the earlier *Code*.

We also read in paragraph 20 that there are (should be?) ''moral limits'' to the exercise of universal papal jurisdiction, but what are they (in view of the present pope's treatment of the bishops and church of Holland, of Hans Küng, of the Jesuits, of sisters who disagree with the pope's position about abortion, the investigation of Archbishop Hunthausen of Seattle, the silencing of Leonardo Boff, the recall of Archbishop Milingo from Zambia to Rome, the disciplining of Charles Curran, and so on)? Who sets these limits (the pope himself?), and who enforces them (the pope? the SCDF?)? Without such limits clearly set in advance, the argument of this paragraph becomes circular, and I think it unlikely that Anglicans will agree that ''the universal primate has the right in special cases to intervene in the affairs of a diocese and to receive appeals from the decision of a diocesan bishop'' (para. 20). It is good to hear (in para. 21) that ''collegial and primatial responsibility for preserving the distinctive life of the local churches involves a proper respect for their customs and traditions, provided that these do not contradict the faith or disrupt communion,'' but who is to decide if the faith is contradicted or communion disrupted (the pope personally? the SCDF?)? My impression is that even most Roman Catholic thinkers today, and certainly most Anglicans, would want clearer limitations to papal jurisdiction than the Commission has provided in this section. The present occupant of the papal throne is generally perceived in the U.S.A., even by Roman Catholics themselves, as ''more conservative than they'' and as wishing ''the church to be more like what it was before Vatican II'' (*N.Y. Times* poll, 25 Nov. 1985, A7), and Anglicans join them in this concern. Surely some public and critical conflict in the church is salutary, and Anglicans would want to ensure that a strong and conservative pope could not arbitrarily suppress it. Even the moderate Pope Paul VI, in concluding the 1974 Synod of Bishops, rejected much of its work and took pains to emphasize that papal "intervention" within the college of bishops "cannot be reduced only to extraordinary circumstances" (*L'Osservatore Romano*, English edition, 7 Nov. 1974, 9). There would have to be jurisdictional room for a diversity of doctrinal opinion within an essential unity of faith, such as the 1931 Bonn Agreement between Anglicans and Old Catholics provides.

True, the *Final Report*, in paragraph 22, calls for the safeguarding of "theological, liturgical and other traditions" which Anglicans value, but these need to be spelled out very clearly and firmly. The papal claim to universal, ordinary, and immediate jurisdiction, for example, was held at Rome in the seventeenth and eighteenth centuries to include the power to suppress national episcopal hierarchies and the structures of national churches, such as that in Holland, and to convert their territories into missionary areas administered directly under the Curia. We would want to ensure that such decisions could no longer be made unilaterally from Rome, if at all, and the present pope's treatment of Dutch Catholicism does not encourage Anglicans to want to risk a similar handling for the Church of England. Recently the agreed statement on "Authority and Primacy in the Church" from the international Anglican-Old Catholic Theological Conference has put the concern in this way:

> The question is, whether it is possible to have a universal primacy in the Roman see without many of the powers which it has acquired over the centuries. It would seem that this could only come about by a carefully limited definition of the authority to be exercised by such a primate and by a constitutional arrangement that he must work within a conciliar setting and in collegiality with other bishops, bearing in mind that the highest authority lies with an ecumenical council.

We may note here the distinction between "powers" and "authority," but the statement on the whole is very close to the ideal of the ARCIC *Final Report*.

The *Final Report* itself, in defining "jurisdiction" as "authority *or power*" (88, emphasis added), has, perhaps unintentionally, equated two terms that are not identical and then described them as being the same. "Is there — in the Christian or any other community — a difference between authority and the legal power to compel obedience or to punish dissent? And if so, is it not the case that legal power may be exercised without authority — or that authority may be exercised apart from the compulsions of power?" asks the *Response* of ECUSA, and it concludes, "Yet the history of the church suggests that papal power has from time to time been exercised arbitrarily and that authority in the Church, misused, *can* stifle freedom of the Spirit. "Therefore the ECUSA *Response* calls for some system of restraints to be explored," lest primacy be exercised heteronomously, to the detriment rather than to the welfare of the body of Christ" (27). An example of such heteronomous exercise of papal authority/power in the view of a vast majority of Anglican bishops from the Episcopal church in the U.S.A., would be the present pope's demand to a group of twenty-three American Roman Catholic bishops on an *ad limina* visit to Rome on 5 September 1983 that they demonstrate their pastoral leadership "by withdrawing all support from individuals or groups who, in the name of progress, justice or compassion, or for any other alleged reason, promote the ordination of women to the priesthood" (*The Tablet,* 17 September 1983, 903). So long as it is possible for the universal primate to make such demands, regardless of the sentiments of the church in a particular region of the world, most Anglicans will not agree even in principle with the concessions about universal, ordinary, immediate jurisdiction made in the *Final Report* by ARCIC I.

What did the Commission make, I wonder, of the assertion of Vatican II, *Lumen Gentium* 22, that the pope has "full, supreme and universal power over the whole church, a power which he can always exercise unhindered"? What are Anglicans to make of the apparent requirement, reaffirmed both in Vatican II and in *Mysterium Ecclesiae*, that even the laity are expected to assent and submit, both in will and in mind, to the teachings of the Roman pontiff even when he is not speaking *ex cathedra?* Consider this text from Vatican II:

> In matters of faith and morals, the bishops speak in the name of Christ, and the faithful (*fideles*) are to accept (*concurrere*) their teaching and adhere (*adhaerere debent*) to it with a religious

assent (*obsequio*) of soul. This religious submission (*obsequium*) of will and of mind (*voluntatis et intellectus*) must be shown in a special way to the authentic teaching authority of the Roman pontiff, even when he is not speaking *ex cathedra*. (Dogmatic Constitution on the Church, *Lumen Gentium* 25, ed. Abbott, 48)

And what must Anglican bishops conclude about the demand placed upon every bishop of the Roman Catholic obedience to constantly agree with and defend not only the pope but even his opinions and teachings on virtually every question of doctrine? Consider these texts from the 1973 Vatican *Directory on the Pastoral Ministry of Bishops* (English trans., Ottawa, 1974, secs. 24 and 44, 18 and 26):

> In matters of faith and morals, the bishop considers it his duty to think with the Church and to agree with the Roman pontiff.

> A bishop also adheres in devoted and religious allegiance to the pope's ordinary magisterium, and by written and spoken word and other means of communication spreads, supports, and, if the need arises, defends it in his diocese.

Such demands seem confirmed in the present time by, for example, the present pope's commendation of Sts. Cyril and Methodius for having "submitted to (the pope's) judgement, in order to obtain his approval" (*Slavorum Apostoli*, 2 July 1985) and by the U.S. Apostolic Delegate's commendation of Archbishop Hunthausen of Seattle (after he had been affirmed following an investigation for liberal views) as having given "clear evidence of your loyalty to the Church and obedience to our Holy Father" (Archbishop Pio Laghi, *N.Y. Times*, 28 Nov. 1985, A14). Is this "obedience" the kind of papal jurisdictional authority that the gospel demands?

Infallibility

Considerable doubt has recently been cast upon the question of infallibility, not the least by recent Roman Catholic debate over research into its historical origins, which may not be so ancient or well founded as has been supposed (see, for example, my summary in *Anglican Theological Review* 58:3, July 1976, 387-390). The eminent Roman Catholic historian Brian Tierney has carefully concluded:

> There is no convincing evidence that papal infallibility formed any part of the theological or canonical tradition of the Church before the thirteenth century; the doctrine was invented in the first place by a few dissident Franciscans because it suited their convenience to invent it; eventually, but only after much initial reluctance, it was accepted by the papacy because it suited the convenience of the popes to accept it. (*Origins of Papal Infallibility, 1150-1350*, Leiden, 1972, p. 281)

Yet, at the official level, this doctrine is still dogma for the Roman Catholic church. "Without infallibility, immediately the most elementary truths of our faith begin to collapse," Pope John Paul II is reported to have said to the bishops of Germany in May of 1980 as he congratulated them on how they dealt with Hans Küng. He also then said that the church needs "a particular certainty about the faith she holds, and we should be profoundly fearful lest our belief in the gift of Christ which guarantees that faith, namely infallibility, be cast in doubt" (*National Catholic Reporter*, 26 February 1982, 28; *The Tablet*, 31 May 1980, 538). Infallibility is certainly the most difficult problem faced in the *Final Report*, and it is noteworthy that on this very point the *Response* of the English Roman Catholic hierarchy says it is "convinced that the Commission has come very close to agreement on the critical issue" (12. para. 34). Anglicans will generally agree with this section of the *Final Report* (91-98, paras. 23-33) when it says that the church as a whole, enabled by the Holy Spirit, is "witness, teacher and guardian of the truth," and that "doctrinal decisions made by legitimate authority must be consonant with the community's faith as grounded in Scripture and interpreted by the mind of the Church, and that no teaching authority can add new revelation to the original apostolic faith" (para. 23), and that "the Church can in a matter of essential doctrine make a decisive judgement which becomes part of its permanent witness" (para. 24), and that, in a united church there will be a need "for a universal primate who, presiding over the *koinonia*, can speak with authority in the name of the Church," and that through his agency (or that of a universal or ecumenical council) "the Church can make a decisive judgement in matters of faith" (para. 26). Here, then, is a large measure of agreement that I think would be accorded by Anglicans, but I think there will be considerable dissent from the Commission's assertion that by such a judgement error is excluded (last sentence of para. 26; cf. *Authority* Venice, 62, para. 19). The *Final Report* is not entirely clear whether by this assertion the Commission is intending to give an affirmative reply to the question it earlier raised in paragraph 23, "whether there is a special ministerial gift of discerning the truth and of teaching bestowed at crucial times on one person." Is there or is there not? Why not give a straight-forward answer to the question posed?

A related question is whether the Roman Catholic doctrine of infallibility is really concerned with "truth" or with "certitude," and here the *Response* of the Church of England is especially cogent:

> The Roman Congregation for the Doctrine of the Faith (*Observations* BIII 3) has criticized the view of the Roman Catholic members of ARCIC by insisting that infallibility "refers immediately not to truth but to certitude." This seems to say that the concept of "infallibility" is concerned with the psychological problem of assurance about truth rather than with doctrinal truth itself. This point may illustrate the fact of diversity of view on the Roman Catholic side. The interpretation here sponsored by the Congregation seems to diminish rather than to increase the divide from Anglican understanding of the relation of teaching authority to the sacred tradition of faith. (95)

With such a criticism, also, the English Roman Catholic hierarchy apparently agrees, for in the infallibility section of its *Response* it urges, "The magisterium is exercised for the strengthening of faith and its infallible exercise brings a certitude that enables the faithful to adhere more serenely to that faith" (12, para. 34). Does this mean, Anglicans will of course want to ask, that the Roman Catholic church really has "certitude" concerning only the two or three doctrines that have been proclaimed infallibly?

In this section of the *Final Report*, the Commission rightly sees that the question of Anglicans (and, I respectfully suggest, of most of the thinking Christian world, even including many Roman Catholics) is whether such authoritative decisions (of the bishop of Rome) are automatically preserved in advance from error or whether they ultimately acquire their authority from the recognition, reception, and assent of the church at large (para. 31, first sentence; para. 29, last sentence). Anglicans cannot accept the claim that "his formal decisions can be known to be wholly assured before their reception by the faithful" (96-97, para. 31, 94-95, para. 29). The Commission rightly cites as an example here the way in which the Marian dogmas were proclaimed in advance as binding (para. 30), and it might have added some comment upon the way these dogmas condemn all who disagree with them. (The proposal of Fr. Avery Dulles, that the anathemas attached to these two dogmas be lifted against those outside the Roman Catholic church who do not believe them, has never been formally accepted: *Origins* 4:27, 26 Dec. 1974, 417-421.)

I suppose the ARCIC I Commission was trying to be faithful to the teaching of both churches on this difficult question of infallibility, but I just wonder if the line of disagreement is too finely drawn on this point in paragraph 29, and if it is not possible to say (as is hinted in the middle paragraph 25) that such decisions of the Roman bishop can be seen as having a sort of "final" authority when they are first announced, simply because they are formally proclaimed, but that such authority is of course inevitably tested in the process of the church's reception? Thus, might it not be possible, in fact is it not the case, that some authoritative decisions of the bishop of Rome have *not* recieved an authoritative reception in the church at large? If reception clearly has a part to play in the ultimate recognition of authoritative *conciliar* definitions, as the *Final Report* hints at many places and as recent historical studies increasingly show to have actually been the case, then why could this not be true also of papal definitions? The *Response* of the Church of England observes:

> If it took three centuries for the Canon of the New Testament to be finally received, and half a century for the Council of Nicaea, should we expect any papal utterances to be accepted

overnight? . . . The Orthodox Churches are as committed to the doctrine of the Church's infallibility as is the Roman Catholic Church, but they equally affirm that the power of such utterance is a gift of the Holy Spirit which, when given, demands recognition and cannot be presumed upon beforehand in virtue of office. (88-89)

Very few Roman Catholic theologians still contend that the Roman bishop's authoritative decisions are *guaranteed* in advance to be free from error, and I respectfully wonder whether the intellectual credibility of this claim was really faced directly by the Commission, at least in its published report. The Roman Catholic members may have felt the need to give public affirmation to their church's official position on so sensitive a question, but who can they cite in support of it? Do they think the Eastern Orthodox will agree to this? Surely this question, the only one on which the Commission does not claim to have reached substantial agreement (para. 29), needs to be aired charitably, in open, published dialogue, rather than covered over for the sake of ecumenical diplomacy. If this was the only major Anglican disagreement with the official Roman Catholic position on papal authority, then we should want to know which published writings led the Roman Catholic members of the commission to conclude that this point alone could not change in their ideal vision of the papacy of the future.

There are still other problems with paragraph 29, one of them being the "rigorous conditions" that it says a judgement of the Roman bishop must satisfy in order to have the advance guarantee of freedom from error. The Commission says that *some* of these conditions that it cites were "laid down by the First Vatican Council" but it does not say which of them were, nor does it reveal the source of the others that it gives. This is puzzling. Then the *Final Report* goes on to state that "when it is plain that all these conditions have been fulfilled, Roman Catholics conclude that the judgement is preserved from error and the proposition true." But the use of "conclude" in this sentence is ambiguous; does it mean that *all* Roman Catholics *do* conclude this (and hence do actually believe it), or *must* conclude this (even if they do *not* believe it), or *ought* to conclude this? I can certainly cite some who *do* not! And paragraph 29 also seems to employ special pleading at the outset in its claim, with example, that "a service of preserving the Church from error has been performed by the bishop of Rome as universal primate both within and outside the synodal process." This may at times have been true, but would the commission want to lead us to believe that the bishop of Rome has never *mis*led the church into *error*? In Elucidation 3 to Authority I, 71, where perhaps less was at stake, the Commission was ready to agree that ecumenical councils have sometimes erred, and to cite examples. But since the Commission is concerned to draw a parallel of papal to conciliar decisions in paragraph 26, then why does it not admit in paragraph 29 that *papal* decisions also can at times be erroneous? Are we to conclude that the authority of the pope is somehow "less erroneous" than that of a council? For me, the Anglican members of the commission have too readily accepted a special pleading for the Roman bishop on this point.

Finally, in paragraph 32, the Commission treats the term *infallibility* itself, agreeing that it "is a term applicable unconditionally only to God, and that to use it of a human being, even in highly restricted circumstances, can produce many misunderstandings." And the Commission explains that this is why, "in stating our belief in the preservation of the Church from error we have avoided using the term." Well and good, most Anglicans and probably many Roman Catholics would say, but then what does the Commission want us to conclude? That this term is *not* necessary, or *is* necessary, for Anglicans, Eastern Orthodox, Lutherans, etc., as a dogmatic requirement in the reunion of these churches with the Roman Catholic church? This question is not directly answered, although it may be significant that infallibility is *not* in the list of items (which does include "universal primacy") that the Commission has specified in its introduction as necessary for "common acceptance" before "full visible communion" is achieved (8, last sentence of para. 9). One is left wondering whether the Commission is in effect proposing that the term be dropped in official Roman Catholic usage now, or whether for some other reason the Commission chose not to reveal its mind on this point. The Commission does recognize that "ascription to the bishop of Rome of infallibility under certain conditions has tended to lend exaggerated importance to all his statements," but if this is so, then should the word be retained?

And yet, need even infallibility be a barrier to the kind of model for unity towards which Anglicans and Roman Catholics should work? John Macquarrie does "not see any way in which this doctrine could ever become acceptable to Anglicans and Protestants" (*Christian Unity and Christian Diversity*, London, 1975, 100), although he does believe "we could all come together on indefectibility." ARCIC does not believe that infallibility can be reduced to the concept of indefectibility, at least in the view of the *Church of England Response* (94; cf. ARCIC *Final Report* 62, para. 18), but it is worthy of note that ARC/ Canada has in fact reached an agreement upon infallibility that does precisely this (cf. *Journal of Ecumenical Studies* 19:1, Winter 1982, 85-93). If Roman Catholics retain the term (concept?) *infallibility* and Anglicans *indefectibility*, though, there is still in Macquarrie's view the possibility of unity with a pope because "it could well be the case that the degree of his authority would be different in different parts of the united church" (101). Certainly if the Orthodox are not expected to accept papal infallibility in a reunion with Rome, neither should Anglicans or western Protestants generally.

The *Response* of ECUSA, however, must be given the final place in these reflections upon the question of infallibility:

The *Final Report* as well as other recent ecumenical statements on the subject of authority raises and deals with the crucial issue (of which infallibility is one clearly defined instance) whether there is an antecedently available "correct answer" for every issue which engages or confronts the Church — an answer which can be more or less automatically "discovered" by resort to certain institutional procedures. For example, in the *Final Report* it is said that "Anglicans do not accept the guaranteed possession of such a gift of divine assistance in judgement necessarily attached to the office of the bishop of Rome by virtue of which his formal decisions can be known to be wholly assured before their reception by the faithful" (*Final Report* 96). In the ecumenical movement a great deal depends, however, on further and more thorough exploration of this sort of issue. If, in principle, we "already know," then plurality of opinion and practice and debate may, in certain circumstances, be tolerable contingencies, but apart from the function of raising questions for authority to settle, they have no licit role in the Church's uncovering or articulation of the truth by which it lives.

If, by contrast, it is not necessarily the case that we "already know," then — despite the embarrassment which may be occasioned for a church by the appearance of uncertainty and the absence of a "united front" — disagreement and debate may turn out to be vehicles by which the Holy Spirit brings the Church to itself and opens the way to a grasp of truth which corrects and deepens the initial positions of all parties to a discussion. To address issues such as these, however, it is necessary to go beyond the present scope of the treatment of authority in the *Final Report* and to ask about the differing shapes that authority can take, about the relationships among them, and, indeed, about the proper function of authority itself. (28-29)

Conclusion

All these critical points, of course, are comparatively minor in comparision to the positive achievement of the *Final Report* as a whole. The overall thrust, direction, and implications of the Commission's findings cannot be denied, and the remaining questions now cry out for solution. Unity with the Roman Catholic church now can be a major ecumenical priority and even possibility on a basis that begins with this *Report*, and I note with approval the Commission's hope (99) to carry along with it not only Roman Catholics and Anglicans but "all Christians" so that what it has done may also "contribute to the visible unity of all the people of God." Surely, after this report, it is now time for those churches such as the Anglican, Old Catholic, even Lutheran, and perhaps Orthodox, whose ecumenical pilgrimages have come to point more in the direction of some sort of authoritative universal primacy for the church as a whole, to sit down together with their Roman Catholic friends and spell out together the contours and limits that such a primacy might have. Perhaps the Congregation for the Doctrine of the Faith should actively enter these dialogues, if it is indeed, as Cardinal Ratzinger says, "the See of Peter speaking through one of its central organs, not indeed in a definitive manner, yet with an authority which carries more weight in the Church than a merely academic publication about the question would" (*Insight*, 1:3, March 1983, 3). Agreement about an authoritative primacy for these churches, at least on a theoretical level, is now within reach. Is a papal primacy, along the contours of the *Final Report* and with the safeguards that I have suggested, desirable? Lambeth 1988 will give the definitive Anglican reply, but what will the Roman Catholic church say?

The Response of the Sacred Congregation for the Doctrine of the Faith

The Standing Commission on Ecumenical Relations of ECUSA has adopted extensive procedural guidelines for official evaluation of and response to agreements, such as the *Final Report*, coming from ecumenical dialogues, a process that involves the active and extensive participation of lay persons, and it was our respectful hope that the process of consideration in our sister Roman Catholic church would also have significant lay participation. What no Anglicans will receive, however, is observations and an evaluation from anything like a Sacred Congregation for the Doctrine of the Faith, and in conclusion I want to suggest what its observations may say about papal authority for Anglicans. At first I was quite annoyed, as were many Christians of both churches, that this "Sacred Congregation" apparently succeeded unilaterally in delaying the release of the *Report* for over two months after the agreed date so that it could release its own commentary at the same time. The SCDF is, in the words of its former secretary Jerome Cardinal Hamer, "the auxiliary of the ordinary magisterium of the Holy Father, with the mission of taking care that the profession of faith be the guide of all the activity of the Church" and it "never issues an important document which is not approved by the pope and whose publication he himself has not ordered" (*La Documentation Catholique*, no. 1691, 1 February 1976, approved English translation, 7). And so, in so far as the SCDF commentary was an extension of the pope's Petrine office, divine right, and universal jurisdiction, and an example of official Roman Catholic response to ecumenical agreements, I thought to myself, Anglicans want no part of it. Many Roman Catholics had similar feelings, one not atypical response labelling it as "devoid of any feeling of sympathy and understanding for the final product of the Commission's labours . . . a frosty Roman document . . . intrinsically, in its reasoning and procedure, a rather disappointing piece of work" (L. Bermejo, S.J., in *Bijdragen* 44:1983, 27).

But as I have reflected upon the various remarks of Cardinal Ratzinger in connection with it, and upon the SCDF commentary, I want to say that I have come to appreciate them, although not on most points to agree with them. I do not see Cardinal Ratzinger or the SCDF as necessarily opposing the cause of ecumenical unity, and hopefully they were not attempting to prejudice the response of the Roman Catholic church in advance. No, I see them as raising important questions and observing that the ARCIC *Final Report* does not quite reach the officially defined Roman Catholic doctrinal formularies that it has inherited from its recent past. (Indeed, most of the references in the SCDF document are made to recent Roman Catholic sources, from Trent to Pope John Paul II, and seldom to the scriptures or the ancient common traditions.) As I understand the Roman Catholic process of authority, it is not the business of the SCDF to suggest that these formularies should now (on the basis of contemporary scriptural, historical, and theological studies) be changed; that is the business of commissions like ARCIC, and of professional theologians who advise the bishops, and then ultimately of the bishops themselves (including the pope) in exercise of their *magisterium*. Even though there is much internal Roman Catholic debate as to the relative teaching authority of the pope, the curia, the SCDF, the international Synod of Bishops, regional episcopal conferences, local bishops, and theologians, I as an Anglican can appreciate this official concern for authoritative expression of doctrine in the Roman Catholic church, a concern that to some extent we lack. And Cardinal Ratzinger himself has insisted that "the dialogue so happily begun should continue," as does the SCDF "since there are sufficient grounds for thinking its continuation will be fruitful." So I think Anglicans should now watch the Roman Catholic process of authority go to work: for Roman Catholic theologians to reflect and then advise the bishops, and for the Roman Catholic episcopal college (with the pope as its head) to consider whether or not the ARCIC *Final Report* is sufficiently consonant with the "substance" of Roman Catholic faith for a significant "next step" to be taken. Perhaps for the future, once an international ecumenical dialogue reaches such critical questions, the SCDF should work more closely at every stage with the Vatican Unity Secretariat, in order that ecumenical partners (such as the Anglican communion) not be misled as to what the Roman Catholic position actually is. I am no less hopeful about the ultimate reception of the *Final Report* in the Roman Catholic church than in my own, but the way the process of the Roman Catholic response is handled will be one clear indication of the future direction of papal authority, at least under the present occupant of the papal throne. Will this direction, will his direction, be the direction in which we want to move?

Catholicity and Authority in Anglican-Lutheran Relations

S. W. Sykes

The premise of this paper is that authority *in* the church must be related to the catholicity *of* the church; authority in the church must proceed from the very nature of the church. In affirming this we simply re-emphasize the importance of a proposition of the much-quoted report to the 1948 Lambeth Conference on the unity of the Anglican communion. Here it is affirmed that authority in the church

> is single in that it is derived from a single Divine source, and reflects within itself the richness and historicity of the divine Revelation, the authority of the Eternal Father, the incarnate Son, and the life-giving Spirit (see the Appendix).

To say that authority in the church is *derived from* God is to make a stupendous claim; in sociological terms it constitutes an apparently unchallengeable legitimation. And yet, as is all too obvious, it is practically intolerable for Christians to claim that ''what the Church does God does.'' The notion of *derivation from* God requires careful elucidation. The direction of that elucidation is already given by the Lambeth report, with its reference to ''the historicity of the divine Revelation.'' There is, I shall argue, both a christological *and* a pneumatological element in the nature of the church, which offer important perspectives upon, and qualifications to, the idea that authority is derived from God.

Authority is related to the nature of the church, and thus to its catholicity. At this point the way in which the word *catholic* is commonly used may well mislead us. Anglicans have accepted into everyday speech the term *Anglo-catholic* to designate those Anglicans with a discernible leaning towards ''catholicism,'' whether in its Roman or (less commonly) Eastern Orthodox form. Thus it has become common to believe that the appeal to catholicity of the church must be an appeal to traditions preserved in those communions. One hears it said, for example, that the

"catholicity of the church" is a ground for opposing the ordination of women to the priesthood. In polemical situations this
misuse of language is understandable; but it is not for that reason
tolerable. It is, in fact, a short hand for an appeal to the practice
of the greater part of Christendom — by no means a negligible
appeal when correctly phrased. But a moment's reflection will
prompt most thoughtful Christians to pause before denying by
implication that the Protestant churches also participate in the
one, holy, catholic and apostolic church. They, too, have a theory
as to the nature of true catholicity which it would be intolerable
to dismiss by verbal sleight of hand. Anglicans, moreover, have
every reason to remember that there is no standard account of
Anglicanism which can permit such usage. The purpose of the
present paper is to focus on the ambiguities of the notion of
catholicity, by means of a critical examination of its use in the
recent dialogues between Anglicans and Lutherans. The discipline
of exposing oneself to a less familiar range of connotations in the
word *catholic* is salutory, not least because it brings Anglicans face
to face with a sister tradition of theological depth and subtlety,
which, in England at least, Anglicans have been more than a little
prone to overlook.

John Howe in his *Highways and Hedges* has rightly draw attention to the fact that the American Episcopal church's careful
negotiations with Lutheran churches is inadequately known in
the Anglican communion outside the U.S.A. and Canada.
Furthermore he offers it as his considered and dispassionate opinion, that "despite the notable progress with Rome it seems prob-
able that common ground there may be less than the Anglicans
have with Lutherans."[1] On the see-saw view of ecumenical relations, according to which tilting towards a Protestant church
entails tilting away from the Roman Catholic and Eastern Orthodox churches, a proposition of this kind would be calculated to
inspire anxiety in the breasts of those most concerned with the
progress of dialogues with the latter. The impact of this grossly
oversimplified model is dissipated as soon as one is exposed to
the quality of Roman Catholic-Lutheran bilaterals, many of whose
conclusions are of considerable moment for Anglican-Roman
Catholic relations. Nonetheless the purpose of this paper is to
review critically the results hitherto of Anglican-Lutheran

bilaterals, and to propose some improvements to them which relate to the issue of catholicity, thus directly to authority in the church.

The procedure I have adopted is first to review the nature of Anglican-Lutheran relations *de facto*. This starting point has been chosen because it is my belief that the way in which Anglicans and Lutherans approach each other is importantly different from the way in which Anglicans have dealings with Roman Catholics, and that these differences can only be elucidated when we take cognizance of certain conditioning factors in our respective histories as denominations. Then, secondly, I shall examine the treatment of catholicity in the reports of the bilaterals hitherto, comparing them briefly with other bilaterals in which Anglicans have been involved. And, finally, the dogmatic problems of catholicity for the whole ecumenical movement will be outlined, and some particular conclusions drawn relating to future Anglican-Lutheran relations.

But first a word must be said about two inherent ambiguities in the notion of catholicity which will be important for what follows. In the first place it is exceedingly difficult to separate the unity from the catholicity of the church. In its original meaning of ''general'' or ''universal'' the word, *katholikos*, lent the phrase, *the catholic church* a sense of totality, that is, of non-particularity. ''Universal,'' of course, contains the numeral one within it. Ignatius, who is the first to use ''catholic'' as a predicate of the church, sees its universality as rooted in the sole spiritual lordship of Christ. Much, therefore, that is said about the catholicity of the church is inseparable from its unity.

The second ambiguity is contained in a change which overtook the term in the early centuries. The idea of the universality of the church spread throughout the world (so *Martyrdom of Polycarp* 19.2) came to acquire a new connotation, that of the great church in contrast to the small heretical sects. The fact that deviations from othodoxy were always local phenomena was held to be proof of their non-catholicity. To this idea was added the notion of universality in time, which is also linked to the eternity of the second person of the Trinity. Catholic Christianity is thus, according to Gregory the Great, the consistent faith of the church both before and after Christ, the proclamation of the mystery of the Holy Trinity.

Avery Dulles, who reviews this and subsequent material in the history of Christian theology, has schematized the multiple aspects of catholicity as follows: catholicity from above, rooted in the Father's self-communication through the Word and the Spirit; catholicity from below in the elevation of the whole of nature and humanity; catholicity conceived quantitatively or horizontally; and catholicity in time.[2] These fourfold dimensions of catholicity lead directly to a discussion of those institutional or sacramental structures which sustain them. The notion of catholicity is, thus, rich and complex, and the combination and interpretation of spiritual and frankly empirical elements give ample scope for diversity of interpretation and for controversy. In what follows we shall draw upon the multiplicity of aspects of catholicity, and return for some guidance in the final section to the discussion of the source of catholicity in the divine revelation.

Anglican-Lutheran Relations, *de facto*

"Anglicans and Lutherans agree in their basic approach concerning the understanding of the Church." The leading proposition of this section on "The Nature of the Church" in the report of the Anglo-Lutheran Regional Commission, *Anglican-Lutheran Dialogue,* agreed at Helsinki in August/September 1982, is a forthright and unqualified statement of "substantial agreement" between sister churches on a matter which closely concerns the fundamentals of the faith. Yet at the same time it could not be said that this and the other statements of consensus or agreement in the same document, leading to the bold affirmation that "there are no longer any serious obstacles on the way towards the establishment of full communion between our two Churches," have been accorded the attention which has greeted the much more obstacle-strewn *Final Report* of the Anglican-Roman Catholic International Commission (ARCIC) of the same year.

There are, doubtless, commonsense reasons why the dialogues with Lutherans are commonly accorded by Anglicans lower prestige, which have to do with size and geographical separation. But it is also possible, precisely because of their respective histories and instinctive outlooks, that they take too much for granted and thus unconsciously impair the impact of agreement over what they already share. There are, it may be suggested, three major ways in which the common experience of Anglicans and Lutherans might cause a deficiency specifically in respect of their grasp of aspects of the catholicity of the church.

In the first place both Lutherans and Anglicans lack organs for the preservation of doctrinal coherence even within their own boundaries. Such a consciousness will inevitably colour the way in which it is felt a plausible understanding of catholicity can be advanced. Thus, for example, in the U.S.A. the Lutheran-Episcopal Dialogue (LED) initially involved on the Lutheran side representatives from three autonomous bodies, the American Evangelical Lutheran Church, the American Lutheran Church, the Lutheran Church in America, and the Lutheran Church-Missouri synod. The joint statement (LED II) issued in 1980 contained a dissenting statement on the declaration concerning the authority of scripture from the representatives of the last named body.[3] Although the American Lutheran Church and the Lutheran Church of America have now entered into a process of unification, the fact is that even in a single country the Lutheran presence is likely to be a federation of autonomous bodies.

In Europe the problem is somewhat magnified. Here the folk-church idea has encouraged Lutherans to develop both separate national churches with their own liturgical and doctrinal identities, and also, in Germany, regional churches constituting individual variations on the Reformed-Lutheran polarity. The Leuenberg Concordat (1973), and the continuing process of convergence deriving from it, constitute a series of complex commitments which Anglicans quickly encounter in any dealings with Lutherans alone.

Anglicanism is somewhat better served regionally by the coherence of its provincial structure, but like the Lutheran churches it lacks an international body which can make decisions binding upon all its autonomous parts. The Lambeth conference of bishops is a consultative body, with the authority of influence but not of coercion. Provincial autonomy can lead to complications and embarassment, as for example when the decision to ordain women to the priesthood in certain provinces overlooked the question of relationship with the churches, such as the Old Catholic church, with which full communion had been established at an earlier date and in different circumstances.

As things stand at the moment, therefore, both Anglican and Lutheran churches lack clear or coherent means for the preservation of unity even within their own boundaries. *De facto* Anglican-Lutheran relations are constrained by the absence of what one might term "organs or instruments of catholicity."

In the second place both Anglicans and Lutherans have to acknowledge the fact of internal diversity. Although it is usually Anglicans who speak more frequently and loudly of doctrinal comprehensiveness, in reality both have "high church" and "low church" parties; both experience the tension between critical liberalism and conservatism; both have histories which include the manipulation of ecumenical relations by one section of the respective churches for internal ecclesiastico-political ends. Agreement between the two denominations on doctrinal matters has always to confront the sometimes hidden agenda of disagreement and conflict inside each body. The problem of the episcopate for example, which has figured so largely in discussion and controversy between Anglicans and Lutherans, has been complicated because of the internal pluralism of both churches. But, as has so often been observed, diverging views on the Christian ministry and sacraments are invariably related to different ecclesiologies, and sometimes even to different understandings of the nature of revelation. The interpretation of internal diversity in both churches in very complex. Many individuals in both bodies will know of the disturbing experience of discovering, in argument with a fellow member, a lack of agreement about the fundamental character of the church. The question immediately arises, How is this related to denominational identity? How can it be that one Anglican finds that, despite being in a state of unquestionable organisational unity with another Anglican, they utterly disagree about how God has revealed himself in and through his church?

Although this state of affairs is not uncommon among Lutherans, Anglicans have a longer and perhaps more bitter and overt history of internal strife. The reason for this has closely to do with the peculiar status, and gradual demotion, of the Thirty-nine Articles, as compared with the Augsburg Confession. The Augustana endures as a contemporary focus of unity for Lutherans, as the heated discussion of its possible "recognition" by the Roman Catholic church revealed. No such discussion of the Thirty-nine Articles would be possible for world Anglicanism, if for no other reason than at least because it is not even mentioned in the constitutions of some Anglican provinces.

Although the symbols of doctrinal catholicity which Anglicans have strongly retained, the Apostles' and Nicene Creeds, are among the most universally acknowledged, they are less articulated than is the Augustana and are thus less capable of being used in contemporary doctrinal dispute. As is well known, in practice Anglicans rely on their ministerial order and their prayer books for the contemporary achievement of unity. But the unity and coherence of these books, which are being constantly revised in every part of the Anglican communion, are more often asserted than demonstrated. Inevitably the weight which Anglicans place upon ministerial order as the one consistently unifying factor (that is, at least, before the ordination of women to the priesthood) increases to fill the vacuum. To surmount internal diversity Anglicans are virtually compelled to celebrate the bare fact of orderly succession, even in the absence of any single (or coherent) theory about the apostolic office.

Thirdly, it is a fact that neither the Anglican not the Lutheran churches can claim anything like geographical universality. As was mentioned above, part of the use to which the concept of "catholicity" was put was intended to distinguish the size, distribution, and internal agreement of orthodoxy as compared with the smallness and parochial character of heretical movements. Evaluation of this geographical claim may legitimately vary, but merely to deny its relevance is unrealistic, especially in a context in which the communications revolution continually reinforces the claim of the largest bodies to public exposure. The Lutheran churches constitute a somewhat larger fraction of the world Christian population than does the Anglican communion, though the Anglican communion is perhaps more widely (and thinly) spread. Both are very closely connected with patterns of immigration and imperial expansion. Both have to make good their respective ecclesiologies against the knowledge that world Christianity is predominantly non-Protestant. In other words, both Anglicanism and Lutheranism look, on an international scale, like highly parochial forms of Christianity.

This situation is apparently not at all threatening to experienced apologists. Richard Hooker advanced in his *Laws of Ecclesiastical Polity* (1593) a justification for the co-existence of autonomous national or regional churches such as the churches of Rome, Corinth, Ephesus, England, Sweden, and so forth, geographically distinct and with their own indigenous forms of church government, but constituting a unity through their "mutual fellowship and society one with another."[4] Fellowship in this case implies that each church worships one and the same Lord, confesses one and the same faith, and performs one and the same baptism. Unfortunately the theory, apart from its negation of the universal claims of the Roman Catholic church, created a host of anomalies, such as the existence of an episcopal Church of Scotland on the geographical territory of the (Presbyterian) Church of Scotland, and utterly broke down through the wholesale pluralism of the denominations in countries settled by European immigrants, such as Australia and North America.

Lutheran apologists generally laid heavier stress on doctrinal purity. The claim of Lutheranism, despite the unfortunate accident of its particular name, is that it represents the truth of the gospel in proclamation and sacrament. Building on the celebrated *satis est* of Article VII of the *Confessio Augustana* ("it is sufficient for the true unity of the Christian church that the gospel be preached in conformity with a pure understanding of it and that the sacraments be administered in accordance with the divine word"), the threat of parochialism is made subordinate to assurance of the possession of truth. Numbers and geographical spread become irrelevant. Inevitably Roman Catholic critics (mis)perceive Lutheranism as teaching that the true church is invisible, and composed only of true believers; that God is concerned only for the salvation of individuals, with the church occupying a subordinate role as the fallible, though necessary means.

Neither apology is intrinsically unjustified; but neither apology precisely meets the charge of parochialism. It is, of course, open to any sect to claim that it, and it alone, teaches the truth. But St. Augustine's demand of the Donatist, Where is the *evidence* of your catholicity? is not easily put out of mind. Anglicans and Lutherans, when in large national majorities, sometimes implicitly make the same demand of some small minority church or sect on their own territories. The claim of a national or folk church to *be* the catholic church of the nation, impressive though it may seem inside the boundaries of that nation, is not validated by the verdict of the whole church. With the (comparatively recent) growth of a sense of global unity that discomforting fact increasingly matters, or should matter, to Anglicans and Lutherans. The universality or catholicity of the church is, or ought to be, an actual matter of some unease.

In making this observation I am attempting to place my finger upon what one might call the social psychology of two medium-sized denominations. Anglicans ought to be conscious of the fact that the universal spread of Anglicanism coincides closely with the exigencies of the British Empire (though the presence of French and Japanese interpreters at the 1978 Lambeth Conference indicates a certain linguistic expansion). Lutherans ought to be conscious of the lack of internal consensus among churches of Lutheran origin. Both Anglicans and Lutherans have established contacts with denominationally near neighbours which complicate their efforts at achieving a broader consensus. For both, therefore, the catholicity of the church is a covert problem, about which they have, or ought to have, a bad conscience. It is in this conviction that the evidence of the dialogues will be subject to examination.

Catholicity in the Anglican-Lutheran Dialogues

The ALIC Report (Anglican-Lutheran International Conversation, 1973; also known as the *Pullach Report*) affirms Anglican and Lutheran adherence to the Nicene characterization of the church as one, holy, catholic, and apostolic. Concerning the unity of the church, the Report envisages, as a goal, "full communion" or "full altar and pulpit fellowship," acceptable to individual members of the churches and supported by "structures which will encourage such fellowship and its acceptance."[5] The goal is phrased in such a way as to be the aim of the whole church, not just the interim intention of Anglicans and Lutherans. But because the report is naturally concerned with the relations between Anglicans and Lutherans the only structures supporting unity to be considered are those which are either agreed, or in dispute between two sides. The most obvious structure, a universal papacy, is overlooked, despite the fact that both sides acknowledge in their other dialogues that the unity of the churches requires its consideration.

The catholicity of the church is treated in the same way. The fullness of the truth of the gospel is committed to the church, which must engage in universal mission to every national race and social class. All aspects of human life are under the dominion of Christ. Anglicans and Lutherans are warned against the deployment of party slogans such as "Catholic fullness" and "the pure doctrine of the gospel." "Fullness, universality, and wholeness," the report concludes, "belong only to the one body of Christ."[6]

The 1982 Report of the Anglican-Lutheran Regional Commission affirms the exposition of the "marks" of the church contained in the *Pullach Report*, and further agrees with ARCIC's description of *koinonia*, which speaks of the church as "the community of those reconciled with God and with each other because it is the community of those who believe in Jesus Christ and are justified through God's grace."[7] By implication this recent agreement of Anglicans and Lutherans is conscious that the mutual recognition for which it argues is only a stage in a much wider process, involving both Orthodox and Roman Catholics. But there is certain danger in the way in which the specific matter of catholicity is treated, on which danger we must now focus.

The interim goal of "full communion" was further defined by the international working group set up to provide an overview of Anglican-Lutheran relations as follows:

> By full communion we here understand a relationship between two distinct churches or communions. Each maintains its own autonomy and recognizes the catholicity and apostolicity of the other, and each believes the other to hold the essentials of the Christian faith.[8]

But what is meant by "catholicity" in this statement? To interpret catholicity in such a way as to offer no challenge to the indefinite perpetuation of denominational autonomy seems to suggest that the Christian church may have catholicity without the inconvenience of unity. A recent report to the General Synod of the Church of England entitled *The Anglican-Lutheran, Anglican-Reformed and Anglican-Orthodox Dialogues: A Background Paper* picks up this point critically. Both the Anglican-Reformed and the

Anglican-Roman Catholic dialogues are said to go beyond the Anglican-Lutheran statement. The report deplores the lack of a multilateral text on ecclesiology, or on stuctures of authority and the goal of union, commenting that ARCIC's picture of:

> the fellowship of the Church held together by structures of collegiality and primacy, the emphasis on the local church, together with the description of the structures and exercise of authority in the statements on authority would seem to suggest a closer-knit structure than that envisaged in the Anglican-Lutheran dialogue. (21)

The implied criticism can be rephrased more sharply. It would be regrettable if, for Anglicans and Lutherans, the catholicity of the church came to be reduced to the elimination of conflict between two expressions of ecclesiastical parochialism. Before we tackle this matter from the standpoint of Christian doctrine, it would be as well to compare the alleged deficiencies of the Anglican-Lutheran dialogue with the results of two other recent international bilateral conversations.

The Anglican-Orthodox Dialogue (The Dublin Agreed Statement 1984) devotes, as one would expect, a not inconsiderable amount of space to the issue of catholicity. Both the unity and catholicity of the church are treated in this report as being actualized and given visible expression in the eucharist. Here the church, gathered round the bishop in common celebration, proclaims Christ's death until he comes. "At each local Eucharist, celebrated within the catholic church, Christ is present in his wholeness, and so each local celebration actualizes and gives visible expression to the Church's catholicity."[9] The communion of the local churches is expressed in a large number of visible forms, meetings, letters, visits, and prayers for each other. The concept of catholicity expressed in this dialogue is that of a multiplicity of local churches each in communion with all other local churches. As Orthodoxy in North America and Australasia has shown "local churches" need not be organizationally unified. But their unity is nonetheless visibly real in the communion enjoyed by their respective autonomous patriarchates. As a goal of a united church, therefore, this dialogue envisages the mutual recognition of self-governing episcopal churches, sharing one faith, realizing their unity in the sacrament of the eucharist, and in a constant state of mutual communication and consultation.[10] Although autonomy is thought of as persisting into the future, this kind of unity differs from that envisaged in the Anglican-Lutheran dialogue in the emphasis placed upon the commonly shared "symbols of catholicity," especially the episcopate and the attention given to communication.

The second bilateral dialogue to which attention must be drawn is the report of the Anglican-Reformed International Commission 1981-1984, *God's Reign and Our Unity*. A more discursive document than other agreed statements, it gives a more articulated picture of the goal of unity.

> We are not simply seeking a *modus vivendi* between two globally organized denominations which would continue their separate though reconciled existence. Since we see the denomination not as by itself "the Church," but as a family or fellowship of churches, we are agreed that Christian unity must in the last resort be discovered and actualized at the local level. Hence we seek the emergence of reconciled local communities, each of which is recognizable as "church" in the proper sense: i.e., communities which exhibit in each place the fullness of ministerial order, eucharistic fellowship, pastoral care, and missionary commitment and which, through mutual communion and co-operation, bear witness on the regional, national and even international levels."

The focus in this statement is, accordingly, upon the "local church," and by "local" the report refuses to accept the customary meanings of "diocesan" or "congregational" supplied by the respective traditions. Rather it urges recognition of the "secular realities of each place," that is to say, the sociological, rather than geographical notion of locality and community. Here again, though not a very high value seems to be placed on global unity (note *"even"* international levels), there is explicit reference to the "symbols of catholicity" ("mutual communion and co-operation") which are to make a reality out of the shared faith. Here, too, emphasis is placed upon the "fullness of the catholic Church" being expressed in the eucharistic celebration of the Sunday assembly of the people of God.

We have, then, in these four bilateral dialogues involving Anglicans some rather different trends and emphases in respect of the idea of the catholicity of the church. It remains, finally, to offer some more systematic reflections upon the same theme.

A Theological Reflection on Catholicity, Christ, and the Spirit

An appropriate starting-point for a doctrinal treatment of the catholicity of the church is the doctrine of the person of Christ, in accordance with the first use of the term in Ignatius of Antioch. When Article VII of the *Confessio Augustana* substitutes the words "one holy Christian Church" for the Apostles' Creed's confession of "one holy catholic Church," not merely is there no polemical intention against the term *catholic* as is still occasionally asserted, it is an interpretation of considerable insight.[12] As Edmund Schlink has finely put it, "because the Church is already catholic in Christ, therefore it ought to be catholic."[13] It is in this sense that the unity of the church is implicit in its catholicity, because there is one Saviour for the whole of humankind. It is the confession of the one Saviour of humankind which is the basis of catholicity; and by confession is meant everything in space and time which points to Jesus Christ, words and deeds, sacraments, and social institutions.

The christological root of the notion of catholicity enables one to identify both an *ad intra* and an *ad extra* dimension of catholicity. *Ad intra* one should speak of the church's enjoyment of the inexhaustible richness of Christ, her grasp of "the breadth and length and height and depth of the love of Christ"(Ephesians 3:18). *Ad extra* one must identify the church's missionary task in space, in time, and across cultures, to realize Christ's saving presence in every corner of the world and every dimension of human life. Both *ad intra* and *ad extra* there are dangers to be overcome and temptations to be resisted. *Ad intra* not merely must the church break out of narrow self-absorption into catholic fullness, it must also preserve a critical sense of the present *kairos*. *Ad extra* it is engaged in a perpetually hazardous dialogue with the problems, concerns, and traditions of particular cultures and sub-cultures. The preservation of the church's catholicity is one aspect of the continuous realizing her own identity. For the church to *be* the Christian church, for Christianity to *be* Christianity, is to testify to her universal Lord and Saviour.

Conceived of as fidelity to Jesus Christ, catholicity becomes the claim and, at the same time, the task of every Christian community or local church. This is why there are such things as "denominational" traditions, that is, claims to catholicity which have acquired over time an identifying denomination. There is Eastern Orthodox catholicity, Roman Catholic catholicity, Lutheran catholicity, Anglican catholicity, and so forth. These amount, in fact, to historical forms of interpretation of what fidelity to Christ consists in. Although such interpretations have often been advanced exclusively in the past, the modern world has seen the rapid growth of inclusive notions of catholicity, that is, of views whose fundamental premise is that the identity of the church is not co-terminous with the boundaries of one tradition, however privileged that tradition may be in its expression of authentic and even normative catholicity.

But the stress so far laid upon the christological component of catholicity needs to be complemented by a pneumatological emphasis. The church has to take seriously her position between Pentecost and the last days, engaged in a complex battle with destructive forces and compelled to rely upon the promised guidance of the Holy Spirit. It is never safe to divorce pneumatology and eschatology. The gift of the Spirit is not, therefore, the promise of immediate infallibility, but of ultimate indefectibility. The gift of the Spirit is not a guarantee that the solution of conflict will be readily identified, but a sign of the seriousness of what is at issue. "Our fight is not against human foes, but against cosmic powers" (Ephesians 6:12).

The characteristic of the pneumato-eschatological approach to catholicity is the recognition that there is a hazardous element in every perceived opportunity for the church. This insight has to be applied equally to contemporary ecumenism, which, as has been frequently pointed out, is not merely a spontaneous movement of the Spirit, but a complex set of responses to shifts in world culture. This is true in two respects. In the first place the church's perception of the need to re-establish the unity implicit in her catholicity has a mundane correlate in the growth of world communication. The ecumenical movement becomes an apparently more urgent responsibility with the development of radio and telephonic communications, which cross geographical and political divisions creating a sense of global unity. That this is in part an illusion is exposed in such phenomena as the jamming of radio broadcasts, the tapping of telephone wires, and the discovery of the politically interested character of the dominant news networks. A church which is not sensitive to the hazardous character of this global movement will come to believe that its work is advanced by means of a good media profile.

Secondly, the shift of contemporary culture is also towards equality. Humanity is pictured as being capable of, or actually of having broken through to, not merely a sense of global unity but also the abolition of barriers of race, sex, caste, or social class. The challenge of ecumenism is conceived, therefore, to be the challenge of unwavering testimony to human equality. The second phase of the ecumenical movement has acquired a sharply political and social character. The prophetic resources of the Jewish and Christian traditions are revived in a crusade on behalf of the poor and oppressed.

A pneumatological sense of catholicity will, however, be alert to certain ambiguities in the Christian response to this new context. It will interpret the church's role eschatologically. Realizations of human brother- and sisterhood will be only partial, small-scale, and inherently flawed pointers to the ultimate realization of the kingdom of God. Secular visions of a "classless society" will be subject to grave suspicion on the score of delusion and deception. Schemes of social engineering will be critically examined for their suppression of human dignity, and denial of the tragic dimension of human life.

The knowledge that the Holy Spirit is given as a sign of the last days will also alert Christians to the pressures exerted by the unredeemed context of all church activity. Article XIX, "Of the Church," of the Thirty-nine Articles expresses in polemical reformation fashion that the historic churches (Jerusalem, Alexandria, Antioch, and Rome are those to be mentioned explicitly) have erred. Notice is thereby given implicitly to other churches, including the Church of England, that it too may fall into error. There is a gulf fixed between the external expression of Christianity and its pneumato-eschatological reality. Here Luther's celebrated distinction between ''spiritual, internal Christendom'' and ''physical, external Christendom'' significantly evokes what may be at issue, the possibility of an institution closed to its own charismatic origins.[14] But Luther's polemical point may have been misinterpreted to imply a doctrine of two different churches, the one having no part in the other. In answer to this the distinguished Lutheran scholar, Vilmos Vajta, has recently argued, however, that although Luther is concerned to underline the possibility that external Christendom may become entangled in abuses, the underlying thought is that of the spiritual-sacramental structure of the church.

> For Luther the concept of the Church is determined, just as that of the concept of the Sacraments, by three elements: the (spiritual) meaning, the (sacramental) sign and the (Spirit-worked) faith which binds the first two together.

This spiritual-sacramental structure guarantees that whatever the criticisms which must be passed of the outer church, it is essentially bound up with the spiritual reality. ''Thus it is impossible to introduce a value distinction between the spiritual and physical church for these form a single unity by the Holy Spirit.''[15]

The theological point may, perhaps, be refined with the help of some exceptionally suggestive proposals of Professor David Martin. He invites us to identify the way in which the fundamental signs and images of the church embodying her hopes have to be defined against the reality of what is. The church stands for the achievement of unity and reconciliation, for equality and the breaking down of barriers, and for universal love. But at once we encounter a series of paradoxes: the abolition of frontiers creates an even more fundamental frontier between the abolitionists and the rest; the challenge to all-pervasive hierarchies in the name of radical brotherhood requires discipline, whose maintenance entails new foci of authority; the universality of love provokes division and sacrifice and initiates a discipleship more intense that the demands of mere toleration.

Though he does not refer to this example these paradoxes may be observed in full expression in the letter of Clement I, where already the need for internal discipline in the face of disorder expresses itself in military, hierarchical terms. The church can achieve nothing if it is not imbued with a discipline analogous to that of the army. Martin puts the process thus:

> Unity has given rise to division and this division is further realised in a complete and comprehensive duality: Church-world, spirit-flesh, body of Christ-body of this death. Without the hope of unity this comprehensive duality could not exist and would relapse into mere inertia, particularly, hierarchy. Division is predicated on unification, just as relativism is predicated on objectivity.[16]

I take this sociological observation to have the following significance for the church's understanding of her own task: there can be no permanent, unambiguous liberation from "the world." The cost which the mundane expression of the Christian hope imposes upon the church in the world is the threat of subversion from within. And yet at the same time this threat is the church's opportunity. It is *because* the structures of human society are themselves vulnerable to the Christian vision of a new transcendent order that the church is liable to corruption. The church is able to infiltrate its images into the culture by means which may in part nullify its impact and expose it to criticism and reformation. Some of this at least Luther may have glimpsed; and as his own movement of spiritual reformation gathered mundane impetus there is enough evidence of his agony at the reoccurrence of the paradoxes. Spiritual Christendom is never finally separable in reality from physical Christendom and its perversions; but this is no grounds for complacency or a failure of critical nerve. It is part of the logic of the theological realm of spiritual unity that it should be confronted inescapably with the duality of the two cities, and be forced constantly into hazardous choices.

Both the christological and the pneumato-eschatological themes expounded above are important for the future Anglican and Lutheran treatment of the theme of catholicity. In the first place future Anglican-Lutheran dialogue will have to avoid all appearance of satisfaction with the parochial goal of mutual recognition. In particular it should inhere in their sense of the fullness of Christ that the issues treated in the bilaterals involving the Roman Catholic and Eastern Orthodox churches will themselves receive the closest attention. The basis for such consideration has already been laid in the Lima text, and the widespread mutual recognition of baptism. The issue should be seen as one which requires the conscious adoption of "symbols of catholicity," that is elements in the worship and practical life of the churches signifying *ad intra* and *ad extra* the determination of the separated churches to point to *one* Lord. Such symbols would include the use of the Nicene Creed (without the *filioque*), adoption of common texts and practices for use in sacramental worship, agreement on fundamental ethical issues, and a conscious attempt to structure the ordained ministry so as to represent the apostolic mission of the whole church.

Secondly, closer and more realistic attention should be given by Anglicans and Lutherans to the communication networks in the separated churches, and to the way in which messages passed in one church can be overheard (and not infrequently misunderstood) in the other. This has a close bearing on the theological problem of authority. Anglicans are occasionally all too ready to give Lutherans the impression that if only their churches received "apostolic succession" (which, of course, some are said already to "possess") then the catholicity of their denomination would henceforth be beyond question. But this is to divorce the notion of what is said to be "catholic order" from the communication of the gospel, as though "apostolic succession" was a genetic strain desirable for the simple reproduction of future bishops. On the contrary the purpose of having a recognized structure in the church is in order that it may realize in space and time its *ad intra* and *ad extra* catholicity. Formal structures as easily conceal and frustrate this process of communication as advance it. The power of the gospel is no greater for its being communicated by a hierarch, if the mode of communication makes it unassimilable. What is of importance to the churches, therefore, is to learn the way in which the *effective* communication of the gospel occurs, and to pay less attention to the theological legitimations of the *formal* structures.

Catholicity, in the third place, entails the practical readiness of the two churches to communicate effectively with each other. Bearing in mind the complexities even of the inner-dominational communication process, considerable effort needs to be expended in allowing inter-denominational speaking and hearing. As was noted above, Eastern Orthodoxy has for centuries practised internal communication by letter. Anglicans in the past decades have created two new organs of communication inside the communion. But the two denominations still behave (as their internal church law doubtless permits them to do) as practically autonomous. They revise liturgies, create constitutions, pass ethical resolutions, exercise discipline, and enact structural reform without pausing to consider the possibility of listening to other voices, except where these are deployed by internal minorities in support of or in opposition to change. Effective communication is, of course, all the more vital where "symbols of catholicity" are involved.

If the above are largely practical issues related closely to the two churches' habits of preserving their own identities in separation from the potential enjoyment of a greater fullness, there is naturally a larger agenda deriving from the problem of the sixteenth-century reformation, on which Anglicans and Lutherans have together an important contribution to make. Thus, fourthly, they should be prepared to work more intensively on the connection between the institutional identity of the church and its reformation, by means of which Lutherans may acquire greater sympathy for the Anglican defense of a ministerial succession, and Anglicans for the Lutheran insistence on the priority of the gospel. But the Anglican-Lutheran dialogue must be seen in a wider context, that provided by the phenomenon of continuous conflict *within* Christianity as the price to be paid for its potential to subvert the cultures in which it is incarnated. Christian identity is not a harmonious state of equilibrium, but one in which paradoxes are continuously arising to provoke disquiet and tension. Insight into these tensions will assuredly not suffice to eliminate them. But it will prevent the ecumenical movement from seeking false goals and specious reconciliations. Anglicans and Lutherans should be provoked by the same insights which illuminate their differences into offering the ecumenical movement more than a mutual recognition of each other's catholicity. For these perceptions could contribute to a profounder understanding of catholicity, in the costly provisionality of the church's institutional identity.

Notes

1. John Howe, *Highways and Hedges* (London, 1985), 213.
2. Avery Dulles, S.J., *The Catholicity of the Church* (Oxford, 1985). The main argument of this important work is that Catholicity can only subsist in reconciled diversity.
3. This was issued "as a matter of conscience" on the grounds that it would "cause confusion and be detrimental to the best interest of the Lutheran Church—Missouri Synod," *The Report of the Lutheran-Episcopal Dialogue, Second Series 1976-1980* (Cincinnati, Ohio, 1981), 31.
4. See Book III, 1, 14 (Folger Edition I, G. Edelen ed., Cambridge, Mass., 1977, 205).
5. Para. 53. See also *Anglican-Lutheran Dialogue*, Appedix 2, where the central theological sections of ALIC are reproduced.
6. *ALD*, 42, para. 55.
7. Quotes ARCIC introduction, para. 8; *ALD*, 21-22.
8. *Anglican-Lutheran Relations*. Report of the Anglican-Lutheran Joint Working Group, Anglican Consultative Council 1983, 25.
9. *Anglican-Orthodox Dialogue* (London, 1984), 11, para. 8.
10. Ibid., 12f, para. 13.
11. *Anglican-Reformed International Dialogue* (London, 1984), 69f, para. 110.
12. Cf. H. Meyer and H. Schütte, "The Concept of the Church in the Augsburg Confession," eds. G.W. Forell and J.F. McCue, *Confessing One Faith* (Augsburg, Minneapolis, 1982), 176.
13. E. Schlink, *Oekumenische Dogmatik* (Göttingen, 1983), 588. Cf. also, Schlink, *Theology of the Lutheran Confessions* (Philadelphia, 1961), 208.
14. *Luther's Works*, American Edition, 70.
15. Vilmos Vajta, "The Church as Spiritual-Sacramental *Communio* with Christ and His Saints in the Theology of Luther," in *Luther's Ecumenical Significance*, eds. P. Manns and H. Meyer (Philadelphia, 1984), 115f.
16. David Martin, *The Breaking of the Image* (London, 1980), 176.

APPENDIX
The Meaning and Unity of the Anglican Communion
(Lambeth 1948)

(Part of a report on the Anglican communion, prepared and presented by sixty-four bishops under the chairmanship of Archbishop Philip Carrington, archbishop of Quebec.)

NOTE: Reports of this kind are said to have the authority, not of the whole Lambeth Conference, but of those bishops who prepare and present them.

The Meaning and Unity of the Anglican Communion

The world is in grievous disorder and needs to be restored to the order which God wills. A perplexed generation is in search of an authority to which to give its allegiance, and easily submits to the appeal of authoritarian systems whether religious or secular in character.

The question is asked, "Is Anglicanism based on a sufficiently coherent form of authority to form the nucleus of a world-wide fellowship of Churches, or does its comprehensiveness conceal internal divisions which may cause its disruption?"

Former Lambeth Conferences have wisely rejected proposals for a formal primacy of Canterbury, for an Appellate Tribunal, and for giving the Conference the status of a legislative synod. The Lambeth Conference remains advisory, and its continuation committee consultative.

These decisions have led to a repudiation of centralized government, and a refusal of a legal basis of union.

The positive nature of the authority which binds the Anglican Communion together is therefore seen to be moral and spiritual, resting on the truth of the Gospel, and on a charity which is patient and willing to defer to the common mind.

Authority, as inherited by the Anglican Communion from the undivided Church of the early centuries of the Christian era, is single in that it is derived from a single Divine source, and reflects within itself the richness and historicity of the divine Revelation, the authority of the eternal Father, the incarnate Son, and the life-giving Spirit. It is distributed amoung Scripture, Tradition, Creeds, the Ministry of the World and Sacraments, the witness of saints, and the *consenus fidelium,* which is the continuing experience of the Holy Spirit through His faithful people in the Church. It is thus a dispersed rather than a centralized authority having many elements which combine, interact with, and check each other; these elements together contributing by a process of mutual support, mutual checking, and redressing of errors or exaggerations to the many-sided fullness of the authority which Christ has committed to His Church. Where this authority of Christ is to be found mediated not in one mode but in several we recognize in this multiplicity God's loving provision against the temptations to tyranny and the dangers of unchecked power.

This authority posseses a suppleness and elasticity in that the emphasis of one element over the others may and does change with the changing conditions of the Church. The variety of the contributing factors gives to it a quality of richness which encourages and releases initiative, trains in fellowship, and evokes a free and willing obedience.

It may be said that authority of this kind is much harder to understand and obey than authority of a more imperious character. This is true and we glory in the appeal which it makes to faith. Translated into personal terms it is simple and intelligible. God who is our ultimate personal authority demands of all His creatures entire and unconditional obedience. As in human families the father is the mediator of this divine authority, so in the family of the Church is the bishop, the Father-in-God, wielding his authority by virtue of his divine commission and in synodical association with his clergy and laity, and exercising it in humble submission, as himself under authority.

The elements in authority are, moreover, in organic relation to each other. Just as the discipline of the scientific method proceeds from the collection of data to the ordering of these data in formulae, the publishing of results obtained, and their verification by experience, so Catholic Christianity presents us with an organic process of life and thought in which religious experience has been, and is, described, intellectually ordered, mediated, and verified.

This experience is *described* in Scripture, which is authoritative because it is the unique and classical record of the revelation of God in His relation to and dealings with man. While Scripture therefore remains the ultimate standard of faith, it should be continually interpreted in the context of the Church's life.

It is *defined* in Creeds and in continuous theological study.

It is *mediated* in the Ministry of the Word and Sacraments, by persons who are called and commissioned by God through the Church to represent both the transcendent and immanent elements of Christ's authority.

It is *verified* in the witness of saints and in the *consensus fidelium*. The Christ-like life carries its own authority, and the authority of doctrinal formulations, by General Councils or otherwise, rests at least in part on their acceptance by the whole body of the faithful, though the weight of this *consensus* "does not depend on mere numbers or on the extension of a belief at any time, but on continuance through the ages, and the extent to which the *consensus* is genuinely free."

This essentially Anglican authority is reflected in our adherence to episcopacy as the source and centre of our order, and the Book of Common Prayer as the standard of our worship. Liturgy, in the sense of the offering and ordering of the public worship of God, is the crucible in which these elements of authority are fused and unified in the fellowship and power of the Holy Spirit. It is the Living and Ascended Christ present in the worshipping congregation who is the meaning and unity of the whole Church. He presents it to the Father, and sends it out on its mission.

We therefore urge the whole Conference to call upon every member of the Anglican Communion to examine himself in respect of his obligation to public worship.

We recognize that our fellow-Churchmen in some parts of the world do not always express themselves in worship according to Western patterns, and that they must have generous liberty of experiment in liturgy; and we therefore reaffirm Resolutions 36 and 37 of the Conference of 1920.

But we appeal to those who are reponsible for the ordering and conduct of public worship to remember how bewildered the laity are by differences of use, and with that earnest care and charity they should be helped to take their full share in liturgical worship.

We consider that the time has come to examine those "features in the Book of Common Prayer which are essential to the safeguarding of the unity of the Anglican Communion" (Resolution 37, 1920) and the Recommendations of Committee IV of 1920.